INCEPTION
AND
PHILOSOPHY

The Blackwell Philosophy and Pop Culture Series
Series Editor: William Irwin

INCEPTION
AND
PHILOSOPHY

BECAUSE IT'S NEVER
JUST A DREAM

Edited by David Kyle Johnson

WILEY

John Wiley & Sons, Inc.

Published by John Wiley & Sons, Inc., Hoboken, New Jersey
Published simultaneously in Canada

For general information about our other products and services, please contact our
Customer Care Department within the United States at (800) 762-2974, outside the
United States at (317) 572-3993 or fax (317) 572-4002.

Wiley also publishes its books in a variety of electronic formats and by print-on-demand.
Some content that appears in standard print versions of this book may not be available in
other formats. For more information about Wiley products, visit us at www.wiley.com.

Library of Congress Cataloging-in-Publication Data:
Inception and philosophy : because it's never just a dream / edited by David Johnson.
    p. cm. — (The Blackwell philosophy and pop culture series)
    Includes bibliographical references and index.
    ISBN 978-1-118-07263-9 (pbk.); ISBN 978-1-118-16889-9 (ebk.);
    ISBN 978-1-118-16890-5 (ebk.); ISBN 978-1-118-16891-2 (ebk.)
    1. Inception (Motion picture) I. Johnson, David (David Kyle)
  PN1997.2.I62I57   2012
  791.43'684—dc23
                                                            2011028933

10 9 8 7 6 5 4 3 2 1

For Zorro, who kept me company through the entire editing process. There will never be a dog better than you. May you always live on in my dreams.

CONTENTS

ACKNOWLEDGMENTS

The Dream Team

The dream that is this book would not be possible without a great many people. It is a shared dream.

I wish to thank the contributing authors for their tireless efforts and philosophical architecture. Like Ariadne, they designed the dream—I just filled it with my subconscious. Hopefully, it didn't turn on them too severely.

My thanks also go to Connie Santisteban, at John Wiley and Sons, for her hard work and dedication. Like Arthur, she makes sure everything runs smoothly. This shared dream wasn't possible without her. Likewise, I would like to thank all the folks at Wiley who work behind the scenes to make this series possible. They are the Saito to my Cobb; their giant bankroll made this book possible. If only I could get them to buy me an airline.

Last, I wish to thank my good friend and colleague William Irwin, for his patience, incredible feedback, and dedication to the cause. I'm very glad, my friend, that we have the shared dream of incepting the public with knowledge of philosophy.

THE EDITOR'S TOTEM

An Elegant Solution for Keeping Track of Reality

I know, I know. An editor's note. Who cares, right? Wrong! Don't skip it. This is important stuff. If you care about understanding *Inception*, and this book, you'll want to hear me out.

Editing this book wasn't easy. *Inception* is so ambiguous, I had to worry about whether the contributing authors interpreted, and thus would speak about, the movie in the same way. One problem, in particular, kept popping up around every corner like Cobol agents in Mombasa. How much of *Inception* is a dream? Is the end a dream? Is everything after Yusuf's basement a dream? Could the whole movie be a dream? If I wasn't careful, the book could have ended up looking like it was about two or three different movies.

So I came up with an "elegant solution for keeping track of reality." Throughout the book, the authors refer to the world in which the inception is planned—the world in which Mal jumps from the window, where Cobb is on the run, meets

Ariadne, and doesn't wear his wedding ring anymore—as *the real world*. The italics are important—they indicate a title, not a description. By the use of the italicized phrase, the authors will not assume that *the real world* actually is the real world (notice, no italics that time). That way, when we need to ignore the issue, we can; and when the issue is important, we can concentrate on it.

Now, that's all you need to know to start reading the book. But if you want to know why we can't just assume that *the real world* of *Inception* actually is real, and you want to gain a much deeper understanding and appreciation of the movie, continue reading.

How much of *Inception* is a dream? Most people think the answer lies in an event just beyond our reach. Does the top fall at the end of the movie after the screen cuts to black? If it does, then Cobb is awake; if it doesn't, then Cobb is still dreaming. A careful examination of the film, however, shows us that this is not the case.

First of all, Cobb's totem is extremely unreliable as a dream detector. Arthur specifically points out, when telling Ariadne about totems, that they work only to tell you that you are "not in *someone else's* dream." So even if the top falls, Cobb could still be in his own dream. Totems have this weakness because, if the dreamer knows how the totem behaves in reality, the dreamer could dream that it behaves that way; and obviously the owner of a totem knows how it behaves in reality. This is why you don't want anyone else to touch your totem. If anyone gets a hint of how it is supposed to behave, they could dream that it behaves that way, and then your totem couldn't tell you that you are not in their dream world.

Despite all this, Cobb tells Ariadne, specifically, how his totem works. When she asks if the concept of a totem was his idea, Cobb says, "No . . . it was Mal's actually . . . this one was hers. She would spin it in the dream [and] it would never topple. Just spin and spin." So the top can't tell Cobb that he is not in Ariadne's dream; she knows how it works. And in fact, since she is the architect of all the dream layers in the inception, couldn't she have (even inadvertently) worked the law "All tops fall" into the very physics of the dreams she designed? How could spinning his top ever tell Cobb that he has left the dream layers of the inception?

And wait . . . what was that? Look at that quote again. The totem was Mal's? Well that's just great! Sure, Cobb thinks Mal is dead; and if she is, then he doesn't have to worry about being in her dream. But Cobb thinks she's dead because he believes the world in which Mal threw herself from the window (*the real world*) is real. The only way he could come to that conclusion, however, is by spinning the top and watching it fall—but wouldn't that be circular reasoning?

Besides, who doesn't know that tops fall after they are spun? We have no idea how Arthur's die is weighted, or how Ariadne's chess piece is supposed to work. But if Cobb spun his top in anyone's dream, wouldn't they dream that it fell? So sure, if the top did keep spinning, after the screen went black, that would tell us Cobb is still dreaming. But the top falling wouldn't tell us anything!

This line of reasoning brings up another problem. Forget the end of the film. Think about the beginning and *the real world* that most of the first half of the movie takes place in—the world where Mal jumps out the window, Cobb is a fugitive, the inception is planned, and the main characters meet. Think about when Cobb and Mal first reentered this world, after leaving Limbo. How could they tell it was real? The top couldn't help, since they both knew how it works; either one of them could have been the dreamer. So how could they tell that world was real? The fact is, they couldn't. There was no way to prove one way or the other. In fact, that was Cobb's problem. There was no way to convince Mal that world was real, and that is why she ultimately threw herself from the window. Now, since that world didn't start to crumble as soon as Mal "died" in it (like the Japanese Mansion dream started to crumble as soon as its dreamer, Arthur, died in it), it's safe to conclude that world was not Mal's dream. But it could still be Cobb's dream. And if it is, Mal is not dead. She didn't commit suicide; she was right. They were still dreaming, and she woke up.

Sure, it's possible Cobb and Mal were still dreaming—but is it reasonable to think they were? Yes! If you pay careful attention to the movie, you will see that it is ambiguous throughout. For the same reasons that the end of the movie might be a dream, the entire movie might be a dream. Let me elaborate.

Whether the top keeps spinning at the end of the movie is an issue because it's not clear whether Saito and Cobb make it all the way back to the real world, after exiting Limbo.[1] Why is this not clear? For one thing, it's never clear. Even when one dream ends, Cobb is always concerned that he merely dreamed that he awoke. That's why he's always spinning his top. But specific elements of the film give us reason to suspect that Cobb and Saito didn't make it back. Think about this: What happens to someone when they exit Limbo? Where do they go? The two clearest examples we have are Fischer and Ariadne, who both exit Limbo by falling off a tall building. Where do they go? Not out to the real world! They go one level up, to the third layer of the shared dream—the snow fortress. (They have to ride the kicks back up to the first layer.) So when Cobb and Saito exit Limbo, wouldn't they go up to that third layer too? If so, wouldn't it have been long abandoned by then? (The other characters make it back up to the first level, while Cobb and Saito's bodies lie motionless in the van.) Given this, wouldn't one of them have simply remade that layer based on their own expectations—to find themselves on a plane, landing in California?[2]

You might think this is inconsistent with the facts of the film, but it says nothing about what happens to someone upon arriving at an abandoned dream level, or whether or not such a thing is possible. We know, at least, that a dreamer exiting a dream layer does not necessarily make it collapse immediately;

we learn this early on in the film, when Arthur exists his Japanese Mansion dream and it continues. So it is possible to inhabit a dream layer, without a dreamer. Arthur even tries to keep Saito under, to keep the dream going. If he had been successful, who knows how long that dream could have continued, or if it would have become Saito's or Cobb's dream.

So, think again of the end of the film. If that third snow fortress dream level was empty when Saito arrived,[3] why wouldn't he dictate a new architecture for that level with his expectations? And, once Cobb arrived, why wouldn't he populate it with projections of his subconscious—his team and his family? They were under very heavy sedation, and according to Cobb and Yusuf, it wasn't going to wear off until after they spent a week on the first layer of the dream (which was six months on the second level and ten years on the third). And the other dreamers made it back up to that level before even an hour had passed in it. Even after exiting Limbo, Saito and Cobb could have almost ten years to live on that third level before the sedative even begins to wear off.

Is it reasonable to worry that Cobb and Saito didn't make it back to the real world after exiting Limbo? Of course it's reasonable—that's why so many people care whether the top falls at the end of the film. But as we listen to Cobb recount his and Mal's story to Ariadne, we realize a very similar problem comes up for them—one where we don't even have to worry about what happens if one arrives at an abandoned dream level.

Cobb and Mal entered Limbo by experimenting with multilayered dreaming. As Cobb recounts to Ariadne,

> We were working together. We were exploring the concept of a dream, within a dream. I kept pushing things, I wanted to go deeper and deeper . . . when we wound up on the shore of our own subconscious [Limbo], we lost sight of what was real.

To exit Limbo, they laid their heads on the train tracks—and woke up on the floor of some house, hooked up to a "dream machine" (PASIV) briefcase, married with two kids. But if their exit from Limbo was like every other, that floor was only one level up—the deepest layer of a multilevel dream, just above Limbo. If so, their fifty years in Limbo was long enough for them to forget this fact, or what the real world was even like. So, even if that world is not real, it's no wonder that Cobb believes it is. Sure, Mal believes it is a dream only because Cobb incepted the idea into her in Limbo. That doesn't mean, though, that Mal's belief is false. She might be right, and if she is, she didn't commit suicide—she woke up![4] If the sedative Cobb and Mal used is nearly as potent as the one used on the airplane, Cobb could be stuck on that level for ten years before he even has a chance to wake up in the real world. Who knows? Cobb and Mal might not even have kids in the real world. They might not even be married; they might have been just exploring the possibility through shared dreaming.

In fact, it seems that Christopher Nolan, the film's writer and director, leaves us some subtle clues to suggest that it is indeed possible that *the real world* is only a dream.

- Through his conversations with Ariadne, Yusuf, and others, we learn that Cobb can't dream anymore unless he hooks into a PASIV device, and that he does so every night. This is, apparently, how he sleeps. Could it be that he can't sleep or dream without the machine because he is already asleep and dreaming?
- Consider the scene in which Mal jumps from the window. Cobb navigates through the room that Mal has trashed, and looks out the window. She is on the opposite ledge, in the open window of another room in the hotel.[5] How did she get there? Wouldn't she have inched out on the ledge, away from *their* hotel room window and thus been on the same side of the building as Cobb? Isn't Mal being on the opposite ledge just the kind of inexplicable thing that happens when dreaming?

- In Cobb's dream in the basement, as he sees images of her laying her head on the train tracks in Limbo, Cobb's projection of Mal tells him, "You know how to find me. You know what you have to do." She says this again, as Ariadne finds him reliving his memories. If the real Mal was right and they were dreaming, Cobb merely has to commit suicide to find her. Is Cobb's projection of Mal calling him to wake up from the dream of *the real world*—by committing suicide—so he can find the real Mal "up above"?

- Consider the chase scene in Mombasa. When Cobb jumps out the bar window, a Cobol "Businessman" is waiting for him and says, "You're not dreaming now, are you?" Yet the chase has dreamlike qualities. Notice, in the overhead shots, how much Mombasa appears to be a maze, a labyrinth—just like Ariadne designs for the Fischer inception. Notice also how businessmen continually appear, around every corner, in just the right place, and for no reason. As the chase begins, Cobb eliminates the two who are chasing him; but as soon as he turns to run, two more are inexplicably right on his tail. When he tries to run out of the restaurant, a businessman literally appears out of nowhere to tackle him from the side. And how about the company they work for—Cobol?[6] Isn't "Cobol" just a little too similar to "Cobb"? Is he chasing himself?[7] And what about that restaurant waiter, who won't get him a "café," but insists on drawing attention to him? And what about when he tries to escape between the two buildings, and the walls literally close in on him? Aren't these the kinds of things that happen while one is being chased in a dream?

- Fischer's subconscious is trained, when Arthur's research shows that it should not be. Could it be trained, because in attacking Fischer, they are actually attacking Cobb—because it's all just Cobb's dream?

- When Ariadne enters Cobb's memory of the night Mal jumped, why does she step on the glass just as Cobb did? Is it because, as a projection in Cobb's dream, she is Cobb?

- Consider the beginning of the movie, when we see Cobb talking to the elderly Saito in Limbo. Saito spins the top, and then we flash back to Cobb speaking to Saito as a young man in Arthur's dream. We then spend the rest of the movie getting back to where we started—Cobb talking to the elderly Saito in Limbo. And, we see, the top is still spinning; it was, in a way, spinning the whole movie! Could this be a symbolic clue, left by Nolan? After all, when the top spins, but doesn't fall, aren't we in someone else's dream?
- Similarly, the running time of Inception is *exactly* 2:28 (in hours and minutes). The song the dreamers use to signal the end of a dream is Edith Piaf's "Non, Je Ne Regrette Rien," the original recording time of which is 2:28 (in minutes and seconds). Another subtle clue? When the song is done, the dream is over.
- And what is the deal with the dream share technology? Not only do we not know how it works, but it doesn't even make sense. Controlling dreams . . . through the arm? The technology working inexplicably is what we would expect if it is just a part of a dream. Not so much, if it is supposed to be technology that could exist in reality.[8]

Of course, you can explain all of this away. Maybe Cobb can't sleep or dream because he is addicted to the dream machine. Maybe Mal rented another hotel room, across the way, and went to it after she trashed the other. Maybe Cobb's projection of Mal is calling him back to Limbo, not back to reality. Maybe Cobb is just unlucky when it comes to Mombasa chases. Maybe Fischer had covert training, and the "movie long spinning top" is just an artifact of the flashback. Maybe the film ending at 2:28 signals that it's time for us to return to reality. Maybe Cobb's memories never change. Maybe a dream briefcase emits some kind of "psychic field" that synchronizes all unconscious brains in the vicinity. Maybe you can't enter layers once they are abandoned, and Saito and Cobb did make it back to *the real world.* Maybe Cobb and Mal didn't use heavy enough sedatives for stable multilevel dreaming, and their suicide in Limbo woke them all the way back up. Maybe, in fact, every dreamlike element of *the real world* is just a way to hint at the fact that Cobb is losing his ability to distinguish dreams from reality. Maybe I'm just anomaly hunting, seeing clues where there are none! I am not arguing that the "Full Dream" interpretation is the right one. I'm pointing out that it is a legitimate, consistent interpretation of the film. (In fact, as we will see, these are not the only clues.)[9]

So you can see the problem. A first viewing of the film leads one to believe that *the real world*—the world in which Mal jumps from the window and in which the inception is planned—is the real world. A deeper look reveals that this might not be the case, however. In fact, the entire movie might be a dream.

It will be helpful, then, to start right from the first chapter by thinking about the issue of how much of *Inception* is a dream. So, stave off your temptation to go watch the movie again and dive right into *Inception and Philosophy*.

NOTES

1. There is even an issue as to whether they exited Limbo at all. But since Limbo is never as populated as the world is in the final scenes in the movie, I think we can assume they at least made it out of Limbo.

2. Besides, even if they did make it back up to the first level, their bodies are strapped into a van that is submerged in water. So, even if they did make it out of Limbo and back to the first level, it seems that they would just die again and fall right back down into Limbo.

3. Since Saito had the gun in Limbo, I'll assume he shot himself first. Since Cobb has the same expectations, if Cobb arrived first, the story works out about the same.

4. Maybe in the real world, but maybe just in another layer of dreaming.

5. If you look behind Mal, you will see the interior of the room is the same as the one Cobb is in—notice the couch and the lamp, among other things. It's just that Cobb's room is trashed. She is not in another part of their suite; she is in the window of another room.

6. Interestingly, the name of Saito's Company is "Proclus Global," and Proclus was a Neo-Platonist philosopher (A.D. 412–485) of minor fame, who played a key role in keeping Platonic philosophy alive by heading the Platonic Academy in Athens. I considered

the possibility that this was another subtle clue that Cobb is dreaming, and looked at Proclus' philosophy. But, alas, I found nothing—although I don't think Nolan chose the name coincidentally. It must be symbolic of something else. Nolan likes symbolic Greek names. Ariadne helped Theseus through the labyrinth to slay the Minotaur. Perhaps Nolan considers Saito to run a company of "cutting-edge thinkers" like Proclus did.

7. Actually, Nolan spoke to this possibility and dismissed it in an article in the January 2011 issue of *Empire* magazine titled "Christopher Nolan Made Our Minds the Scene of the Crime." When asked whether the name "Cobol Engineering" is a giveaway that the whole plot's a subconscious fabrication since its first syllable matches Cobb's name, he said, "That unfortunately I would have to confess is definitely not the case. For legal reasons I had to rename Cobol Corporation about ten times. So that one I can shoot down as being not indicative of anything in particular." One wonders, however, despite his original intention—could it still be a clue? For more on whether an author's original intent sets the meaning of a film, see Ruth Tallman's chapter in this volume.

8. This last point deserves some elaboration. It could be that an aside about how the technology works would just get in the way of the story, so Nolan left it out. This is actually how my favorite modern sci-fi television show, *Doctor Who*, handles such things. It simply explains away funky technology and time travel paradoxes by saying "It's wibbly-wobbly, timey-wimey stuff," and moves on. Unlike *Star Trek* fans, most *Doctor Who* fans care about the story and characters, not the technical specifics, so this seems perfectly acceptable. But the problem with *Inception*'s dream technology goes a little deeper. How the dream share technology works is not only unexplained, it's inexplicable. Dreams are caused by brain activity, and for a device to synchronize a group of people's dreams, it would have to make their brains' neurons fire in similar ways. Perhaps the machine could find some arm nerves to hook into, but synchronizing brain activity with arm nerves would be like trying to program a computer by using only the "shift" key. There is no way to control the mass action of the brain through the arm.

9. For more such clues, see Ruth Tallman's and Jason Southworth's chapters in this volume.

INTRODUCTION

Plato's Academy Award

Inception didn't win the 2010 Academy Award for Best Picture. But if they gave an Oscar for philosophical depth—call it Plato's Academy Award—*Inception* would have taken home the statue (which would look like Rodin's *The Thinker*). Indeed, no film in recent memory raises philosophical questions quite like *Inception*.

The screen cuts to black before we see whether the top falls. If we can't know whether Cobb is dreaming, can we know that we ourselves are not dreaming? And if we can't, how exactly should we deal with the angst such uncertainty brings? This problem has been considered by philosophers as far back as Plato (c. 428–347 BCE), and it raises questions about *Inception* itself. If we can't know whether Cobb is dreaming, can we really know how much of the movie is a dream? Maybe Cobb is still in Yusuf's basement. Maybe Mal was right, and the whole movie is a dream! When it comes to works of art, is there even a way to settle such matters and determine what *Inception* means?

What if someone offered you a life in Limbo? Would you take it? Imagine living in a world that you control, where you can have any experience you want: a utopia. Sure, they aren't real experiences—but what if you didn't know that? What if, like Mal did in Limbo, you thought it was real? Would you take it then? Or would there be something pitiful about being a prisoner in Limbo, forced to think that your dream was real? Would you really want to live in Limbo anyway? Is a utopia even possible? If not, why do we strive toward one? Perhaps because it's important to dream?

What about inception itself? You might think it's impossible, but isn't it just implanting ideas in other people's minds in a way that makes them think they came up with the idea themselves? Isn't that a big part of what advertisements, news media, songs, television shows, preachers, teachers, and even movies like *Inception* do? In fact, *Inception* seems to be an allegory for moviemaking—Cobb is the director, Eames is the actor, Yusuf is special effects. Does this mean that movies are as dangerous, and as immoral, as inception? Does real-world inception violate our free will?

What exactly are dreams? Do they really occur while we sleep? Might they occur in another world? Is it possible to act immorally in our dreams? What exactly is a mind, and could we really share ours—share our dreams? In *Inception*, time moves slower the deeper you go into multilayered dreams. Even in reality, though, dreaming messes with our sense of time. What might our dreams tell us about the nature of time itself?

Cobb, Saito, and Mal are all asked to take a leap of faith. Mal leaps twice, once right out a window. Saito, too (it seems). Cobb does not. He "knows" what's real. So when, if ever, should we take our own leaps of faith?

The questions don't stop there. Regret, self-knowledge, paradox—unlocking *Inception*'s secrets with Asian philosophy. We have already designed the dream. So get out your big silver briefcase, pull out the tubes, hook them up to your arm, put your finger on the big yellow button, and get ready to tackle all these issues, and more. We are about to enter the dream world of *Inception*.

PART ONE

WAS MAL RIGHT? WAS IT ALL JUST A DREAM?: MAKING SENSE OF *INCEPTION*

WAS IT ALL A DREAM?: WHY NOLAN'S ANSWER DOESN'T MATTER

Ruth Tallman

> Your world is not real. Simple little thought that changes everything. So certain of your world, of what's real. Do you think [Cobb] is? Or do you think he is as lost as I was?
>
> —Mal

Inception is anything but straightforward. If nothing else, the fact that the final scene cuts to black before we see whether the top falls leaves the movie open to many interpretations. Of course, figuring out whether Cobb is still in a dream is not the same as figuring out the "meaning" of the film. But the two questions are closely related, as are the questions one must ask in order to answer them. It seems that the movie doesn't give us enough information to settle these questions, so how will we find answers? Where do we look? Is there a single answer?

If Christopher Nolan, the director of *Inception*, told us what he thought, would that settle it?

These questions are not new, nor are they unique to this particular film. Good works of art are usually not straight-forward. They challenge us, confuse us, and leave us wondering what we "should have" or "were supposed to" get from them. We worry that we might have missed the point, or misunderstood, or made a mistake in our understanding of the artwork. And when we have these concerns, when we disagree with one another about the "right" understanding of an artwork, quite often the go-to solution is to find out what the artist intended the work to mean. So, many people think, if Christopher Nolan thought the top fell, then we have our answer—the top fell. The idea here is that the artist, as the creator who gave life to the work, is privileged to determine the meaning and proper understanding of the artwork; if anyone has the authority to say, "Sorry, you just got it wrong," it's the artist. This position, known as intentionalism, will be discussed below.

But is this right? Does the creator of an artwork have such power over his creation? Let's look at this question. After considering some views and arguments, I think you will agree that the answer is no. In fact, I think you'll see that Christopher Nolan would agree as well.

The Major Interpretations

Determining whether or not the top fell at the end of the movie should, it is believed, indicate whether Cobb and Saito made it out of Limbo. But this is only the tip of the iceberg. Remember when they went to that basement full of men who shared forty hours of dream-time every day? Cobb tried Yusuf's heavy sedative, and the dream was so deep that Cobb spun his top in the bathroom to make sure he had come out of the dream. But if you recall, he knocked the top over before it fell on its own. The whole rest of the movie could be a dream!

In fact, the entire movie could be a dream. After all, Mal and Cobb entered Limbo while "exploring the concept of a dream within a dream." What assurance do we have that when they exited Limbo, they didn't simply rise into a second or third layer of dreaming—like Ariadne and Fischer did when they exited Limbo at the end of the film? Consider that after Cobb assures his Limbo projection of Mal of his knowledge of reality, she retorts, "No creeping doubts? Not feeling persecuted, Dom? Chased around the globe by anonymous corporations and police forces? The way the projections persecute the dreamer?" Even part of Cobb, it seems, is not really sure *the real world* is real. Maybe Mal was right. Maybe she didn't commit suicide. Maybe she woke up.

All in all, it seems that there are four major interpretations of *Inception*.

> **The "Most Real" Interpretation:** Cobb and his crew exist in waking time except for when we are clearly told they are entering dream states. Cobb's wife, Mal, is dead, having killed herself as she tried to "wake up" from her real life, which she believed was a dream. The movie ends with Cobb and Saito exiting Limbo and Cobb finally able to return home to his children in reality.
>
> **The "Mostly Real" Interpretation:** Just like the most real interpretation, except that Cobb and Saito do not fully awake into reality, but into some other part of Limbo or some other dream. Thus, Cobb does not make it back to his children in reality.
>
> **The "Mostly Dream" Interpretation:** What Cobb thinks is reality is reality, including Mal's death. However, when he tries out Yusuf's heavy sedative in his basement, he gets trapped in a dream that is the rest of the movie.
>
> **The "Full Dream" Interpretation:** The entire movie is a dream, which takes place on several different dream levels, all in Cobb's head. When Cobb and Mal woke up from

Limbo, they only woke up into a layer of dreaming they had created to enter Limbo in the first place.[1] They spent so long in Limbo that they forgot, and only because Cobb had incepted Mal in Limbo did Mal think it was a dream, attempt suicide, and wake up. (Perhaps she woke up in reality, perhaps in another layer of dreaming.) None of the other characters are anything but projections of Cobb's subconscious. Even if Cobb did return to what he thought were his real children, in *the real world*, he is still only dreaming.[2]

So which interpretation is correct?

Clues from the Work

One method used to determine which interpretation of an artwork is "correct" involves an internal analysis of the work—what clues does the work itself offer? Sometimes the work gives us a pretty clear-cut answer, but a blessing and a curse of *Inception* is its ambiguity. Proponents of the Most Real view will point out that Cobb's children, Phillipa and James, are played by actors who are two years older in the final scene, and that their clothing is also different in the last shot, lending credence to the view that the children have aged and Cobb really has made it home.[3]

Defenders of the "Mostly Real" hypothesis will argue that the children may only dress differently and look older because Cobb expects them to, and that his expectations determine the content of his dream. In addition, we never see Cobb or Saito commit suicide in Limbo, and the final sequences of the movie seem dreamlike (the film is very slow and jumps from scene to scene with no explanation). Last, the top seems to spin for much longer than is natural.

Proponents of the "Full Dream" hypothesis will point to the many dreamlike elements that *the real world* possesses. Cobb himself informed us, through a conversation with the dream architect, Ariadne, that a way to know that you're dreaming is that you can't explain how you got to your present location.

We see such jumps quite often in *the real world*, including when Cobb mysteriously enters his father-in-law's classroom in Paris without opening the door. In this same scene, Cobb's father-in-law, Miles, implores him to "come back to reality." Of course, we might be meant to take that as a metaphorical reality check. And maybe Cobb opened the door so quietly that Miles didn't hear it. But wait a minute—how did Mal get to the ledge *across* from the hotel room she and Cobb frequented? Are the two ledges connected? Who's to say? That's actually the problem, right?[4] When two careful viewers struggle with the same data and cannot agree on an answer, chances are that one of them is simply getting something wrong. But that's not what we're dealing with here. We're dealing with thousands of viewers, many of them very careful, repeatedly studying the work and struggling to find "the answer." Yet disagreement persists. It seems that Nolan simply has not given us enough information to determine "*the* correct understanding" of the film. Nolan himself addressed this issue in an interview. After acknowledging how many viewers have asked him for "answers" regarding the correct understanding of the film, he says:

> There can't be anything in the film that tells you one way or another because then the ambiguity at the end of the film would just be a mistake. It would represent a failure of the film to communicate something. But it's not a mistake. I put that cut there at the end, imposing an ambiguity from outside the film.[5]

What Nolan Says

So an internal analysis tells us that the film is ambiguous, and Nolan says he made it that way on purpose. Yet Nolan claims to have an "answer" to the meaning of the film. He says:

> I've always believed that if you make a film with ambiguity, it needs to be based on a sincere interpretation.

If it's not, then it will contradict itself, or it will be somehow insubstantial and end up making the audience feel cheated. I think the only way to make ambiguity satisfying is to base it on a very solid point of view of what you think is going on, and then allow the ambiguity to come from the inability of the character to know, and the alignment of the audience with that character.[6]

Clearly, Nolan thinks part of the magic of an ambiguous artwork is that the audience, like the characters, and like real-life human beings, must decide what to believe in the face of incomplete evidence. A work of art from a God's-eye view, in which there is no question about how events are to be understood, rings far less true than a work that forces us to make decisions without full knowledge. And this is part of the beauty of *Inception*. Yet many viewers are still wedded to the idea that there is an answer, a secret to be unlocked, and that the answer lies in Nolan's intention when he created the work. Even if he refuses to tell us what it was, these viewers feel, since Nolan intended a particular interpretation when he created the film, that's the right answer and any view that runs contrary to that is incorrect.

Why We Shouldn't Care What Nolan Says

Again, figuring out the "meaning" of *Inception* is not the same thing as figuring out how much of the movie is a dream. The meaning question, and how it relates to the dream question, is an entirely different issue. But what philosophers have said about meaning, and how to grasp the meaning of art, can help us determine how to interpret the plot of *Inception*.

Many philosophers accept *intentionalism*, the view that the artist's intention determines the meaning of the artwork.[7] But I think that such an approach fails, for three reasons. First, the intentionalist view leaves us with an epistemic (knowledge-related) problem regarding many artworks; many end up either having an unknowable meaning or no meaning at all, both of which are quite counterintuitive conclusions. Second, intentionalism forces us to understand artworks as interpretively static, when they don't seem to be. Third, intentionalism is inconsistent with the view that the concept of art is a social convention that, properly understood, means that artworks are the collective property of the art world.

The Epistemic Problem

This objection stems from the problem that if the meaning of an artwork is rooted in the intention of the artist, we are left with an interpretive hole regarding many works of art. Nolan tells us that he has an answer regarding *Inception*, but that he plans to keep it a secret. This means that if Nolan gets to set the meaning of the work, the rest of us will simply never know the "right answer" regarding the way we ought to interpret the film. Now, maybe one day Nolan will crack and give us his answer (I doubt it), but what's worse is that many artists report that they simply did not intend any particular meaning when they created their works, arguing that their only intention was for each viewer to find her own meaning in the piece (J. R. R. Tolkien made this claim regarding *The Lord of the Rings* in the introduction to that work).[8] Regardless of that intention, if artworks really obtain their meaning through artist's endorsement, we're forced to conclude that these works are simply meaningless, because their artists didn't see fit to give them one. And that doesn't seem right.

Another problem is that some artists appear to change their interpretive account of their works over time, perhaps because they themselves are unsure of the meaning or perhaps because they perceive some benefit from rewriting their account (maybe to accord with a particular political agenda or to cash in on a new trend). In fact, they may even change their mind about how they think the work ought to be understood, or come to view it in a new way. (For instance, Christopher Nolan claimed in an interview that he never detected the connections between filmmaking and the dream-sharing technology in the film—the relationship has to do with simultaneous creation and observation—until it was pointed out to him by his brother.)[9] Regardless, these types of cases raise further concerns regarding the intentionalist view. Do we really want to say that the meaning of artworks can change at the whim of the artists but that they cannot be changed for any other reason? This gives a strange amount of power to the artist and runs contrary to a social understanding of art.[10] (We'll talk more about that below.)

Not to pile on, but some works of art are of unknown authorship, making their meaning forever unknowable on this account. The gravity of this problem should be clear when you consider that many portions of the Bible—certainly a work of art, whether or not you believe it to be divinely inspired—are of unknown or disputed authorship. And even those works with known authors typically do not come packaged with an authorial account of meaning, which leaves the majority of viewers, who lack knowledge of the author's intent, in the dark about the meaning of the work. The intentionalist view forces us to conclude that all of those viewers simply cannot know the meaning of the work or, if they do, they merely lucked into it and don't know that they know it. The epistemic problem with the intentionalist view, then, is that many artworks—including *Inception*—are either meaningless or are interpretive mysteries.[11] And this is quite counterintuitive. Most of us believe that we can derive meaning from a work, even if we do not know what interpretation the artist had in mind, and we don't think the meaning we derive is in some sense wrong, or flawed, if it doesn't accord with the artist's intentions. A position that commits us to believing that most viewers cannot know the meaning of most works of art is therefore one that ought to be rejected.

The Interpretively Static Problem

Setting aside the epistemic problem, even if the artist's intended meaning were knowable in all cases, the intentionalist view would still face the problem of forcing us to the position that artworks are interpretively static. On this view, once the artist has set the meaning of the work, that meaning is fixed for the life of the artwork. This view thus denies one of the features that we tend to value about art. It is generally held that one of the marks of a great work of art is that it continues to be relevant to audiences long after its original context has faded into history, and we tend to fault works that quickly become "dated." Sometimes modern viewers will read an interpretation into a work that the artist could not possibly have intended. There is no way that Sophocles intended for *Oedipus Rex* to be read with a Freudian psychoanalytic spin, but do we want to say that such an interpretation is wrong because the author didn't intend that interpretation? On the contrary, it is typically held that the power and immediacy with which *Oedipus Rex* continues to hit new readers is a mark in its favor, rather than an indication that all of us today are simply involved in a huge misunderstanding of the work.[12]

Despite its success, it is too early to tell whether *Inception* will stand the test of time, and if our great-grandchildren will be arguing about whether or not the top fell. But if viewers are still watching and trying to understand this film in fifty years, it is quite reasonable to suppose that those future audiences will find meaning in the work, connecting it to events or perhaps new ways of thinking or new understandings of dreams and the subconscious that Nolan could not possibly have anticipated. Do we throw out those views as incorrect, and insist that the only way to know the work is to situate it rigidly in the context of its original creation? This runs counter to a fluid understanding of art, one that allows the audiences to impact future understandings of the work, just as the work impacts the audience's future understanding of their world. If we value the ability of an artwork to continue to exist as a dynamic piece, immediate and powerful to ever-changing audiences, we cannot privilege the author with the ability to set the work's meaning for all time.

The Collective Ownership Problem

A third reason why we should believe that artists lack the authority to impose a singular meaning on a work stems from the very definition of art as a social convention. Some philosophers argue that artworks must be understood in relation to other artworks. This view requires a clear rejection of the intentionalist view of artwork meaning because, in this view, the meaning of a work comes partially from *other works*, rather than from the artist. For instance, think of the way music and lighting cue you to anticipate a particular kind of narrative turn as you watch *Inception*. We experience Pavlovian responses to ominous music, such as the "drum drum" in the introductory score of *Inception*—which, interestingly, is really just a sloweddown version of the song (Edith Piaf's "Non, Je Ne Regrette Rien") that is used to time kicks throughout the film—because years of movie watching have primed us regarding the way we should encounter films. Think about something as basic as understanding *Inception* as a work of fiction in which we are invited to suspend our disbelief and suppose, for the duration of the film, that such a thing as dream-sharing is possible. This would not be the effortless transition out of everyday life that it is for us, smoothly executed as we move through the dimming aisle with our popcorn, were we not schooled in the art of film-watching.

Some philosophers place less emphasis on the role of other artworks in setting the stage for our understanding of a work, arguing instead that the concept of art exists because a subset of society, typically referred to as the "art world," has agreed to accept the concept and to set its parameters. To put it a bit more concretely, George Dickie explains that artworks are the kind of things that are deliberately presented to an audience for the purpose of appreciation.[13] This is what sets objects of art apart from ordinary objects—the art objects are the ones that have been purposely held up with an invitation to attend to them, it is hoped with positive results. On this view, there is no such thing as a private work of art. Why? Because it is the act of presenting the object to the audience that transforms it from a private sketch, musings, or experimentation into an actual work of art.

Arthur Danto takes the audience's role with regard to artworks even further, arguing that artworks, as opposed to non-aesthetic objects, engage the audience by inviting them to "finish" the work by shading in the interpretative gaps that have been left in the artwork by the artist. After all, that is why the artists left them there—to be filled in by the audience as part of the aesthetic experience.[14] When we understand an artwork as something that is by definition public in nature, the artist necessarily relinquishes control of the work when he sets it free in the world. The work then becomes the shared property of its society, and everyone is invited to impose their interpretation on it. For instance, one particularly interesting take on the movie comes from Devin Faraci, who argues that *Inception* is a movie about making movies.[15]

In this view, the artist's possession and control of the work end when he presents it to the world as a work of art. Any restrictions regarding acceptable interpretations of the work must be built into the work itself, and to the extent that the artist leaves the work interpretively open, he has surrendered his ability to define the work. This seems to be precisely what Nolan had in mind in telling us that he purposely left the film ambiguous. He appears to be advocating the position that it is each viewer's task to decide what to make of the confusion of information that they receive when they view the film. *The* right answer does not exist, and were Nolan to reveal "his" answer, it would not make a bit of difference, as the whole point of the film is for each of us to discover an answer for ourselves.

So What's the Alternative?

My view, multiplism, says that more than one interpretation of an artwork could be valid, or "correct." Thus, in addition to not giving the intentionalist view priority, *no* one view necessarily gets priority—there could be multiple, equally valid interpretations of an artwork. A common concern regarding this type of view is that it leaves artwork interpretation too open, allowing for an "anything goes" approach to artworks.

For example, we don't want a view that says that an acceptable interpretation of *Inception* is that it is about a troubled guy with parental abandonment issues who dresses up in a scary cape and haunts rooftops seeking to bring bad guys to justice. We'd want to say such an interpretation is acceptable for other Nolan films, such as *Batman Begins* and *The Dark Knight*, but is unacceptable as an interpretation of *Inception*. Fortunately, the view I am defending does allow us to reject such interpretations, for it allows us to dismiss interpretations that are inconsistent with the facts of the film itself. As a result, the artist does have a way to restrict interpretations of his work. Our understanding of an artwork, if it is to be proper, must be consistent with the information the artist chooses to give us.[16] So we are bound to the view that Cobb is highly motivated by the desire to be reunited with his son and daughter, James and Phillipa. It would be inconsistent with the facts of the film to think that his motivation is instead to take over both Saito's and Fischer's energy companies and rule the world. And had Nolan wanted us to be further committed to the views that Phillipa loves ponies and James has a stuffed dog named Sir Barks-a-lot, he would have needed to put that information into the artwork itself, in such a way that any interpretation to the contrary would be inconsistent with the facts internal to the film.

Even once we leave the domain of information that is set by the work itself, we can still evaluate different interpretations, rule out ones that seem wildly implausible, and argue in favor of those that offer the most coherent reading of the film or that are the most helpful depending on the interpreter's particular point of view. In chapter 2, Jason Southworth does just this. Even though he admits to the ambiguity of the film, he offers up his own preferred interpretation of *Inception* and his reasons why it ought to be accepted over other views.

Of course, whatever Nolan's interpretation is, it should be given equal weight with any other equally plausible account. It's just not the only one—or even the most authoritative one. Now that we realize artists don't determine the meaning of their artworks, each of us will have the freedom to take on the task of figuring out *Inception* and other artworks for ourselves.

NOTES

1. Another possibility is that the entire movie is a failed inception on Cobb, performed perhaps by Miles, to trick him into waking up into reality. Andrew Terjesen, a contributor to this volume, favors this interpretation and articulates it in his chapter.

2. As multiple authors and the editor point out many times in this volume, Cobb's top spinning and falling in *the real world* does not actually tell him, or us, that he is not dreaming. There are multiple reasons, the most obvious of which is the fact that Arthur tells Ariadne (and us) that totems tell you only that you are not in someone else's dream. They cannot tell you that you are not in your own dream.

3. http://clothesonfilm.com/inception-jeffrey-kurland-costume-qa/14317/.

4. There are many other dreamlike qualities of *the real world*. For a thorough rundown, see "The Editor's Totem" and Jason Southworth's chapter in this volume. A complete list is also in the appendix of this volume: "A Safe Full of Secrets: Hidden Gems You May Have Missed."

5. Brad Brevet, "Nolan Offers New 'Inception' Insight Prior to Its Debut on Blu-ray and DVD," *Rope of Silicon*, www.ropeofsilicon.com/article/nolan-offers-new-inception-insight-prior-to-its-debut-on-blu-ray-and-dvd, December 2, 2010.

6. Ibid.

7. See Paisley Livingston, *Art and Intention: A Philosophical Study* (Oxford: Oxford University Press, 2007), and William Irwin, *Intentionalist Interpretation: A Philosophical Explanation and Defense* (Westport, CT: Greenwood Press, 1999).

8. Some intentionalists would say that this itself is an intention. See E. D. Hirsch Jr., "Meaning and Significance Reinterpreted," *Critical Inquiry* 11 (1984): 202–225; see also Irwin, *Intentionalist Interpretation*, p. 117.

9. "Dreaming/Creating/Perceiving/Filmmaking: An Interview with Writer/Director Christopher Nolan," interviewed by Jonathan Nolan, in *Inception: The Shooting Script* (San Rafael, CA: Insight Editions, 2010), p. 19.

10. Many intentionalists would say, however, that it is only the original intent that matters.

11. Many intentionalists, however, would say that the text is never meaningless because its meaning is always derived from the artist's original intent. They would admit, though, that sometimes the meaning of a text is forever lost to us, but in this respect works of art are no different than texts of any other kind, including bits of conversation that leave us forever wondering what was truly meant.

12. One way to respond to this worry would be to draw a distinction between meaning and significance, and suggest that meaning is static, but that significance is not. Although the meaning of a work will always remain the same, its significance can alter as culture changes. An example of significance would be the interpretation of *Inception* as a film about filmmaking. See E. D. Hirsch Jr., *Validity in Interpretation* (New Haven, CT: Yale University Press, 1967), p. 8, and also Irwin, *Intentionalist Interpretation*, pp. 46–50.

13. See George Dickie, *Art Circle: A Theory of Art* (Louisville, KY: Chicago Spectrum Press, 1997).

14. For a full explanation of his account, see Arthur C. Danto, *The Transfiguration of the Commonplace: A Philosophy of Art* (Cambridge, MA: Harvard University Press, 1981).

15. Devin Faraci, "Never Wake Up: The Meaning and Secret of Inception," chud.com, July 19, 2010, www.chud.com/24477/NEVER-WAKE-UP-THE-MEANING-AND-SECRET-OF-INCEPTION/. Also, for more on how *Inception* parallels moviemaking, see Daniel Malloy's chapter in this volume.

16. For an opposing intentionalist view see Noël Carroll, "Art, Intention, and Conversation," in Gray Iseminger ed., *Intention and Interpretation* (Philadelphia: Temple University Press, 1992), pp. 97–131. Carroll argues that internally consistent interpretations can be wrong. For example, *Plan 9 from Outer Space* can be consistently interpreted as a parody, though certainly it is not a parody.

LET ME PUT MY THOUGHTS IN YOU: IT WAS ALL JUST A DREAM

Jason Southworth

Cobb: I know what's real.

Mal: What are the distinguishing characteristics of a dream? Mutable laws of physics? Tell that to the quantum physicists. Reappearance of the dead? What about heaven and hell? Persecution of the dreamer, the creator, the messiah? They crucified Christ, didn't they?

Cobb: I know what's real.

Mal: No creeping doubts? Not feeling persecuted, Dom? Chased around the globe by anonymous corporations and police forces? The way projections persecute the dreamer?

—*Inception: The Shooting Script*[1]

In chapter 1, Ruth Tallman argues that there is not just one legitimate interpretation of *Inception*—or of any film, for that matter. I completely agree. But if that is correct, where does it leave us? Are all interpretations equally valid? Is it impossible to offer reasons for preferring one to another? That doesn't seem right, either. I think there can be a "best," or at least a "better," interpretation of some films, and in the case of *Inception*, the best interpretation is this: the entire film—from the opening scene to the closing scene—takes place in Dom Cobb's dream.

A Stalemate between Views

In "The Editor's Totem" you've already learned why the "Full Dream" interpretation of the film is legitimate. Cobb and Saito might not have awoken from Limbo into *the real world*, but instead have awoken just another layer up, in a dream. In the same way, though, Cobb and Mal, after their exit from Limbo, might not have awoken in reality, but just awoken another layer up, in a dream. After all, just like Saito and Cobb, Mal and Cobb arrived in Limbo after going through a layer of dreams under heavy sedation. And where one goes when one exits Limbo is far from clear. (Fischer and Ariadne simply went one level up, to the third layer of dreaming—the G.I. Joe Snow Fortress—when they exited Limbo.) So why do I think that the "Full Dream" hypothesis is the best interpretation?

Most people argue in support of a particular interpretation of a film by pointing to a series of events and scenes that support their position. My favorite example is an extremely subtle clue. When Cobb is explaining to Ariadne how dreams work, he mentions that, when dreaming, "we create and perceive our world simultaneously." What is interesting about this scene is that Nolan chose to start it asynchronously. The audio for the scene starts several seconds prior to the video. Cobb begins talking as a voice-over to the previous scene, where Arthur is setting up the room in which they are dreaming. We as the audience are watching the creation of the dream room at the same time that we perceive the dream environment (the conversation actually taking place in the dream). Nolan appears to be giving us a visual metaphor of the phenomenon that Cobb is describing.

A less subtle example comes from the conversation between Cobb and his father-in-law, Miles. After Cobb spends some time discussing how he has found a way to come home, Miles simply responds, "Come back to reality." If Cobb is dreaming, Miles would be speaking as a manifestation of his own subconscious, reminding him that all of his current experiences are simply a dream.

Two significant visual clues involve Eames. Recall that when Cobb first meets him in Mombasa, Eames is sitting at a dice game, fiddling with (according to the script) "his last two chips."[2] He bets and loses them, but then he goes to cash out and "mysteriously produces two stacks of chips."[3] Where did they come from? Cobb's comment ("I see your spelling hasn't improved"), while looking at one of the chips, clearly indicates that the chips are Eames's forgeries. But Eames didn't have time to make new chips on his walk from the table to the cashier. It seems that, as Cobb's "dream forger," Eames has produced two stacks of forged chips, by pure will, within Cobb's dream. Similarly, Eames supposedly lifts Fischer's passport when they cross paths on the plane.[4] But watch closely—he doesn't do it. In no way does Eames reach anywhere near any of Fischer's pockets. Yet inexplicably, after the next cut, Eames just "produces" the passport and gives it to Cobb. Is Eames "dream-forging" once again?

These examples, and the dozens of others like them,[5] are not conclusive, however. All of these examples can be explained in a way that is consistent with the view that says everything that happens in *the real world* actually is real—the "Most Real" view. Maybe it's just a voice-over. Miles's comment about returning to reality might be meant to be taken figuratively. Maybe those weren't really Eames's last two chips. Perhaps Eames is just that good at lifting passports, or it's an editing mistake.

The same point can be made for the clues that support the "Most Real" view. Proponents of this view like to point to the fact that when Cobb finds his children at the end of the movie, they are wearing different clothes, appear older, and are even played by different actors. This suggests that his children have aged in real time while Cobb has been out of the country, whereas if he was still in his dream it would be likely that the children would look just as they did the last time Cobb saw them. Another bit of evidence comes from Cobb's wedding ring. He doesn't wear it in *the real world*, but does while he is dreaming. The absence of his wedding ring at times is seen as a clear indication of when he is awake, and this includes the end of the movie (although you have to look closely to notice it).

While interesting, none of these points conclusively proves anything. The children, as a part of Cobb's dream, could be dressed differently and appear older simply because Cobb believes that he has returned home after a long time and thus believes that his children should be dressed differently and appear older. A different wardrobe could have been selected, and different actors could have been cast, to achieve this effect. The same could be true of Cobb's ring. Perhaps Cobb dreams that he doesn't wear his ring in that world because Mal no longer appears there, and he believes her to be dead in that world. After all, he did wear the wedding ring in that world before Mal jumped out the window.

Other people argue that the change from reality to dream happens in Yusuf's basement when Cobb tests the drugs. The chief support for this interpretation is the fact that Saito interrupts Cobb when he is checking his top, and we don't see it fall. To this point, we can argue that the totems are simply red herrings. Cobb can construct a reality where the top falls just as easily as one where it does not. In case this point wasn't obvious to you, Arthur comes right out and says a totem can only tell you that you are not in *someone else's dream*, since they don't know how the totem behaves and you do. The top failing to fall would be sufficient evidence that Cobb is in a dream, but the top falling does not give us the same level of confidence that he is not in a dream. As Tallman points out in chapter 1, there is no clue that definitively proves one interpretation over the other.

How to Go Beyond the Evidence

What we are dealing with is the problem of *underdetermination of information*—there is not enough information to prove one hypothesis over the other. This is a common problem that comes up most often in the sciences. The problem arises when the available evidence adequately fits more than one hypothesis. Consider the classic example of Earth's place in the cosmos.

In ancient and medieval times, it seemed obviously true that Earth was stationary and at the center of the universe. It did seem a bit odd that the planets sometimes doubled back on themselves in orbit, but this was easily explained. Ancient thinkers suggested that the planets orbited around points that themselves were orbiting Earth—thus, you would expect to see retrograde motion every now and again.

This geocentric (Earth-centered) view was first defended by Ptolemy (ca. AD 90–ca. 168), in the second century. When Copernicus (1473–1543) came along, however, he suggested that the Sun was the center of the universe.[6] He thought Earth was just another planet that orbited around the Sun and that retrogrades were an illusion created when Earth passed or was passed by another planet in orbit. The problem was, both Ptolemy and Copernicus made the same predictions about where you would see the planets each night, and neither made any unique observable predictions that would prove who was right.[7] Just like the "Full Dream" and "Most Real" interpretations of *Inception*, which theory was true was underdetermined by the evidence. So how did we end up rejecting one and favoring the other?

It took some time, but the heliocentric view was eventually accepted because of its simplicity and scope.[8] "Simplicity" here means observing the principle of parsimony, also known as Occam's Razor. The heliocentric view makes fewer assumptions—there is less "stuff" in it. To work, the geocentric model requires retrogrades, and even retrogrades on retrogrades. The whole thing is quite complex. The heliocentric model requires none of this—just elliptical orbits around the Sun. The greater "scope" of the heliocentric model means it explains more; it answers more questions, making it a more comprehensive theory. An unanswerable problem for the geocentric model was why there were no solar or lunar retrogrades when every other body orbiting Earth doubled back on itself. The heliocentric model gave us the power to solve this problem. There's no solar retrograde because its apparent motion is caused by Earth's rotation, and no lunar retrograde because the Moon orbits Earth. Problem solved.

Unfortunately, the principle of parsimony is not going to help us decide between interpretations of *Inception*. What would it even mean for one interpretation of a movie to be simpler than another? Is it simpler to think everything takes place in one dream plane, or is it simpler to think everything Cobb believes is happening is actually happening? Which interpretation "makes fewer assumptions"? I haven't a clue. Worse yet, *Inception* is a complex film, with a complex narrative structure, dealing with complex issues. A complex explanation might be appropriate. We favor simplicity in science because of the belief that simpler explanations are more likely to be true. This is not the case with fiction, however. We know writers and directors often intend complexity in their films, and in the case of *Inception*, the work was intentionally designed to be ambiguous, adding to the complexity.

So we will have to look elsewhere for a reason to favor one interpretation over another.

A Helpful Principle

The principle that will be most helpful to us is the principle of charity. In a nutshell, the principle says that when a statement is ambiguous and thus has multiple interpretations, we should choose the interpretation that is most charitable. That is, we should choose the interpretation that is kindest to the author of the statement. Not only is this principle "nicer" than one that would choose the unkind interpretation, but using it gets great results.

Suppose someone gives an unclear argument, and there are multiple interpretations of what that person meant. In one interpretation, the argument is good; in another, it is clearly bad. What interpretation should we accept? First, we should attempt to find out what the person intended—preferably by asking him. If, however, the person's intention is unavailable (because he's dead, absent, or unwilling to discuss the matter further), we can't just assume the bad interpretation. As philosophers, we're concerned with truth—not just "winning the day"—so we should interpret the speaker as charitably as we can. In other words, we should assume that the speaker meant to give the best possible version of the argument. After all, if we only show that the weak version of the argument is faulty, we have not shown that the conclusion is unfounded. In short, when possible, we should assume that the arguer does not make stupid mistakes.

Applying the principle of charity when interpreting art, including films, we should prefer interpretations that see the work as a success rather than as a clear failure. To do this, we should pay close attention to criticisms of the work and question whether they are fair, or if there is a way to see these "flaws" as intentional artistic choices that actually make the work stronger and more interesting. With this in mind, let's take a look at some of the major criticisms of *Inception*.

Avoiding Criticism

Watching *Inception* with a critical eye, we can see that there are some serious potential problems with the film. Consider the film's character complexity and development. With the exception of Cobb, all of the characters seem one-dimensional. All we really know about them are their roles in the dream world and the basic elements that motivate the plot. Yusuf is the chemist, Eames is the brains, Arthur is the old friend, Ariadne is the new architect—these characters don't even have last names! When there is slightly more depth, it seems irrelevant. Why are we told Eames likes to gamble, even though it never comes into play? The characters don't grow or change, and their actions appear unmotivated. As a result, it's hard to care about them.

This criticism is compounded when we consider the quality of the writer/director involved. In his other films, Christopher Nolan has proven to be very good at characterization. In *Batman Begins* and *The Dark Knight*, even supporting characters like Jim Gordon (Gary Oldman) and Alfred Pennyworth (Michael Caine) are shown to be robust individuals with complex characters and well-formed motivations. The actors playing the supporting roles in *Inception* are also skilled at their craft. Michael Caine, Ellen Page, Joseph Gordon-Levitt, and Tom Hardy are all excellent performers and have a history as strong supporting actors. With all of these talented artists, from writer and director to actors, it is surprising that *Inception* would be such an epic failure regarding characterization. Given how unlikely that would be, we should look for an interpretation that can explain the lack of characterization as something other than a mistake or flaw of the film.

A second serious issue appears to be sloppy editing. Traditionally, films, especially American films, share a certain visual language. This is not to say that all directors shoot films the same way, or that all editors put films together the same way, but there are conventions to which most filmmakers adhere. One of these conventions is that if people are moving in a scene, they are shown to move, rather than just having them stand in a different place every time the camera cuts. This makes it easier to follow what the characters are doing. With that in mind, go back and pay careful attention to Cobb's time in Paris. When he visits Miles, you see Cobb watching him from outside a closed classroom door. The camera then cuts, and Cobb is inside the room, with the classroom door still closed. Keep watching. A minute later, when Cobb meets Ariadne, there is another odd cut, when in midconversation they move from inside to outside.

No evidence beyond Nolan's *Memento* (2000) should be needed to establish that he is skilled at putting together a film. That film, more than any other in recent years, is all about editing and sequencing. All of the tension and emotional impact of *Memento* come from the ordering of the scenes. Additionally, *Inception*'s editor, Lee Smith, has been editing feature-length films since 1986, averaging about one a year (he was nominated twice for best-editing Academy Awards, once for his work with Nolan in *The Dark Knight*). Given these points, it would be very surprising if *Inception*'s unusual edits were the result of ineptitude or laziness.

Going along with the sloppy editing, there appear to be weak writing choices. During the chase scene in Mombasa, Saito just happens to appear, out of nowhere, at exactly the right time, saying, "Care for a lift. . . . I'm here to protect my investment." Really? Seems pretty unlikely. When Fischer's father gets sick, they replace the desk in his office with a hospital bed. To what end? It seems far more likely that he would be getting personalized care from the best hospitals in the world. Late in the second act Saito buys an airline, instead of bribing a single stewardess. (How is that neater?) These problems sting twice as hard because we know that Nolan is a strong filmmaker who writes tight, methodical scripts.

Thinking back to our aesthetic principle of charity, we should favor interpretations of the film that see these points of criticism as intentional choices by the artist, made to enhance the film, rather than elements that make the film worse. Ultimately, the only interpretation that can do this is the "Full Dream" interpretation. (Unfortunately, for most movies that make such mistakes, the "Full Dream" interpretation is not available.)

Let's deal with the one-dimensional characters first. The film tells us explicitly that characters in dreams are just a manifestation of the dreamer's subconscious, and that these manifestations lack the subtle intricacies of real people. Cobb tells us this toward the end of the film, when he explains to his projection of Mal that she's only a "shade" of his real wife; that's how he knows she is not real. So under the "Full Dream" interpretation, we should expect the characters to seem flat and lacking in nuance. We should also expect that, as manifestations of Cobb's subconscious, the characters would be focused on Cobb, and that is exactly what we get. They unquestioningly follow his orders, seeming to have no goals of their own, and no motivation other than to help Cobb accomplish his goals. Consider Ariadne, who goes out of her way to aid and protect Cobb, at significant risk to herself, even though she has no prior relationship with him and stands to gain nothing of substance. Not only that, but Cobb clearly takes Ariadne's participation for granted, even predicting "She'll be back" when she quits the team after Cobb's manifestation of Mal stabs her. (And, of course, he was right. What he expected to happen, happened—just like in a dream.)

The dream interpretation also makes sense of the sloppy-editing criticism. Cobb's explanation to Ariadne of how dreams work gives us the tools to resolve that criticism. In discussing how dreams often have their own logic that is slightly askew, Cobb explains, "It's only after you wake up that you realize it was strange." The same is true for these "sloppy edits." When you are just watching the film passively, enjoying the journey, you don't notice them. When you stop to reflect on the film (or when you're taking notes while watching it to write a chapter in *Inception and Philosophy*), these cases jump out at you.

This is not a case of reading too much into a line of dialogue, either. The film sets up a visual language that your nose is rubbed into during sequences that we know are a dream. Our introduction to Mal in Saito's dream is a clear example of this. Cobb meets her on the walkway overlooking the ocean. In the middle of that conversation, midsentence, there is a cut, and Cobb and Mal are suddenly in a room and Cobb is preparing to rappel down the side of the building. As previously noted, Ariadne's introduction (which happens in *the real world*) worked the same way—in midconversation, they just appear somewhere else, where the conversation is still going. (In fact, the script describes both of those cuts with the same words—"moments later"—suggesting we should treat them the same. This gives us good reason to think that both scenes take place in a dream.)

Now consider the script problems. Surely, if he'd wanted to, Nolan could have written a better solution to the Mombasa situation than for Saito to show up, out of nowhere, and he certainly could have come up with a better excuse than "I have to protect my investment." Charitably, we should see this as a subtle clue that Cobb is actually dreaming. He dreamed himself into a jam and, deus ex machina, he dreamed himself back out of it.

No set of clues establishes the truth of the "Full Dream" interpretation, but if it is true, *Inception* is a much better movie. And for this reason, the principle of charity demands that we favor it.

"You Never Really Remember the Beginning of a Dream"

A further reason to believe that all of *Inception* is a dream comes not from applying the principle of charity to the film, but from an expectation that Nolan and the others who helped create the film have consistent beliefs.

The most interesting thing about *Inception*, and the reason I think it is a great film, has nothing to do with the story but with how the story is told. Nolan takes many of the stale conventions of action movies that often distract from the narrative and uses them to advance his story. Let's start with the use of slow motion. For almost as long as there have been action movies, there have been slow-motion action sequences. Heroes jump, fall, punch, and shoot in slow motion. This is done to heighten suspense. The longer the slow motion, the longer our feeling of hope, fear, or expectation. The slow motion in *Inception* has the same effect on the audience, but it also literally indicates a difference in the passage of time. When things happen in slower motion in the upper levels of nested dreams, it is to remind the viewer that things are happening more quickly on the lower levels. For example, the van falling into the water is always shown in slow motion because everything that happens on the snow fortress level, from the time of the avalanche to when the snow fortress collapses, happens in the few seconds it takes the van to hit the water.

Another visual trope of action movies is jump-cutting, in which there are a series of quick cuts in a row, some not lasting longer than a second. While not from an action film, the most famous example of this is the shower scene in *Psycho*. Jump-cutting heightens action, often making things appear faster and more chaotic than they were when they were actually shot. Your mind fills in the gaps between these cuts, and you may perceive things that don't actually happen.[9] In *Inception*, however, these cuts are also used to show us what is happening in each of the dream layers at roughly the same time. Jump cuts are the only way to convey this information, as the cuts have to be short to suggest that the events are simultaneous.

Most filmmakers exploit the fact that songs or pieces of scoring make us feel something viscerally. Think of the notes in *Jaws* that signal the shark is coming. We as viewers then see the scene in light of the feeling the music is giving us. *Inception* uses music not just to convey feelings but also to convey story information. When the Edith Piaf song "Non, Je Ne Regrette Rien" plays in the background, we know that there is only a short time left in the dream. And what makes this different from *Jaws* is that in this case, the tone and mood are not set by our visceral reaction to the music. Rather, our conscious recognition of what the music signifies is the key, thus turning the musical convention on its head. Even more to Nolan's credit, both the characters and the audience are aware of the significance of the music, so we are sharing in the emotional response with them.

The obligatory fight scenes play a complex role in *Inception*. Arthur's zero-gravity fight scene in the hotel, for example, is not just one of the most visually compelling fights in movie history, it also plays a role in the narrative. The characters are in free fall because the kick in the first dream happened earlier than expected. Since Arthur is in free fall in the first dream, there is no gravity in the second dream. Again, it looks incredible, but it isn't just cool to look at—there is a point to it.

With all that in mind, consider another cinematic convention that Nolan uses: having the audience join a scene that is already under way. This story-telling technique has been around forever, but it has been used and abused often in films since the mid-1990s, when it was popularized by Quentin Tarantino. The way it works is that rather than the viewer following a scene from the start, a cut puts the viewer in the middle of a scene or a conversation. When this is done effectively, the boring and unnecessary parts of the scene are eliminated (walking into the room, introductions, and so on), and it makes exposition more exciting because we as audience members have to play catch-up to figure out what's going on. *Inception* opens in this way, with Cobb on the beach; it happens again when that scene cuts to Cobb attempting to sell Saito mental protection; and it is repeated again and again.

Knowing that the other conventions are being repurposed in service of the story and expecting consistency give us reason to prefer the interpretation that treats this technique as something that motivates the narrative, rather than just a worn-out movie trick. As Cobb tells Ariadne in her first trip to the dream world, "You never really remember the beginning of a dream . . . you always end up right in the middle of what's going on." So for the sake of consistency, we should see the continued use of the start-in-the-middle-of-the-scene trick as Nolan's way to communicate something to us—that *the real world* is really just a dream.

Is Dreaming Worse?

You might be tempted to think, however, that the "Full Dream" hypothesis makes the movie worse, by negating the "stakes" that we've been caring about throughout the movie. Thus, you might think that the principle of charity calls us to favor the "Most Real" hypothesis. After all, what reason do we have to care about the characters, or anything about the film for that matter, if it is all just a dream? If that thought has crossed your mind, stay tuned for chapter 3. Andrew Terjesen thinks you should still care, even if I am right and *Inception* is, from start to finish, all Cobb's dream.[10]

NOTES

1. Christopher Nolan, *Inception: The Shooting Script* (San Rafael, CA: Insight Editions, 2010), p. 196.

2. Ibid., p. 76.

3. Ibid.

4. He lifts Fischer's wallet in the hotel dream while posing as the blond "lovely lady" in the same way.

5. For more such examples, see "The Editor's Totem" and Ruth Tallman's chapter in this volume.

6. The knowledge that ours is merely one of many solar systems was not discovered until much later.

7. Actually, the heliocentric theory predicts parallax, and the geocentric theory does not. Distant stars should appear in slightly different places during different seasons if we orbit around the Sun. At the time the theories were competing, we didn't have powerful enough telescopes to observe such differences. We do now, and parallax is now a well known phenomenon.

8. There are, of course, more criteria to look at when comparing hypotheses. A good scientific hypothesis is also testable (makes observable predictions), fruitful (gets those predictions correct), and conservative (does not contradict things that we already think we know). This is, for example, why creationism and intelligent design shouldn't be taught in science classrooms—they fail to make successful predictions, they raise more questions than they answer, they invoke extra mysterious forces when none are needed, and they conflict with numerous established facts. Evolution, on the other hand, has made countless successful predictions, explains phenomena in every area of science, requires no mysterious entities (just sexual reproduction and time), and doesn't contradict anything we know to be true, but in fact coheres with our knowledge (for instance, the fossil record). For more on how to use scientific criteria for comparing hypotheses in everyday life, see Theodore Schick and Lewis Vaughn's *How to Think about Weird Things: Critical Thinking for a New Age*, 6th edition (New York: McGraw-Hill, 2010).

9. Like in the example of the scene in *Psycho*, where people thought they saw Janet Leigh's nipple, which was not there.

10. I would like to thank Ruth Tallman and David Kyle Johnson for their helpful comments on previous drafts of this chapter.

EVEN IF IT IS A DREAM, WE SHOULD STILL CARE

Andrew Terjesen

It's never just a dream, is it?
—Dom Cobb

Inception is highly ambiguous and open to interpretation. In fact, it's possible that the entire movie is a dream. Some critics, though, have suggested that it diminishes the movie to think that it's all a dream. They contend that since we don't ultimately care about what happens in our dreams, we don't care about a movie that only depicts a dream. As we'll see, though, such critics are misguided. It's absurd to say, "I can't care about this movie because it was a fictional dream instead of a fictional reality."

Dreams Don't Matter?

I favor the interpretation of *Inception* that says *the real world* is a dream in which Cobb has become trapped.[1] The Fischer inception was a Trojan horse for the real inception organized by Miles (Cobb's father-in-law) to try and create the idea in Cobb's head that he has become trapped in a dream so that he'll finally respond to his kick and wake up. Ariadne could be Cobb's daughter trying desperately to get him out (after all, what proof do we have that his daughter is as old as she appears in his memories?) or a projection of his subconscious. In my interpretation, it doesn't matter whether the totem falls or not at any point in the film. Even if it does, Cobb could still be dreaming. The totem was Mal's, after all, so there is no reason why it would be a reliable anchor to reality for Cobb. Remember, the whole point of the totem is that it should be something that no one else has touched; for it to work, only the owner can know its weight and feel.[2]

Of course, you might feel equally strongly about a different interpretation of the events in *Inception*, and that is part of the movie's appeal. Christopher Nolan has said that it was his intention to make a film that was ambiguous and that produced heated but ultimately irresolvable conflicts.[3] The ending of the *Inception* script just reads: "Behind him, on the table, the spinning top is STILL SPINNING. And we—FADE OUT. CREDITS. END."[4] It's just not meant to be resolved.

When *Inception* premiered it provoked a polarizing response among the critics, dividing them into two main camps. Not between those who thought the movie ended in *the real world* and those who thought it ended in a dream, but between those who thought the movie was a satisfying film and those who thought it was emotionally empty. Most people who fell into the latter camp complained that the film's basic premise made it impossible to create an emotionally satisfying narrative. As the review in the *Village Voice* summed it up:

> There's no push-pull around Leo's torrid emoting, and when the "We're awake now—*or are we?*" kicker catches you in the pants, who cares? It's obvious that Nolan

either can't articulate or doesn't believe in a distinction between living feelings and dreams.[5]

The *Wall Street Journal* more clearly attributes the problem to the premise of the story (as opposed to Nolan's directing):

> Dreams and movies have a kinship as old as cinema itself. . . . Both dreams and movies provide an alternate reality. . . . But "Inception" reneges on the implicit deal: By convoluting the various planes of experience, by overlapping and obscuring ostensible realities and ostensible dreams, Mr. Nolan deprives us the opportunity of investing emotionally in any of it.[6]

For most of us, the stacking and blurring of levels of dreaming are what make *Inception* so enjoyable, as we find it rewarding to untangle the different threads of narrative. For a small but vocal group of critics, though, it makes the movie impossible to care about.

Spinning, Falling, or Perpetually Wobbling, It's Still Just a Movie

It might not seem very philosophical to talk about these critics' dislike for *Inception*, but the issues they raise about the film present an interesting paradox. Look at what the Toronto *Globe and Mail* had to say about the film:

> Our eye may be dazzled by the surreal sights, but our mind tends to shout in protest, "Stop. This is a cheat. Since the movie has abandoned even the pretense of realism, traded in for a realm where everything is possible but nothing is palpable, where even a fired gun lacks any true consequence, then I've lost any reason to believe and, with it, any motive to care. If the dreamer feels nothing, neither do I." . . . So blind to the big fat

problem that won't go away—you can't feel for anyone when nothing feels real.[7]

I suspect that the critics who reacted this way to *Inception* are probably not fans of science fiction films in general.

Still, *Inception* seemed to provoke an especially strong response, and it wasn't just the usual problem that things were too fantastical on the screen to seem real. The nature of *Inception* created a level of uncertainty that can only occur in a specific kind of science fiction film. As other chapters in this book point out, there is no way to tell whether *the real world* of the film is actually real. There is no totem or other marker that signals, for sure, if or when all dreaming has ceased—when the setting of the events of a scene we are watching is actual reality.[8]

That's the thing, though. It's a movie; regardless of what interpretation you like, none of it is actual reality. Even if the film somehow made it clear that Cobb was awake while planning the inception, the world we inhabit doesn't contain dream-sharing briefcases. So even if he and his dream team are awake, they aren't in the real world—the world we occupy. Even if our world did contain dream-sharing technology, it would still be a fictional story. That's what's so paradoxical about the critics' negative response to *Inception*. Since they know they are watching a film and that none of it is real, why should it matter whether the film takes place in a fictional dream world or a fictional *real world*? It's not real, either way.

These critics seem to believe that only some fictional worlds can be emotionally moving (even though we know they aren't real). Before we can figure out what separates the fictional world of *Inception* from the fictional world of, say, Todd Solondz's *Life during Wartime* (a movie that came out in the United States at the same time as *Inception* and was mentioned as the right kind of movie to care about in more than one negative review of *Inception*), we need to consider the more basic problem of why we care about anything that is not real. This is the paradox of fiction.

The Paradox of Fiction

The philosopher Colin Radford (1935–2001) explored this problem in the context of Anna Karenina.[9] According to Radford, there seems to be a problem when we become worried about the fates of fictional characters like Anna Karenina or Dom Cobb. The problem is that our fear for Dom's safety when he is being chased through the streets of Mombasa is a fear that he will be hurt or killed if he gets caught. Dom isn't in any danger, though (and I don't mean because I think he is *actually* asleep in some lab with a worried Mal hoping he will finally wake up). Dom is not a real person, so Dom by definition can't be hurt. Worrying about Dom's safety makes about as much sense as worrying about whether Santa Claus will get cancer from the hole in the ozone layer. Nonexistent entities can't feel anything and can't experience anything.

The paradox of fiction consists of three claims that can't all be true. Here they are illustrated using a movie-watcher's fear upon seeing the locomotive bearing down on Cobb and company in level one of the Fischer inception:

1. Feeling fear requires a belief that the locomotive barreling down a city street is a threat to one's safety. (Let's call this the "Threat Claim.")
2. People do not believe that the locomotive they see on the screen is a real threat because they believe that it doesn't exist. (Let's call this the "Nonexistence Claim.")
3. People are *actually* scared by the locomotive they see on the screen. (Let's call this the "Fear Claim.")

The most obvious way to get rid of the paradox is to reject the Nonexistence Claim. People sometimes refer to this as "suspension of disbelief." When we are in the theater, we forget that we don't believe that what is happening is real. As Radford and others have pointed out, though, this just doesn't seem to be a credible response. If you believed that the locomotive was real, you should have been running out of the theater to avoid getting hit by it when it was coming at you. Besides, how does one suspend disbelief? How do you will it so that you believe something or that you no longer believe it? In order to will it, you'd have to be aware (somewhere in the back of your mind) that it wasn't real. So Radford doesn't want to reject the Nonexistence Claim.

Yet Radford is also convinced that the Fear Claim is true. People do cry during emotional scenes in movies, which seems to be a display of genuine emotion. All that is left is the Threat Claim. Does Radford reject it?

No. To support the Threat Claim, Radford gives the example of someone being told about the plight of a neighbor. As the details of the situation are described, we are moved to pity. But then imagine that we find out that the whole story is made up— that the neighbor described is made up, the circumstances never happened, and so on. Radford claims that we would immediately feel our pity dissipate on learning this. It seems, then, that we need to believe in the existence of something in order to feel for it.

Since Radford accepts all three premises, he admits that he sees no solution to the problem—it's a paradox of fiction. Because our fear at the locomotive involves a set of inconsistent beliefs, Radford states that the response is irrational. Not surprisingly, a lot of philosophers take umbrage at the idea that they are irrational if they are moved by something like Fischer's reconciliation with his father.

Don't Worry, You're Not Really Scared

An influential line of thought on the paradox of fiction argues that the Fear Claim is false. We don't experience actual emotions when we engage with fiction. According to philosopher Kendall Walton, we're not really afraid for Mal's safety when she is dangling on a ledge.[10] Walton, however, cannot deny that we act as if we are scared (the actions that Radford mistook for evidence of real emotions). So he needs to explain what we are experiencing when we are watching Mal on the ledge.

According to Walton, we know that Mal is not real. There is no "suspension of disbelief" where we forget that we are watching a movie in a dark theater. We know that the scene is being acted out by Marion Cotillard and Leonardo DiCaprio on a sound stage. So when we're watching *Inception* we pretend that we are seeing a real confrontation between Mal and Cobb. We make believe that it's possible to enter people's dreams and get lost in a dream reality. It's our ability to act *as if* there is a woman who thinks she is still trapped in a dream threatening to really kill herself that enables us to exhibit the behaviors that Radford confuses with real emotions.

This may seem to be a strange view because it sounds like we are constantly playacting while we watch a movie (or read a book), but that is not what Walton means when he says we're not genuinely afraid for Mal's safety. Pretending that we see a woman in front of us about to jump out a window causes us to have a reaction. The pretense can get our heart rate going, cause us to shout out, or cry. According to Walton, though, this reaction is not the same as genuine fear. It is merely quasi-fear, because it has some of the features of fear but is not fully experienced the way we would feel fear if we were watching a woman in real life hanging out a hotel window. After all, while a movie can provoke some reactions in its audience, we don't do everything we would do if we were really afraid for Mal. Certainly, no one is calling 911 to report a suicide attempt. That's just one of the most obvious examples of the difference between genuine fear and quasi-fear. If you reflect on your own experiences, you can probably detect other differences as well.

While Walton's view has persuaded a number of philosophers, it also has its staunch opponents. According to Walton's critics, the biggest problem is that he is not very clear about what makes something an example of quasi-fear as opposed to genuine fear.

The Art of Feeling about Art

The philosopher Noël Carroll offered a different take on our reaction to movies in his book *The Philosophy of Horror, or Paradoxes of the Heart* (the paradox of fiction was one of two paradoxes he dwells upon in the book).[11] Carroll does not deny that people are experiencing real emotions when watching a horror movie. Instead, he rejects the Threat Claim. We don't need to believe that some real object poses an actual threat in order to provoke a reaction in the audience. Carroll argues that we can react to ideas as well as things.

According to Carroll's "thought theory" (so as to distinguish it from Walton's "make-believe theory"), when we are watching Fischer experience a happy resolution in his relationship with his father, we react to the idea of joy that the scene presents. The idea of joy presented by the scene produces an emotion in us that is a genuine feeling. Carroll is very careful, however, to classify our reaction to the film as an example of an "art emotion." Art emotions are still emotions, but they are emotional reactions to ideas, not to things. Imagine that Fischer is a friend of yours and you witness him finally coming to terms with all the expectations his stern father placed on him. As you see him pull the revised will and the homemade pinwheel out of the safe, you feel joy at his epiphany. Your joy would be a physical sensation directed at your friend Fischer, and it would undoubtedly have a visceral feel. Contrast that with how you feel when I tell you the story of someone who lived a long time ago and stopped living under his father's shadow. Your joy would have a more detached, abstract quality. It would be an example of art joy.

The thought theory explains our investment in the ending of *Inception*. Depending on whether the totem falls or not, the viewer is presented with different ideas in the film. If the totem falls, then you could view the film as being about the importance of letting go of one's guilt. If it keeps spinning, then it might be about the tendency we have toward self-deception. We care about what the movie is depicting because it determines the appropriateness of our emotional response. Our art relief (as opposed to genuine relief) at seeing Cobb come to terms with Mal's death will seem disingenuous if it turns out that the film is meant to end with Cobb trapped in a dream.

Although he has tried to leave the movie open-ended enough for different interpretations of what happens (how much of the movie is a dream), Nolan has weighed in on what he thinks the movie is about and how that is reflected in the final scene. In an interview Nolan said,

> I put that cut there at the end, imposing an ambiguity from outside the film. That always felt the right ending to me—it always felt like the appropriate "kick" to me. . . . The real point of the scene—and this is what I tell people—is that Cobb isn't looking at the top. He's looking at his kids. He's left it behind. That's the emotional significance of the thing.[12]

Nolan admits that this particular interpretation says as much about him as the film. He claims, "I choose to believe that Cobb gets back to his kids, because I have young kids. People who have kids definitely read it differently than those who don't."[13]

Nolan's emotions toward the film seem to be rooted in ideas that could affect us regardless of whether Cobb is still dreaming. Even if he doesn't wake up, we can be moved, like Nolan, by his decision to focus on his children. At the same time, this kind of emotional response seems to rely upon the belief that things worked out in *the real world*. Nolan's claim that he imposed ambiguity, and that he chooses to believe Cobb returned to his children, suggests that he finds it difficult to connect with the film without seeing it as having "really" happened.

Maybe We Just Can't Help Ourselves

Although Radford continues to defend his position that our emotional responses to fiction are irrational, most philosophers have chosen to side with some variation of Carroll's or Walton's proposal. There is a small (and growing) minority who think that the whole paradox is misconceived, as it is based on a very specific idea of emotion. Both Carroll and Walton describe emotion as something that we experience on a conscious level, which is why Walton thinks our responses to fiction don't qualify as real emotions and Carroll thinks that emotions can be produced by conscious thoughts. Many things that we call emotions are not experienced consciously, however. Fear can be experienced as a physiological response (sweating, heart racing, and so on) without any conscious thoughts concerning the cause of our fear. The ambiguity in the word "emotion" creates a paradox where there is none because the emotions referred to in the Threat Claim and the Fear Claim are not necessarily the same thing. If our fear of the locomotive on the screen is understood as a physiological response and the claim that our fear reactions must be motivated by things that we perceive to be real threats is a requirement only for conscious emotions directed at real objects, then all three claims can be true without contradicting one another.

Philosopher Norman Kreitman follows this line of reasoning and claims that our emotional responses to fiction are real, even though we know that what we are seeing is not.[14] If we are upset when we see Saito get shot, it's not because we are upset that someone called "Saito" was really shot. Instead it is because we are upset at people being shot. Even if no one in the world has ever been shot, we could still be upset imagining someone getting shot. Kreitman argues that our emotional responses to fiction are mediated by our imagination, and recent neuropsychology suggests a new explanation for why we are upset about Saito being shot.

Neuroscientific evidence suggests that all our thoughts contain emotional components, which help us sort through information quickly.[15] A fear of guns, for example, is a much quicker and more efficient way to recognize that a situation is dangerous than trying to calculate the odds of getting hurt or killed when we see a gun. Since our thoughts have ties to our emotions, those thoughts also cause us to feel the emotions they are connected with. The particular situation might affect how we think, and that explains why fiction or fantasy does not usually stir up the same response as a real event. The thought that "there is a loaded gun pointed at me or my loved one" will be connected to a very visceral response prompting us to act immediately, while the thought that "there is a prop gun filled with blanks pointed at the character Ken Watanabe is playing" will be connected to a weaker feeling of discomfort because that kind of thought does not require immediate action.[16] Also, the association between particular thoughts and particular emotions is something we learn over time and through experience. That means that different people could develop different responses to seeing Saito shot and dying.

As Kreitman describes it, the particular properties of the scenes in *Inception* resemble aspects of our real-world experiences and consequently play on the emotions we associate with those aspects. This may sound very similar to Carroll's "thought theory" because it involves thoughts and ideas about fiction provoking emotional responses. It is not exactly the same view, however. First of all, Kreitman uses "thoughts and ideas" in a very broad sense to include automatic reactions with no conscious component. You might not be aware that guns scare you, but seeing one gets your heart racing. Second, Carroll thinks of the emotions produced by art as being a specific kind of "intellectual" emotion, so-called art emotion. Kreitman, by contrast, equates our stress at seeing Saito getting shot with our stress at seeing a real person getting shot.

Can You Relate?

It's a stereotype of philosophers that we don't provide any answers (if anything, we just create more questions and confusion), and to a certain extent I am going to feed that stereotype. I have presented several viable solutions to the paradox of fiction, but I can't say that one of them is obviously the right answer. Despite not knowing what view is correct, though, I can tell you that Radford's view is incorrect. Our emotional response to Saito being near death is not irrational just because we know Saito isn't real.

Even though I cannot present a definitive solution to the paradox of fiction, there is an interesting trend in the debate that suggests a convergence on at least part of the paradox. And it's the part that is most pertinent to our central question: Why is it that some critics think that the world of *Inception* is more fake (and therefore less emotionally engaging) than the fictional world of, say, a Wes Anderson or a David Fincher movie?

In defending the positions of Carroll and Walton, proponents have increasingly turned to the process of imaginative simulation. Make-believe is obviously imaginative simulation. Art emotions also depend on our ability to imagine what it would be like if it were happening to us. The strength of our imaginative simulation in either case is going to depend on how well we can imagine what it would be like to be in that situation or to be that character. Most people rely on their own experiences to predict what it would be like to be in a fictional situation. If the situation or character they are trying to imagine is too far removed from everyday life, then they can't create that quasi-emotional response. Kreitman's solution to the paradox also relies on how closely the world of fiction resembles the world that we consider real. If it seems real enough, it can "trick" us into experiencing a physiological response.

So even though we can't say for sure who has the right view concerning how we are moved by fictions, all of the plausible views converge on this point: our engagement with fiction is dependent on our ability to relate to the situation. We don't have to believe that something is real (or even could happen at some underdetermined point in the future), we just need to think that there is something relevant to our existence in the fiction we are watching. This is akin to what happens to dream-sharers in the movie. They know it is a dream.[17] And, at least in the world of *Inception*, you cannot die in a dream. It should be the case that the dream-sharers are not scared of oncoming locomotives or being shot, but they are, because it hurts to be shot or hit by a runaway train. And, as is the case in the main heist, if they die they will fall into Limbo and might never wake up. They are never afraid, however, that a real locomotive could hurt them. What moves them to action is what the locomotive represents. The pain that locomotive would cause them (even in a dream) makes the situation relevant to them through the possibility of experiencing pain. We are moved by fictions because something is at stake for us, or at least because they remind us of a time when something was at stake.

For almost all of us, thinking that we are watching something that *could* really happen is enough to engage our emotions. For some reason, though, a number of critics find it much easier to relate to a story of a family trying to move on after their pedophile father has been released from jail (part of the plot of *Life during Wartime*) than the story of a man trying to forgive himself for past mistakes and return to his children. This shows us that what engages us depends entirely on what we choose to focus on in a fictional story. Some critics were much more interested in the nihilistic and dark themes of Solondz's film than they were in the more uplifting resolution of Nolan's film.[18] It's probably not a coincidence that the superhero film that has received the best overall critical response was Nolan's own *The Dark Knight*, with its morality in shades of gray and tragic ending. A lot of critics must not lead very happy lives.

A Failed Inception

The ambiguity at the end of *Inception* makes it impossible to say for sure what the film is really about. But ambiguous endings are nothing new to fiction. Does anyone ever triumph over the villain in a horror film? Freddy Krueger, Michael Myers, and Jason Voorhees are always waiting to pop up again at the end to remind us it's not over. Or what about another ending with a very well placed cut, the end of *The Sopranos*? Was Tony whacked at the end or not? Was *The Sopranos* showing us how a criminal life always ends badly or showing us that sometimes the criminals do get away with it?

To take issue with *Inception* because its premise has an inescapable ambiguity is unfair to the film. In the end, we choose to engage with fictions because we look for ways that they connect with our concerns and ideas. It seems true (as Kreitman points out) that we are hard-wired to respond more easily to some fictional situations than others, but that is not a reason to discount the value of situations that require more effort. After all, we seem to be hard-wired to find fart jokes and other scatological humor funny, but that doesn't make them superior to sophisticated humor. If anything, we have greater appreciation for the things that require greater effort.

If nothing else, critics should appreciate how *Inception* is crafted; it has all the features of a dream as described in the movie. While we assume there is action between the scenes we see, that's no different from a dream where we jump from one significant moment to the next, thinking that something must have gotten us from point A to point B. When Ariadne is in the Paris bistro, she thinks she knows how she got there. It's only when Cobb presses her on it that she realizes the truth—the bistro is a dream. When we first saw the scene, we assumed that they had traveled there off-camera. We later realized how Nolan's careful editing tricked us. Couldn't the same careful editing of scenes on a plane, in an airport, and at a house with his children give us the erroneous impression that Cobb made the trip across the ocean in *the real world*? To make a film with so many ambiguous scenes is a lot harder than the prevailing formula (in most of those "realistic" indie dramas that critics fawn over) of giving every character who seems to have a perfect life a dark secret.

Many critics, even those who liked *Inception*, had problems with its final act in the mountains. Their attitude seemed to be: why is that there now? As if it made no sense that things would be a bit surreal in the part of the movie that (without needing to check one's totem) was depicting a dream. Every character at that level knew it was a dream. It would be unusual if it weren't surreal. Besides, Ariadne needed to create an environment that had a safe where Fischer's secrets were hidden, that Fischer would want to break into. If critics can't open themselves up to that aspect of the film, it's not surprising that the rest of *Inception* had difficulty reaching them emotionally. It's as if the film was a failed inception for them—an inception that would have taught them to not take fiction so seriously.

NOTES

1. I constantly waver on whether I think that Mal was right and she escaped or that she really died and afterward Cobb retreated into a dream surrounded by memories.

2. See the "The Editor's Totem" and Ruth Tallman's and Jason Southworth's chapters for more reasons to think that the entire film is a dream.

3. Jeff Jensen, "Christopher Nolan on His 'Last' Batman Movie, an 'Inception' Video Game, and That Spinning Top," *Entertainment Weekly*, http://insidemovies.ew.com/2010/11/30/christopher-nolan-batman-inception/. Retrieved January 10, 2011.

4. Christopher Nolan, *Inception: The Shooting Script* (San Rafael, CA: Insight Editions, 2010), p. 218.

5. Nick Pinkerton, "The Dream Is Dead: *Inception* Fails to Get Inside Our Head," *Village Voice*, www.villagevoice.com/2010-07-13/film/the-dream-is-dead-inception-fails-to-get-inside-our-head/. Retrieved January 10, 2011.

6. John Anderson, "'Inception': To Dream, Perchance to Sleep," *Wall Street Journal*, http://online.wsj.com/article/SB10001424052748703394204575367412265057270.html?mod=WSJ_ArtsEnt_LifestyleArtEnt_2. Retrieved December 18, 2010.

7. Rick Groen, "As Dreamy Looking as Its Star, but Not a Dream of a Movie," *The Globe and Mail*, www.theglobeandmail.com/news/arts/as-dreamy-looking-as-its-star-but-not-a-dream-of-a-movie/article1641429/. Retrieved March 14, 2011.

8. As has been pointed out to me by my skillful editor, some people think that Cobb's wedding ring is the "real" totem. I must admit, I hadn't paid much attention to that detail. I won't rule out the possibility that that was Nolan's totem for the audience (much like the color red in *The Sixth Sense*), but the same problem remains: It's hard to see clearly whether Cobb is wearing his wedding ring or not at the end. More important to the point I'm making, Cobb's wedding ring may only symbolize *the real world* where Cobb thinks Mal is dead; there is no way to prove that *the real world* isn't a level of dreaming.

9. Colin Radford and Michael Weston, "How Can We Be Moved by the Fate of Anna Karenina?" *Proceedings of the Aristotelian Society, Supplementary Volumes* 49 (1975): 67–93. It's worthy of note that, despite appearances, this article is not coauthored, but was published as a discussion between Radford and Weston. The argument and ideas discussed above are wholly Radford's.

10. Kendall Walton, "Fearing Fictions," *Journal of Philosophy* 75.1 (1978): 5–27.

11. Noël Carroll, *The Philosophy of Horror; or, Paradoxes of the Heart* (New York: Routledge, 1990).

12. Jensen (November 20, 2010).

13. Robert Capps, "Inception's Director Discusses the Film's Ending and Creation," *Wired*, www.wired.co.uk/magazine/archive/2011/01/play/inception-director-lives-the-dream. Retrieved January 24, 2011. This quote might make one think, contrary to the claims of the first two chapters of this book, that Nolan has revealed his answer to "Was it all a dream?" If Nolan believes that Cobb really gets back home to his children, mustn't he also think the real world to which Cobb returns is real? But it's unclear whether, in this quote, Nolan is stating the interpretation he had in mind as he made the film or whether he is saying how he chooses to view the film now that it is complete. Since he uses the word "choose," it seems that he is describing how he, as a member of the public to which his film has been presented, reacts to the film—not how he intended the film to be interpreted.

14. Norman Kreitman, "Fantasy, Fiction, and Feelings," *Metaphilosophy* 37 (5) (2006): 605–622.

15. The neuroscientist Antonio Damasio did a lot of research on the connections between our thoughts and our emotional states. He argued in his book, *Descartes' Error: Emotion, Reason and the Human Brain* (New York: HarperPerennial, 1995) that our physiological states become connected to different concepts and thoughts in order to assist us in efficient decision-making. He further developed this thesis about the connections between emotion and reason in his later books.

16. I know that we wouldn't normally describe our thoughts about a movie that way, but if the Nonexistence Claim is true and we don't believe the movie is real, then we are implicitly thinking a thought like the one I described.

17. I'm ignoring those who have become lost in the dream, as Cobb may have. Those dream-sharers are akin to those who truly experience "suspension of disbelief" and reject the Nonexistence Claim. They don't know that what they are experiencing doesn't actually exist, but there is no paradox in fearing what you think will kill you.

18. Admittedly, it is up to the actors to make these themes salient to us. Some critics who panned *Inception* put the blame on DiCaprio and the rest of the cast for not emoting enough, but I think that those critics were already inclined against caring about those themes that would put a much larger burden on the cast than if it had been a more realistic film.

THE UNAVOIDABLE DREAM PROBLEM

James T. M. Miller

> Dreams feel real while we're in them. It's only when
> we wake up that we realize something was actually
> strange.
>
> —Dom Cobb

At its heart, *Inception* is a film about dreams and reality. Are we experiencing a real external world or merely one that our (or someone else's) subconscious is filling? *The Matrix*, *eXistenZ*, and *Vanilla Sky* all involve characters believing the world is real, when it is not. *Inception* flips this trend on its head with a character who believes the world is a dream, when it is not. Mal, Cobb's wife, jumps out a hotel window believing that *the real world* is in fact a dream from which her death will cause her to wake.

But can we *know* that Cobb was right, and Mal was wrong— that the so-called *real world* of *Inception* is real? Other chapters in this book look at the movie for clues, but here we consider a broader question. Can we know that we are not dreaming, like Cobb supposedly did? As we will see, what at first seems like a trivial, somewhat silly, philosophical puzzle is a real cause for concern—a real threat to our knowledge. If we can't know whether Mal was dreaming, we can't know whether we are dreaming.

The Dream Problem

The issue of whether we can know that we are not dreaming is fundamental to epistemology—the branch of philosophy that studies knowledge. The possibility that Mal is right points to *radical skepticism*, the view that knowledge is impossible. Why would anyone take this position? Consider the hypothesis that you are, right now, asleep and vividly dreaming of reading this book. How would you prove this isn't happening? You might firmly grip this book (or your Kindle) to verify it is solid, ask someone near you if you are awake, or even pinch yourself. But the very experiences these "tests" produce—the feeling of solidity, hearing the words "Yes, you are awake," and not awaking after a pinch—can also be dreamed. So these tests do not prove anything.

But isn't it obvious that you are awake? After all, no strange dreamlike things are happening. But of course, we have all had that dream that was just as obviously real as our waking life. We may have even considered the possibility that we were dreaming and dismissed it, because the dream was so obviously real. Of course afterward, we may have wondered how we could have thought this. But, as Cobb pointed out in the quote that begins this chapter, while dreams are happening they do not seem strange. "It's only when we wake up that we realize something was actually strange." In fact, the reason bad dreams often wake us up is that they seem real. So the non-strangeness and obvious reality of the real world cannot be used as evidence that it is in fact real. Dreams can have these same qualities.

And if we can't be sure we are even awake, what can we be sure of? Certainly not the host of other things that are less obvious than the existence of the real world—the existence of other minds, the existence of God, the ethical beliefs we hold dear. Even things like $1 + 1 = 2$ are subject to doubt. You think this is true—obviously true—even true by definition. But isn't it possible that you have been deceived by something like the Matrix into thinking that "$1 + 1 = 2$ is obviously true by definition," when in reality 1 and 1 total 3? In fact, anything that is false could be dreamed to be true—so, it seems, we can be certain of nothing at all. How can we know anything? This is radical skepticism.

Christopher Nolan knows that we will instinctively feel that Mal must be mad and that Cobb is sane. But radical skepticism undermines that instinct. Maybe Mal was not so crazy after all.

Ways Out of Skepticism:
(1) Descartes' Solution

The philosopher René Descartes (1596–1650) attempted to refute radical skepticism by establishing one piece of absolute certainty as a foundation stone upon which all other human knowledge could be built. If he was successful, we can use his argument to eliminate our own doubts; perhaps we can even establish that Cobb was right in believing that he was awake and that Mal was wrong in believing that she was still dreaming.

Descartes raised skeptical doubts in several ways, by realizing that his senses sometimes deceived him, that he could be dreaming, and that he could be deceived by an evil demon (a scenario updated to virtual reality in *The Matrix*). For example, he knew his senses had led him astray in the past— like when they told him that a stick placed in a cup of water was bent, when in fact it was straight. What assurance did he have that his senses were not always leading him astray?

Ultimately, Descartes realized that there was one thing he could not doubt—his own existence.[1] Why? Because in performing the very act of doubting, he must exist. He cannot persuade himself that there is no world unless he exists. An evil demon cannot fool Descartes, unless he exists to be fooled. So, "the proposition, *I am*, *I exist*, is necessarily true whenever it is put forward by me or conceived in my mind."[2]

If Descartes is right, each one of us can be sure of the existence of our thoughts and ourselves. But if this is all that we can ever be sure of, what use is it? Can it be used to prove the existence of the external world or that we are not dreaming? It would seem not. This is Mal's problem. She believes in her own existence, but cannot prove that she is not dreaming, and it leads her to jump out a window.

Descartes, though, believed there was a way to move beyond the knowledge that he existed as a thinking thing. He had an idea of a perfect being, God, which he believed could not simply have been created by his own imperfect mind. In fact, the only thing that could create such an idea was the perfect being itself. So, Descartes concluded, God, a perfect being, exists.

How does this get us knowledge of the world? If the world is not real, then Descartes is being deceived on a grand level. But if he is being deceived, that perfect being must either be doing the deceiving or at least allowing Descartes to be deceived. But a perfect being would never do either of these things because "all deception or fraud involves some imperfection."[3] So, Descartes concluded that what his senses tell him clearly and distinctly must be true. Since the senses incline him to believe that the world is real, belief in the existence of the world is justified. Knowledge of the world is grounded.

There are problems, however. Descartes' argument for the existence of God relies on the supposition that something less perfect cannot create something more perfect. Descartes thinks this is clearly and distinctly true, but cannot this be doubted? Can't we imagine a scientist creating a robot that far exceeds his own perfection? To create the idea of God, all one needs is to experience a being and something getting better. From there one could conceive of a being that cannot get better—a perfect being. In fact, many evolutionary psychologists suggest that belief in God comes from humans anthropomorphizing impersonal natural forces. Of course, they might be wrong. But in order for Descartes' argument to work, they have to be necessarily wrong; a perfect being has to be the only possible source of such an idea. Clearly this is not the case.

We can still be wrong about what we believe; we could be dreaming or otherwise deceived. Descartes' arguments cannot save us from the radical skepticism that Mal suffers from. So we still lack a principled reason to think that Cobb is correct.

Ways Out of Skepticism:
(2) Modern Science and Reality

Perhaps modern science can secure our knowledge of reality in a way that Descartes could not. The successes of science are apparent all around us, from the development of quantum physics to the technological advances that we enjoy. "Scientific realism" holds that science accurately describes the world and is moving toward its goal of a complete description of the true nature of reality. Since our senses *broadly* correlate with science and its findings, we can infer that our senses must be accessing the external world. And so, it seems, our senses are reliable—they are accessing the external world, and thus it exists.

This is one way to think about the view that Cobb takes. The use of his totem, the spinning top, tests whether the scientific picture of the world that he has—one that includes certain beliefs in certain physical laws acting upon a spinning top—matches up to what he experiences. For him, if the top keeps spinning, then what he "knows" to be correct within physics is contradicted, and thus he concludes that he must be dreaming. Conversely if the top falls, then the scientific picture of the world that he takes to be describing reality correctly is justified, and so he must be awake.

Cobb's belief in the correctness of our scientific picture of the world, and its physical laws, provides a basis for him to conclude that he is not dreaming when the totem falls.[4] This is best illustrated in the final sequences when the cut to black deprives the audience of a sure answer to whether the totem falls. We are left unsure of whether Cobb is in a dream precisely because we are bound up in this scientific realist view of the world; if the physical laws (as described by current science) are broken—if the top keeps spinning—then we conclude that Cobb must still be in a dream.

The intuition that scientific realism is correct is not enough to support a philosophical position, though. We need an argument, such as Hilary Putnam's "no miracles" argument, roughly reconstructed as follows:

1. There are scientific theories that are empirically successful.
2. It would be a miracle if the theories were successful and *not* approximately true.
3. The best explanation of the empirical success of these theories is that the theories are at least approximately true.
4. Therefore, successful scientific theories are approximately true.[5]

This argument suggests that because science seems to be successful, can explain and, more importantly, predict, what will happen in the world around us, then it must at least be approximately true. The truth of scientific theories indicates that they must be describing reality. This is enough to support the realism that Cobb needs to justify his belief that he is in the real world, and thus that Mal's skepticism is unfounded.

Putnam qualifies his statements with the concept of "approximate truth" because he realizes that scientific theories are rarely (if ever) wholly complete. They are constantly being updated and revised given new discoveries and data. Even if parts of a theory are mistaken, and may be dropped or changed in future versions of the theory, this does not mean that the theory does not accurately describe reality to some degree. Take, for example, Copernicus's view that the Sun is the center of the universe and that the planets revolve around it in circular orbits. Surely this view could be said to accurately describe reality—at the least, it was much more accurate than the existing "Earth-centered" model—even though it was later discovered that planetary orbits are elliptical, and that the Sun is the center of the solar system only (not the entire universe).

So it seems that science has stepped in and shown that radical skepticism is avoidable. Some philosophers, though, have raised doubts about this and questioned the scientific realist position, taking an "antirealist" position. Some antirealists argue that science is a tool through which we seem to be able to manipulate the world, but that it cannot help us *know* the world. Others suggest that science is too caught up in the fallibility of humans; due to our finite abilities, we could never possibly *hope* to know truths about reality, nor could we *even* recognize them if they were presented to us. If, as the antirealist will hold, the realists' arguments are not sufficient to show that science is in fact describing reality, then this defense against the radical skepticism will fail, leaving us again with no way to argue against Mal's doubts about the world.

So let us reconsider the "no miracle" argument. The argument makes a step from the empirical success of a theory, via the claim that there are no miracles, to the conclusion that the theory must be approximately true. So, one wonders, is the empirical success of a theory sufficient to indicate that there is an element of *truth* in the theory? When we consider how science has changed throughout history, we are tempted to think that it is not.[6] Throughout the history of scientific investigation there have been many theories that were, at the time, empirically successful but later turned out to have completely inaccurate descriptions of the world.

An oft-cited example is the phlogiston theory, which explained combustion and rusting. Phlogiston was posited as a substance that was lost from combustible substances when they burned. Predictions made by the theory were in line with the evidence of the time, including the fact that covering a candle with a cup would make it go out. (It was thought that the air in the cup could only "handle" so much phlogiston. Once it was full, the candle could no longer "put out" phlogiston.) The theory was later dropped, however. First it was discovered that some metals, like magnesium, actually gain weight when heated—how could that happen, if they were losing phlogiston? Defenders of phlogiston scrambled to explain away such evidence by insisting that sometimes phlogiston has "negative weight." But this was clearly just an excuse to save the theory. The discovery of oxygen, the development of oxygen-based theories of combustion, and the realization that such theories were much simpler (and that one doesn't have to make silly excuses to save them), led to the demise of the phlogiston theory.

It is undeniable, however, that phlogiston theory fit the evidence of the time. It was empirically successful at both explaining and predicting the behavior of substances undergoing combustion. If we had applied the "no miracles" argument to it, and thought the argument valid, we would have concluded that the theory of phlogiston accurately described the world. Yet clearly it did not.

Worse yet, if two competing theories make the same successful predictions, the miracles argument would force us to conclude that both theories accurately describe the world. This was the case with Newton's theory of gravitation and Einstein's theory of relativity for a while; they both made all the same observable predictions.[7] But they said fundamentally different and opposing things about the nature of the universe; they couldn't both be right. But by the lights of the "no miracles" argument, they would have to be. So something must be wrong with the "no miracles" argument.

The danger here for scientific realism is that we cannot know that our current scientific theories are not like phlogiston theories—that they will not also be proven incorrect by future evidence. Quantum mechanics, the general theory of relativity, and other areas of current fundamental physics (as well, of course, as other scientific theories) are currently empirically successful. If, however, we cannot know that they will always be successful, and as we have seen, *current* empirical success is not capable of supporting the claim of approximate truth, then the "no miracles" argument fails.

This means that Cobb's reasoning behind thinking that a totem proves that he is not dreaming fails. And this is not too surprising; it turns out that the top is not very reliable as a totem anyway. It does not tell him whether he is in his own dream; he knows how it works. But so do, for that matter, Mal (it was hers originally) and Ariadne (he told her). In fact, don't we all know that a top does not spin forever? Why would anyone dream that it did? The totem clearly is not up to the task of differentiating dream from reality.

Ways Out of Skepticism:
(3) Pragmatism, the Last Resort?

Science and philosophy have been unable to produce arguments that would convince Mal the skeptic that we live in the real world, and therefore that we are not dreaming. Are we thus forced to conclude that Mal was right after all, that she and

Cobb were dreaming? Are we forced to conclude that we are dreaming? If so, perhaps we should all follow Mal out the hotel window.

No, please, back away from the window. There are a couple of reasons such a conclusion is not justified. First, Mal oversteps the bounds of skepticism by concluding that she is in a dream (though this overstepping is painted by the director as being caused by the lingering and ever-growing effects of her skepticism on her psychology). The skeptic's position is not that we are in a dream; that is not the conclusion of the dream argument. The point was that we cannot tell whether we are awake *or we are dreaming*. Mal, however, says that she knows that she is dreaming and that, if she dies, she will wake up in the real world. The skeptic would argue that she cannot know either of these things any more than Cobb can know that he is awake. Maybe she is awake. Maybe she is dreaming, but the shock of dying in the dream would kill her in the real world. She does not know, and that is the skeptic's point. We still cannot know that Cobb is right, but we also do not know that Mal is right. Thus, it is clearly not a good idea to follow her out the hotel window.

Are we stuck then, not knowing what to believe about whether the world is real? No. Fortunately, pragmatism can step in and save us.

Concerning knowledge, pragmatism asserts that we should not think of ways to doubt things that we seem to just intuitively know and would otherwise accept without question. Charles Sanders Peirce (1839–1914), one of the key figures in the promotion of pragmatism, wrote, "Let us not pretend to doubt in philosophy what we do not doubt in our hearts."[8] What would Peirce say about radical skepticism? He would ask, "Do we naturally feel that the world we experience is the real world?" Of course, the answer is yes. And since we feel intuitively that the external world is real, and we experience it at least roughly as such, Peirce would conclude that we should not doubt its existence, nor seriously consider the sort of radical skepticism that would lead us to be convinced that we are dreaming. At least in everyday life (rather than philosophical study) this would seem to suffice. If we cannot know for sure one way or the other whether we are dreaming or not, then the sensible conclusion would be the one that follows our natural instincts on the issue: believe we are not dreaming.

What would Peirce conclude about whether Cobb or Mal was right? On the pragmatic level, the radical beliefs that led Mal to extreme actions and risks are sufficient to explain and support our intuitive feeling that Mal is mistaken and Cobb is correct. Thus, it would seem, we can conclude that Mal was indeed driven insane by doubts, at least from a pragmatic viewpoint. We cannot prove that she was wrong, but that she was wrong does seem to be the sensible view.

We still have no concrete provable answer to the question of whether Mal or Cobb was correct. (Further investigation into the movie might actually prove that our initial "pragmatic" reaction was wrong.)[9] Nor do we have provable answers for whether we (outside of the fictional life of film) should begin to doubt our own experiences in the way Mal does.

Within the realm of everyday life, however, pragmatic considerations are compelling. Life in a state of radical skepticism is impossible; you would not be able to function properly if you seriously doubted that the objects that you are interacting with are not real.[10] Furthermore, if the way to "wake up" is to die in the dream in which we live, then the risk of being wrong would lead most people to think it was not worth it. We cannot prove the issue one way or another, but living as though the external world is real produces far fewer complications. Put simply, we may not (ever) be able to *prove* that we are not dreaming, but I would not jump out of a window to test the hypothesis.

NOTES

1. Ironically, the famous line "I think therefore I am" does not actually appear anywhere in Descartes' *Meditations*. But it is an accurate summary of his reasoning, in the opinion of many scholars. This is probably why it is so popular. The line does appear in his *Principles of Philosophy*, Part 1, Article 7 (Whitefish, MT: Kessinger, 2004).

2. René Descartes, *Meditations on First Philosophy*, was originally published in Latin in 1641. This quote is from an English translation, found in the Second Meditation, eds. Charles Adam and Paul Tannery (Paris: J. Vrin, 1904) VII 25; CSM II 16–17. There is debate among Descartes scholars about whether or not Descartes derived his existence from the existence of his own thoughts (which were indubitable), or whether he thought that his existence itself was indubitable. For more on this debate, see chapter 10 of Harry Frankfurt, *Demons, Dreamers, and Madmen: The Defense of Reason in Descartes Meditation* (Princeton, NJ: Princeton University Press, 2007).

3. René Descartes, *Meditations and Other Metaphysical Writings*, trans. Desmond Clarke (London: Penguin Classics, 1998), p. 44.

4. More precisely, it's only supposed to show him that he is not in someone else's dream. But we will ignore that detail here.

5. Hilary Putnam, *Mathematics, Matter and Method*, Vol. 1 (Cambridge, UK: Cambridge University Press, 1975), p. 73.

6. For more on this, see Larry Laudan, 1981, "A Confutation of Convergent Realism," *Philosophy of Science* 48: 19–49.

7. How Einstein was eventually proven right is a fascinating story. He predicted that light would bend around the Sun; Newton did not. An observation of stars that should have been concealed by the Sun during an eclipse showed that Einstein was right.

8. Charles Peirce, "Some Consequences of Four Incapacities," *Journal of Speculative Philosophy* 2: 140–157.

9. See Jason Southworth's chapter in this volume.

10. And, as the pragmatist would argue, this skepticism would most probably not be sustained at all times as the person would instinctively slip into the natural attitude of believing in the existence of the external world.

PART TWO

IS THE TOP STILL SPINNING?: TACKLING THE UNANSWERABLE QUESTION

THE PARABLE OF THE SPINNING TOP: SKEPTICISM, ANGST, AND COBB'S CHOICE

Katherine Tullmann

Cobb: If I were to do this, if I even could do it, I'd need a guarantee. How do I know you can deliver?

Saito: You don't. But I can. So. Do you want to take a leap of faith, or become an old man filled with regret, waiting to die alone?

As it turns out, Dom Cobb can and does perform the inception. When he returns home, though, Cobb worries that he is still dreaming, that none of this newfound happiness is real. So he gives the top a final spin. If it falls, he will believe that all this is real; if not, he will know that he is still trapped in a dream. But before he can determine whether or not the top falls, Cobb becomes distracted by his children and walks away from the still-spinning top.

Inception invites the audience to question its own reality. How can you be certain that you are not dreaming right now? Sure, it feels like you are not. But, as Ariadne learns, that is the distinguishing feature of a vivid dream.

> Ariadne: How could I ever acquire enough detail to make them think that it's reality?
> Cobb: Well, dreams, they feel real while we're in them, right? It's only when we wake up that we realize that something was actually strange.
>
> . . .
>
> Ariadne: I guess I thought that the dream space would be all about the visual, but it's more about the *feel* of it.

The realization that we might be dreaming, and thus that we might not be certain about anything, gives rise to a kind of anxiety—what Duncan Pritchard called an *"epistemic angst."*[1] (He got the name from the word "epistemology," which is the study of knowledge.) Once you realize that you can't be certain of anything—what then? How do you go on living? What is the proper way to deal with this angst? Defeat it? Embrace it? Ignore it? Jump out a window?

Angst and Meaningfulness

To consider how angst might arise, let's consider a skeptical argument. We will use Cobb as the subject, the possibility that he is dreaming as the skeptical hypothesis, and the assertion that he has two children, James and Phillipa, as the proposition that he wishes to know:

1. Cobb does not know that he is not dreaming.
2. If Cobb does not know that he is not dreaming, then Cobb does not know that he has two children, James and Phillipa.
3. Therefore, Cobb does not know that he has two children, James and Phillipa.[2]

Cobb makes it clear throughout the film that his children are his top priority, his main motivation for wanting to go home. The fact that he can never really know beyond a doubt that his children actually exist must be a staggering thought, certainly one that would cause him a certain amount of angst.

According to the skeptical argument, we can substitute any proposition for "he has two children, James and Phillipa." This means that Cobb might not know anything. In his Second Meditation, the philosopher René Descartes (1596–1650) describes feeling something like angst after he's begun to question his reality: "I feel like someone who is suddenly dropped into a deep whirlpool that tumbles him around so that he can neither stand on the bottom nor swim to the top."[3] Consider also Ariadne's reaction when she finds out that she is dreaming in the Paris street scene. She panics: the glasses on the table begin to shake; books, fruits, and vegetables fly off their stands; window glass explodes around her. The dream worlds that we create can be very unstable. When Mal and Cobb are in their world (dream Limbo), they are able to knock over several buildings just by toppling their sand castles. This instability adds to the feeling of anxiety that Cobb and other dreamers might feel.

Another negative consequence of epistemic angst is the belief that because we cannot really know anything, our experiences are in many ways meaningless. If Cobb's children are really just projections of his subconscious, then it doesn't matter if they are happy or sad, or even if they live or die. We must be careful, however, about drawing a value conclusion from an epistemological premise. We cannot really say that existence is meaningless based on the idea that we do not know whether our world exists. It is possible that even the dream world is meaningful in some way, but we do not or cannot know what that meaning might be. Nevertheless, we may come to *believe* that our lives lack meaning if we cannot know anything about our world, even though belief and knowledge are not the same things.[4]

The skeptic's uncertainty shapes both thoughts and actions. Cobb, Mal, and Yusuf's "basement dreamers" illustrate different possible responses to epistemic angst. Alternatively, one can try to eradicate doubt by rejecting the skeptical hypothesis, as philosophers throughout history have attempted to do. So let's see what might work.

The Philosopher's Response: Denouncing Skepticism

Descartes provides one of the most famous attempts to eliminate epistemic doubt. In the *Meditations*, he notices that: "Because I may be dreaming, I can't say for sure that I now see the flames, hear the wood cracking, and feel the heat of the fire; but I certainly seem to see, to hear, and to be warmed."[5] Further, Descartes accepts that an evil demon might be controlling his world and everything he perceives. Nevertheless, Descartes has a way out of his skeptical dilemma, a way he can prove without a doubt that he is not dreaming or being deceived. He has clear and distinct ideas, including an idea of a perfect and immutable God that he could not have simply imagined.[6] Because this God would not directly put ideas into his mind or deceive him, Descartes argues, most of his ideas must come from somewhere else. Thus, Descartes concludes that the physical world must exist and that it was, like himself, created by God.[7]

There are two main problems with applying Descartes' apparent solution to Cobb's situation in *Inception*. The first is that it relies on a flawed argument for the existence of God, as James Miller shows us in his chapter. The second is that Descartes' "way out" of the skeptical hypothesis does not apply to Cobb. It is not God who creates the dreams into which Cobb and the extraction team enter, but humans, who are unpredictable, dangerous, and fallible.

One might respond, however, that Cobb *does* appear to have a reliable way to tell whether or not he is in someone else's dream: his totem, the top. So the top might be Cobb's way out of the skeptical scenario. During Ariadne's training, Arthur explains to her the significance of the totem: "You need a small object, potentially heavy, something you can have on you all the time . . . it needs to be unique . . . only I know the balance and weight of this particular loaded die. That way, when you look at your totem, you know beyond a doubt that you're not in someone else's dream."

The value of the top is dubious, though. The top was originally Mal's totem. "This one was hers," Cobb tells Ariadne. Worse yet, right after that, he tells Ariadne how it works. "She'd spin it in a dream, and it'd never topple." If this is the case, and a totem is effective if only you know how it works, then how can Cobb use the top as his own? Furthermore, the totem falling would only tell Cobb that he is probably not in someone else's dream. And it's possible, even if it falls, that he is stuck within his own dream.

The attentive viewer may spot another solution, though. Pay attention to Cobb's left hand in each scene. You'll see that in *the real world*, Cobb stopped wearing his ring sometime after Mal's death, but he wears it in his dreams—where Mal is still "alive." So perhaps his wedding ring, not the top, is his totem. At least, the ring could be the viewer's totem—a clue telling us which scenes are real and which ones are dreams. When Cobb appears to wake up after completing his final mission, you can see (if you pause the movie) his left hand; it's clearest when he is handing his passport to the INS agent.[8] And he is not wearing his ring!

As conclusive proof that he is not dreaming, however, this evidence is insufficient. After all, Cobb wears his wedding ring in dreams because in them he believes Mal is still living. (Recall his hesitation to shoot Mal at the snow fortress, despite Ariadne's reassurance that she was not real.) Cobb may not wear the wedding ring in *the real world* merely because in that world he believes Mal is dead—not because he is not dreaming. In fact, this is exactly what you would expect if *the real world* actually is a dream—Cobb's dream—from which Mal awoke when she jumped from the window. The point is that no matter how we choose to interpret the film, we have no evidence that would definitively establish one conclusion over another. There really is no way for us to tell if he is dreaming at the end of the film.

We can now begin to see how the problem of skepticism persists: even if we have a rational "tool" with which we think that we can dispel our doubt about our reality, we have no reliable way to tell if that tool is working as it's supposed to. This leads to a regress of sorts; we must always find further justification of whatever evidence we think we have.

Other philosophers have tried to reject the skeptical hypothesis in other ways, but these, too, are open to debate.[9] Even if these other philosophers succeeded, however, they still might not rid you of epistemic angst. Imagine that you confide in your friend, a wise epistemologist, that you doubt the reality of your experiences. He pulls out a pen and paper, and perhaps several texts, to support his claim, and writes out a proof, explaining step by step why it is extremely unlikely that you are dreaming. Do you think that this explanation will calm your fears? Perhaps for some people it might, but for many it won't. Even if a philosopher logically proves that you are probably not deceived about reality, this knowledge will not eradicate your angst. After all, he still could be wrong; your feeling that he is right could merely be part of a dream. In the end, there may not be a logical way to escape the feeling of angst. Let's turn, then, to the other possible responses that the film presents.

The Basement Dreamers' Response: Escape Reality

As Cobb and Arthur explain the intricacies of the inception job to the rest of the team, Ariadne comes to the stunning conclusion that in the third dream level, they will have as long as ten years to complete their mission. Time in the dream world acts differently than in *the real world*! She asks: "Who would want to be stuck in a dream for ten years?" to which a grinning Yusuf replies: "Depends on the dream." If our experiences are all that matter, and we get the best experiences when we dream (for example, Cobb would get to be with Mal and his children), then why wouldn't we want to be in that dream forever? This, essentially, is the question put forward by Robert Nozick (1938–2002), who formulated a thought experiment to help us decide whether we would want to live in a dream of sorts. "Suppose there were an experience machine that would give you any experience you desired," Nozick muses:

> Superduper neuropsychologists could stimulate your brain so that you would think and feel you were writing a great novel, or making a friend, or reading an interesting book. All the time you would be floating in a tank, with electrodes attached to your brain. Should you plug into this machine for life, preprogramming your life's experiences?[10]

Nozick provides several reasons why we normally would not wish to plug into the experience machine. The moral that he draws has to do with our desire to truly live our own lives: "Perhaps what we desire is to live (an active verb) ourselves, in contact with reality. (And this, machines cannot do for us.)"[11] Nozick's scenario is not quite the same as in *Inception*. Dreamers are not entirely passive, as Cobb notes, if their minds are working to create a world, and dreams are not always purely pleasant—but the moral is the same. We do not want to always be dreaming, despite what Yusuf says, because we wish to be agents in our own lives, and to have "contact with reality."

Consider the dreamers in Yusuf's shop, the ones who have "plugged in." The basement dreamers are no longer able to dream on their own, so they go to his shop daily to "share the dream." Their epistemic angst is different from Cobb and Mal's: they believe that they are not dreaming, but wish that they were. Because of the pleasant experiences they have in their dreams, they no longer wish to remain in *the real world*. As Yusuf's elderly attendant says, "The dream has become their reality. Who are you to say otherwise, sir?" Their angst has to do with the disparity between what they expect life to be and what it really is. In the end, their dream lives are more real to them than their real lives.

"Perhaps you will not want to see," Yusuf warns Cobb, Eames, and Saito before showing them the semi-comatose dreamers. What reaction do we have toward them: pity? disgust? moral consternation? There certainly seems to be something pitiable and cowardly about those who exchange their real lives for a dream world. Why are they choosing to escape reality? What are they running from? These dreamers might also be morally blameworthy: people *should* live in the real world and not engage in escapist activities. These are important issues, and the reader can turn to the chapters by Dan Weijers and Bart Engelen to read more about them. For now, it is enough to note that we can value other things in our lives besides the dream. Contact with reality seems, intuitively, to be something valuable in and of itself.

Mal's Response: Forget the Dream

Mal and Cobb's explorations eventually land them in dream Limbo, a place of unstructured dream space where a minute feels like hours and the dreamer completely loses track of what is real. Mal and Cobb happily created a world for themselves in Limbo, growing old together before Cobb decided that it was time to get back to their real lives. Before this, however, Mal, too, made a choice about facing reality. Cobb relates the story to Ariadne: "[Mal] had locked something away, deep inside her, the truth that she had known, but chose to forget." Mal hid her totem, the top, in one of the deep recesses of her subconscious (the safe inside her childhood bedroom), thereby shutting herself off from "the truth that she once knew"—the truth that she was actually dreaming. Why didn't Mal want to leave Limbo, like Cobb? Presumably, she was very happy there living "like gods." As Cobb said, "We created, we built the world for ourselves. We did that for years. We built our own world." After a while, Cobb could no longer "live like that"; he could not live knowing that his world wasn't real. This is real angst, and Mal felt it, too. But she dealt with it in a different way. Mal hid the truth away and "Limbo became her reality."

This angst is a bit different from ours. Mal and Cobb knew they were dreaming, but questioned the meaningfulness of such a life—a fake existence. Mal's angst returns when Cobb plants the idea in her mind that her world isn't real; he cracks open the safe in her childhood bedroom, sets her top perpetually spinning, and locks the safe back up. Again, though, this is different from the angst we feel. She did not merely doubt the reality of her experiences, wondering whether they were accurate. She believed them to be inaccurate; she believed that she was dreaming. Unfortunately, even after she awoke the top was still spinning in the safe of her subconscious, so in *the real world* she still believed she was dreaming. As Cobb says to Ariadne, "I never knew that that idea would grow in her mind like a cancer, that even after she woke, that even after [she] came back to reality, that [she'd] continue to believe that [her] world wasn't real." Believing that her existence was meaningless, and that the only way to wake up was to die, she threw herself from a hotel window.

Compare Mal to the basement dreamers. Both Mal and the basement dreamers engage in a form of escapism, but what makes Mal's situation more severe is that she succeeds in forgetting that *the real world* is her reality. The basement dreamers always wake up to reality, no matter how little they wish to do so. Mal never would, if not for Cobb's inception. Insofar as Mal chose to forget her reality, she is at least as blameworthy as the basement dreamers. It was Cobb's tampering with her totem that led to her angst in *the real world*, though, where her response to her angst is not blameworthy. Because she not only doubts, but is convinced that the only way to return to reality is by dying, jumping off the ledge of the hotel window seems reasonable. After all, isn't that how Cobb helps them escape from Limbo in the first place—by lying down on the tracks in front of an oncoming train? Isn't that what Cobb convinces Saito to do at the end of the film? Commit suicide? Yet the moral of Mal's story is that we should value our contact with reality enough to face its difficulties—she shouldn't have hidden her totem. In the end, forgetting which of her experiences were real did not lead Mal to any greater happiness. Likewise, forgetting about our own doubt—just ignoring the skeptical problem altogether—may not be the best idea. If we care about knowledge of the world, we can't simply ignore the problem that suggests we don't have it.

Cobb's Response: Choosing Reality

Choosing not to plug into a dream is easy enough if we have a firm grasp on reality. But what if, like Cobb, we struggle to tell the difference between dream and reality and as a result feel great angst? Furthermore, we have already seen how skeptical hypotheses can not only contribute to our anxiety, but also make us question the meaningfulness of our lives. This leaves us in a bind. How is it possible to continue with our day-to-day pursuits in the face of epistemic angst and the possibility that everything that we value isn't real? Why not just plug in where we are happy? Pritchard suggests that a certain degree of angst is inevitable; we cannot return to our blissfully ignorant state once we begin to doubt our reality.[12]

The philosopher David Hume (1711–1776) had a commonsense way of dealing with angst:

> Most fortunately it happens, that since reason is incapable of dispelling these clouds, nature herself suffices to that purpose, and cures me of this philosophical melancholy and delirium, either by relaxing this bent of mind, or by some avocation, and lively impression of my senses, which obliterate all these chimeras. I dine, I play a game of backgammon, I converse, and am merry with my friends; and when after three or four hours' amusement, I would return to these speculations, they appear so cold, and strain'd, and ridiculous, that I cannot find in my heart to enter into them any farther.[13]

Hume's pursuits—backgammon, friendly conversation, and so on—are trivial occupations to take his mind off what bothers him. Perhaps, though, the more significant parts of our lives can distract us even more effectively, despite the *possibility* that they aren't real. Recall how Cobb walks away from the spinning top at the end of the film, completely distracted by his children. Earlier in the film, Miles implores Cobb to "Come back to reality," to which he replies: "Reality. Those kids—your grandchildren—they're waiting for their father to come back home. That's their reality. And this job, this last job, *that's* how I get there."

This, it seems, is Cobb's choice. He chooses happiness with his children and success from the mission over the perpetuation of his anxiety. He chooses life (and doubt) in an uncertain world with his children over happiness with Mal, where he might also end up mistaking dream for reality. As stressed throughout the film, this decision is a *choice*. While in dream Limbo with Ariadne, Mal accosts both her and Cobb:

> Mal [to Ariadne]: So certain of your world, of what's real. Do you think he is? Or do you think he's as lost as I was?

Cobb: I know what's real, Mal.

Mal [to Cobb]: No creeping doubts? Not feeling perse-cuted, Dom?—chased around the globe by anonymous corporations and police forces, the way the projections persecute the dreamer? Admit it. You don't believe in one reality anymore. So choose. Choose to be here. Choose me.

Notice that it is while Cobb is in Limbo—when he is dreaming—that he is convinced that he "knows what's real." It's only when he believes that he is not dreaming that the doubt creeps in. Cobb doesn't choose to plug in, so to speak. He fights to escape Limbo, where he could be with Mal, and he recognizes the limitations of his dream creations. Cobb chooses not to let his angst overcome him. It's not that Cobb doesn't care whether or not he's dreaming, but rather that he decides that there are other things worth living for, other things worth caring about. He realizes that *this* Mal is merely a projection, and that he had already spent a lifetime with her in Limbo. Now he wants to be with his children. Cobb chooses what seems to be reality, even if he can't be sure. This is a subtle difference from plugging in, perhaps, but it is an important one. Like Hume, Cobb finds that his existential questions do not matter as much once he believes that he is reunited with his real children. He may also, like Hume, return to these questions—return to check the top—at a later time, if the story were to continue. But at the moment, Cobb seems content with his choice.

Taking the Leap

Right before Mal jumps to her death, while sitting on the windowsill of the hotel, she asks Cobb to "take a leap of faith." Mal believes that when she dies she will return to her real life. Her "leap" is into the belief that she will escape the dream world and return to reality. Indeed, the concept of a "leap of faith" runs throughout the film. It is the central metaphor of the "train riddle" that Mal tells Ariadne during Cobb's dream:

> Mal: You're waiting for a train, a train that will take you far away. You know where you hope this train will take you, but you don't know for sure. But it doesn't matter—how can it not matter to you where that train will take you?
> Cobb: Because we'll be together.

The train represents the sudden transition that Cobb and Mal wish to take place. If successful, the train will take them back to reality. If not, they will die. For Mal, it was more important that she and Cobb remain together, in a dream or in reality. As we've seen, Cobb, in the end, chooses reality.

The concept of a leap of faith is also a theme in the works of the Danish philosopher Søren Kierkegaard (1813–1855).[14] Taking a leap of faith might strike one as a fundamentally religious concept: our reason cannot convince us of the existence of God, so we must let some other force guide us to this conclusion. The leap, however, can be understood as any sort of transition between two very different ways of life.[15] Often, the leap occurs at a "crucial and decisive moment"[16] in our lives, shaping and defining who we will become.

Cobb takes his own leap of faith at the beginning of the film when Saito asks him to take the inception job. At that moment, Cobb decides what is most important in his life—what is worth the risk of such a dangerous task. In this decisive moment, Cobb chooses to accept the mission. But where does this leap leave him? Near the end of the film, Cobb remains in Limbo to save Saito. He confronts the aged businessman and picks up his gun—but does he shoot? Do he and Saito wake up?

Remember that in the first dream layer both Saito and Cobb remain inside the sinking van, still sleeping, when the others swim out. Because we don't see Saito or Cobb leave Limbo, we cannot know whether they ever woke up.

This is the final mystery of the film, and it provides a lesson that we can apply to our own lives. We must take our own leap of faith. Our interpretation of the film is largely a matter of choice because we cannot know, in the end, whether or not Cobb is still dreaming. And we can apply the same reasoning to our own lives. Since we cannot know beyond a doubt that our world is real, we are left with a choice: do we sink into despair, or continue to live and thrive? We can learn from Cobb's choice how to handle our own epistemic angst: find what really matters to us, and continue to live.

NOTES

1. See Duncan Pritchard, "Skepticism, Epistemic Luck and Epistemic *Angst*," *Australasian Journal of Philosophy* 83 (2005): 185–205, and "Absurdity, *Angst* and the Meaning of Life," *The Monist* 93 (2010): 3–16.

2. The basis of this skeptical argument is taken from Pritchard (2005), p. 187. He uses a brain-in-a-vat hypothesis, but the idea is the same. Note also that many philosophers have found ways to refute this skeptical argument, thus undermining skepticism itself. See Hilary Putnam, "Brains in a Vat," in K. DeRose and T. A. Warfield, eds., *Skepticism: A Contemporary Reader* (Oxford: Oxford University Press, 1992). See also the *Stanford Encyclopedia of Philosophy*'s entries on "Brains in a Vat" and "Skepticism" for further information: Tony Brueckner, "Brains in a Vat," *The Stanford Encyclopedia of Philosophy* (Fall 2008 edition), edited by Edward N. Zalta, <http://plato.stanford .edu/archives/fall2008/entries/brain-vat/>; Peter Klein, "Skepticism," *The Stanford Encyclopedia of Philosophy* (Summer 2011 edition), edited by Edward N. Zalta, <http://plato .stanford.edu/archives/sum2011/entries/skepticism/>.

3. Rene Descartes, *Meditations on First Philosophy*, was originally published in Latin in 1641. This quote is from an English translation of his Second Meditation by Jonathan Bennett. It, along with his translation of every one of Descartes' meditations, can be found online at www.earlymoderntexts.com/de.html.

4. See Thomas Nagel, "The Absurd," *Journal of Philosophy* (1971): 716–727; and Pritchard's (2010) response, for more on questions surrounding the meaning of life.

5. Pritchard (2010), p. 6.

6. See Descartes' Third Meditation for Descartes' first proof of the existence of God.

7. See Descartes, Sixth Meditation for Descartes' argument for the existence of the physical world.

8. The other two times are around 2:17:32, when Cobb takes the immigration form from the flight attendant, and 2:20:00, as he spins the top for a final time.

9. See Pritchard (2005), for some responses.

10. Robert Nozick, *Anarchy, State and Utopia* (New York: Basic Books, 1974), p. 42.

11. Ibid., p. 45.

12. See Pritchard (2010), section 4.

13. David Hume, *Treatise of Human Nature*, Book 1, Part 4, Section 7. Quoted in Nagel (1971), p. 724, footnote 3.

14. While there is no Danish equivalent for "leap of faith" in Kierkegaard's writings, the basic idea of a transition from one state to another is a central theme in his work. See M. Jamie Ferriera's "Faith and the Kierkegaardian Leap," in *The Cambridge Companion to Kierkegaard*, eds. Alastair Hannay and Gordon D. Marino (Cambridge: University Press, 1998), pp. 207–234.

15. Ferriera, p. 207.

16. Ibid.

REALITY DOESN'T REALLY MATTER

Dan Weijers

The dream has become their reality. Who are you to say otherwise, sir?

—Elderly bald man

So you're leaving the movie theater—you've just been blown away by *Inception*—and your mind is whirling. Everyone's asking each other: "Does Cobb's spinning top fall?" The screen cut to black before we could tell. You discuss it with your friends and wonder if there were any clues that you missed. You can't wait for it to come out on DVD, so you can watch it again more carefully. But even after watching *Inception* seventeen times, the movie retains many mysteries, especially about what happens to Cobb in the end. How frustrating! The success of Cobb's plan to get back home to his children, and to keep his grip on reality in the process, seems to be determined by whether or not he is really dreaming at the end. The whole point of the movie seems to hinge on whether or not Cobb's top keeps spinning. With no way to answer that question, the point of the movie seems to be forever beyond your grasp.

Fortunately, this view of the movie is inaccurate. Perhaps Cobb's spinning top falls and he gets to see his kids in *the real world*, and perhaps it doesn't and Cobb ends up living in Limbo. (For the purposes of this chapter, unless otherwise stated, we'll assume that the real world is reality.) But either way, Cobb is happy. Cobb himself realizes this; this is why he walks away from the top while it's still spinning. The experience of being with his kids is what he cares about most, not reality. The correct answer to "Does Cobb's spinning top fall?" is: "Who cares!" Reality doesn't really matter. And this is the point of *Inception*. It's our experiences that really matter, not whether we are living in reality.

Limbo Is Great, *the Real World* Ain't

If the closing scenes of *Inception* are showing Cobb enjoying a dream about reuniting with his kids, then Saito is probably behind it. Saito agreed to enable Cobb to see his kids again if Cobb could successfully pull off the inception on Robert Fischer, which Cobb did. So it makes sense that Saito would hold up his end of the bargain.

If Saito did choose to reunite Cobb with his kids in a dream, he would probably create a new world for Cobb in Limbo instead of in a shallower dream. (In fact, that may be how Saito originally intended to hold up his end of the bargain. How else could Saito fix Cobb's situation with one phone call?) The depth of Limbo combined with a Yusuf-esque super-sedative would ensure that Cobb couldn't be kicked out of his dream. So, what would Cobb's Limbo world be like? Limbo is unstructured dream space. Anyone sharing the dream could create the world as they please, with their unconscious minds filling in the blanks. Saito, and anyone Saito wanted to employ, could create the Limbo world in which Cobb now resides. They could also arrange the course of events in the Limbo world by manipulating people and places.

Saito's employees might take advantage of Cobb's sub-conscious when creating the Limbo world. The influence of Cobb's subconscious memories and desires would help to create the world so that it would be both familiar and suitably predictable for Cobb. By combining their talents with Cobb's subconscious in this way, Saito's employees could make the Limbo world indistinguishable from *the real world* for Cobb. Since the Limbo world would be designed by Cobb's subcon-scious and Saito's (presumably highly skilled) employees, it would seem impeccably real. Everything would be just as Cobb remembered, and all future events would be partly based on Cobb's desires and expectations, giving him no reason to ques-tion them. Recall Cobb's comments to Ariadne: "You never really remember the beginning of a dream, do you? You always wind up right in the middle of what's going on." So Cobb's transition to Limbo (whenever it might have occurred) would have been too smooth for him to notice.

In addition to being indistinguishable from *the real world*, Cobb's Limbo world could even be far superior to *the real world*. After spending time catching up with his children, Cobb would need to start living a normal life again. He would need to find a job, make new friends, and plan for his children's future. In *the real world*, Cobb's lack of references and (legal) job experience might mean that he could only find a job as a cleaner or, if he's really unlucky, a bathroom cleaner. In Limbo, though, Saito's employees could concoct a plausible scenario that results in Cobb landing a cushy act-ing job in an upcoming blockbuster movie—perhaps starring as a plucky rogue who stows away on the *Titanic* and then falls in love. If Cobb lives in Limbo, instead of *the real world* he could achieve much better results in all of the important areas of his life. In Limbo, Cobb's friends could be more fun and generous, his work life could be more stimulating and fulfill-ing, and his children could go to Ivy League colleges instead of bathroom-cleaning school.

Given the obvious advantages a life in Limbo has over a life in *the real world*, it's a wonder that Cobb didn't just ask Saito for a Limbo life instead of a life in *the real world*, right? Well, not quite. If Cobb had asked to be reunited with his kids in Limbo, rather than in *the real world*, then he would probably always be burdened by the thought that he was living in a dream. Fortunately for Cobb, if he did end up in Limbo, he has no idea. So, at least in terms of what Cobb would experience, we can see that ending up in Limbo is probably better for Cobb than ending up in *the real world*.

Hold on, did I just say that living in a dream is better than living in reality? No, just that in this example the total of Cobb's life experiences would probably be better in Limbo. But this raises a very interesting question: Are experiences the only things that matter for how well someone's life goes for them?

Why All the Hoopla about Reality?

I believe that only what we experience matters for our well-being. Events that we do not become consciously aware of in any way (directly or indirectly) cannot have any impact on how well our lives go for us. So I think that Cobb would be better off living in a more enjoyable Limbo (and believing it's real) than living in *the real world*.

You might not agree with me, though. Perhaps you think that Cobb's life would be better if he lived it in *the real world*, despite the fact that his experiences would be more enjoyable in Limbo. If this is the case, I have some questions for you. How is it possible that something can make your life go worse for you if you never become consciously aware of it in any way? Can you explain the causal process by which Cobb's not living in reality would make his life go worse for him, without referring to impacts on his conscious states? If not, can you make some other argument as to how something can affect how well our lives go for us without affecting our consciousness in any way?

These are certainly difficult questions. Fortunately, the hard work has already been done. In fact, thanks to philosophers with an interest in well-being (the good life for the one living it), there is a veritable mountain of philosophical musings relevant to these questions.

At the top of this mountain are works based on renowned philosopher Robert Nozick's (1938–2002) pioneering and powerful argument that more than just our experiences matters to us.[1] Nozick maintained that living a life in reality is preferable to living a more enjoyable but unreal life. His argument is almost always referred to when philosophers want to claim that reality does matter. So let's use Nozick's argument to see if Cobb should care if his spinning top falls.

Imagine that Cobb is on the plane with the others after completing the inception on Fischer. Saito leans over and whispers two options in Cobb's ear. Saito is giving Cobb the choice between either reuniting with his kids in *the real world* or in Limbo. Saito makes it clear that all of Cobb's experiences will be much more enjoyable in Limbo. Saito also mentions that if Cobb chooses Limbo, he will slip Cobb a pill that removes his memory of this offer so that Cobb will never realize that he chose Limbo. Saito also guarantees that the Limbo world has been so carefully crafted that Cobb will never realize it is not real. Now, remember, we are assuming that *the real world* is real. So, considering only what is best for himself, what do you think Cobb should choose: *the real world* (that is, reality) or Limbo?

Most people think that Cobb should reunite with his kids in reality. They acknowledge that the Limbo life might be more enjoyable in some ways, but they also think that choosing it just doesn't feel right. Cobb never getting to see his real kids again seems like a bum deal. Of course, if Cobb did choose the life in Limbo, he would never realize that he was lovingly raising projections instead of his real children. But most people argue that this doesn't really matter because Cobb doesn't want to reunite with projections that seem real; he wants to see his real children again.

The idea of living the rest of our lives in Limbo might seem both exciting and depressing. Many of the differences would be fun, but one difference would ruin it all for most of us. Since Limbo is not real, our actions would have no significant impact on any real person, and our lives would be, in some ways, meaning-less. We have plans that are important to us, and we want them to come to fruition. The vast majority of these plans include having an impact on real people, such as lovingly raising our real children. In Limbo, we couldn't succeed in these plans. So the hoopla about reality seems to be that without reality, we can't achieve many important and meaning-giving goals. This seems like a good reason to think that reality matters (even if it never affects our consciousness) and to choose reality over Limbo (even if we won't realize we're in Limbo). This also seems like a good reason to care if Cobb's totem will keep spinning; his life will be more meaningful, and therefore better, if it drops.

Turning the Tables

Actually, the hoopla about reality is as bogus as one of Eames's impersonations. As convincing as they might seem, the reasons given for why most of us choose reality over Limbo for Cobb are just guesses, bad guesses, in fact. Let's consider a reversed scenario to see why.

Again, imagine that Cobb is on the plane after successfully completing Saito's job. Saito leans over and tells Cobb that he has actually been in Limbo all along, that Cobb's whole life up to that point has been a dream. (So, in this scenario, the assumption we have been making so far in this chapter is false; the real world is not reality.) Saito gives Cobb the choice of either remaining in the world that he has been experiencing as real all this time (*the real world* that is not actually real) or living in reality. Again,

Saito gives Cobb a pill so that Cobb can erase his memory of the conversation if he wants to. Saito also guarantees that if Cobb remains in the dream, he will never become aware that it is a dream. Cobb asks what his real life is like, and Saito replies that it is both very different from this life and much less enjoyable. Only considering what is best for Cobb, do you think that Cobb should choose to spend the rest of his life in the realistic dream or in the less enjoyable reality that he knows nothing about?

This time, most people think Cobb should take the pill and stay in Limbo. Why? This new scenario is a reversal of the original one. In the first scenario, you were asked if Cobb should choose the reality he knew over a more enjoyable dream. In this second scenario, you were asked if Cobb should choose the dream he knows over a less enjoyable reality. Most people think that Cobb should choose to remain in reality in the first scenario and to remain dreaming in the second scenario. But if reality is so important, why don't most people think Cobb should choose reality in the second scenario, as they did in the first? The only thing that changed between the scenarios is where Cobb spent the majority of his time—what Cobb had become familiar with.

Could it be that sticking with what we are familiar with matters more to us than what is real? Is it perhaps the case that we are irrationally biased toward the familiar? Is this bias the main reason that we choose reality over Limbo in the first Nozickian scenario? The answers to these questions are "yes," "yes," and "yes" (respectively).

Familiarity Breeds Approval

Psychologists are well aware of the human tendencies to prefer things to remain the same and to favor what they are familiar with over unfamiliar things of equal or even greater value. These tendencies are collectively referred to as "status quo bias" and are considered irrational because they can make us miss out on beneficial changes of circumstance.

You may not realize it, but mere exposure to a person can make you think that they are more attractive. If you happened to live in the same town as Ellen Page (Ariadne) and had caught a glimpse of her here and there, then you would prefer to look at a picture of her rather than one of an equally attractive person. Psychologists recently demonstrated this by planting several equally attractive models in a class, each a different number of times, making the students familiar with each of them to a different degree. The students were then asked to rate pictures of the models, which they did, scoring the models they were more familiar with more highly.[2]

In another experiment, three classes of students were rewarded for completing a task. In the first class, the students were given a mug and then (a short while later) asked if they wanted to swap their mug for a chocolate bar. In the second class, the students were given a chocolate bar and then (a short while later) asked if they wanted to swap their chocolate bar for a mug. In the third class, the students were given a choice between a chocolate bar and a mug. Despite only having to raise a piece of colored paper to accept the offer to switch gifts, only 10 percent of students from the first two classes chose to do so. This is unusual because about half of the students from the third class chose the mug and the other half the chocolate bar—indicating that the bar and the mug had similar value. It can't be that 40 percent of the students in classes one and two were just too lazy or shy to swap their reward. Psychologists think that the students didn't want to swap their rewards because they had created irrational attachments to them—they overvalued them because they had become familiar with them.[3]

Even more recently, the philosopher Felipe de Brigard demonstrated how status quo bias can affect our decisions about which kinds of lives we would choose for ourselves. Using scenarios similar to those we have been considering, de Brigard revealed that the less familiar we are with a life, the less likely we are to choose it even if it is more enjoyable or more real.[4] The point of all this is to show that we tend to overvalue what we are familiar with, including when we evaluate potential lives.

Landslide on Mount Nozick

So, are we victims of status quo bias when we consider Cobb's choice between Limbo and reality? Sure, most think that Cobb should choose reality over the dream in the first case; but remember, reality is also what is familiar in the first case. In the second case, most think Cobb should choose the unreal world, and in this case it's the unreal world that is familiar. So most think Cobb should choose to reunite with the kids he knew, regardless of whether they were more real or more likely to bring him happiness. This shows that the judgment that Cobb should choose a real life over a dream life in the first scenario isn't as heavily impacted by our concern about reality as we first imagined. What we care about is familiarity. And if familiarity is the main reason most people chose reality in the first scenario—instead of because it is real—then Nozick's argument fails to show that reality is important.

Where does the failure of Nozick's argument leave us? It certainly becomes much less clear whether reality matters and why it should matter. We are returned to the problem of how living in Limbo could make Cobb's life go worse for him, despite never becoming aware that he is not in reality and never experiencing any negative consequences from living in Limbo. You might worry that his real desires are not being satisfied in Limbo, but there is still no good explanation for how this actually affects him. If Cobb ends up in Limbo, then, as far as he is concerned, his desires do get satisfied and his life is meaningful. In fact, the advantages of Limbo, such as providing Cobb more fulfilling work and better friends, would mean that from Cobb's perspective, his life would be more enjoyable and more meaningful than if he had ended up in reality. Since we are interested in what is best for Cobb, why should any other perspective be more important than his subjective one?

But what about the people who think that Cobb should choose to avoid Limbo in both scenarios? Let's call these people die-hard fans of reality (not because they attend all the reality conventions in their reality-branded T-shirts, but because they still think living in reality is better for us). They can plausibly claim to be relatively unaffected by the status quo bias, since they didn't choose the familiar life in both scenarios. These people presumably chose reality over Limbo both times precisely because they think there is something valuable about reality even if it never, directly or indirectly, affects our consciousness. As we shall see, these die-hard fans of reality are in the grip of a couple of pernicious assumptions.

The Problem with Reality-Spotting

Die-hard fans of reality probably assume both that they can really know when they are in reality and that they are in reality right now. Most people have probably never given either of these assumptions much thought. Fair enough, too, considering that most of us haven't had much reason to question them in the past. Seeing *Inception*, though, generally makes people want to dig a little deeper into these issues.

How do you know when you're dreaming and when you're awake? It might seem obvious when you wake up . . . until you wake up again! Just like Saito, when Cobb is performing the extraction on him, you could be in a dream, within a dream, within a dream. Of course, right now you think it is obvious that you are awake. But has it not been equally obvious, while in a vivid dream, that you are awake? As other chapters in this book have pointed out, the sensation of "not dreaming" can be dreamed—so it can't guarantee that you are not dreaming.

We think there are telltale signs that help us to know when we are dreaming. It's said that trying to read can let you know you are dreaming; the text won't sit still or will look garbled. The movie *Waking Life* suggests that you can't turn off the lights in a dream. If I am just waking up, but wondering if I am still dreaming, I check for the drool patch—it's never there if I'm still dreaming. Others will try to control the dream, say by flying or making others in the dream do what they want. Successfully doing any of these things may very well tell you that you are dreaming.

But does failing to do these things necessarily indicate that you are not dreaming? If you can read, if you can shut off the lights, if the drool patch is there, if you can't fly or control others—presumably all of these things are true right now (except maybe the drool)—are you certain you are not dreaming? Haven't you tried to fly in dreams before and failed? Failing such tests could simply be a part of your dream, and thus would not necessarily let you know that you are not dreaming. Mal points this out to Cobb when he is trying to convince her, in their kitchen, that they are not dreaming. He asks, "If it's my dream, why can't I control it?" She replies, as if it's obvious, "[Because] you don't know you're dreaming."[5] We can't control every dream, especially vivid ones we think are real. So even though controlling a dream might tell us we are dreaming, failing to control one doesn't tell us that we aren't.

Consider Cobb's totem—his top. If he spins it and it doesn't fall, this lets Cobb know that he is dreaming. But if it falls, is that a certain indication that he is not dreaming? No. Arthur explains to Ariadne that when entering someone else's dream your totem will act differently because the dreamer does not know the specific features that make it unique. So a totem's usefulness relies on only its owner knowing its precise characteristics, and even then totems only tell you whether you are in someone else's dream. They cannot tell you whether you are in your own dream. Of course, if all the talk about, and making of, totems occurs within a dream (if, say, the entire movie is actually Cobb's dream), then totems cannot be trusted at all. If totems are made in a dream, then their precise characteristics cannot be secret.[6] Similarly, if Cobb ends up in Limbo and his subconscious is partly responsible for populating the world with objects, then he can't trust his totem because one of the dreamers (himself) knows how it works. This is a good reason not to care if Cobb's spinning top falls or not, but it also helps make a very important point: just as Cobb can never be sure that he is not in a dream, neither can we.

So die-hard fans of reality, who are adamant that actual reality (not just the experience of it) is important for well-being, should be feeling a little uneasy now. They probably thought they knew how to tell when they were dreaming. Now, however, they must admit that they can't be sure. And if reality is so important to die-hard fans of reality, then their inability to really be sure that they are not dreaming should make them worry about whether they are missing out on something very important.

When die-hard fans of reality avoid Limbo in both of the scenarios because reality matters so much, they are making two big mistakes. First, they have assigned reality special value for Cobb—they value reality over the additional enjoyment and sense of meaning in Limbo. They have even assigned this special value to reality in scenarios when it's impossible for reality to affect Cobb's consciousness in any way.

Second, die-hard fans of reality are making the mistake of placing great value on something that they can never be sure of. Even if reality (that never affects our consciousness) is more valuable than extra enjoyment and a sense of meaning in life, actively valuing it and pursuing it is a choice that would seem to lead to a worse life. Someone who has seen *Inception* should realize that they can't be sure of whether the life they are familiar with is actually a real one. So anyone who remains a die-hard fan of reality after seeing *Inception* is likely to be made worse off by worrying about whether they are in fact living in reality. And since there is no way for them to be certain that they aren't dreaming, this worry could plague them for the rest of their days.

Some philosophers have argued that knowledge doesn't require certainty. We can know that we are not dreaming because it is the best and most justified explanation of our experience. Still, I contend that we cannot be certain, and lack of certainty is still something significant to worry about.[7] I can in fact have certainty about something else. I can be certain of my own experiences—of how they feel, how they seem, of which ones are enjoyable and which ones are not. Even if I am dreaming, I know what kind of dream I want to have.

When we take the uncertainly about whether *the real world* is actually real into account, it is clearly a mistake to think that Cobb should make his choice based on valuing reality rather than valuing enjoyment and a sense of meaning in life. In choosing *the real world*, he would be gambling that *the real world* actually is real, but this is a bad bet because the stakes are very high and the payoff is uncertain. Even if *the real world* is real, it's not clear that reality can actually impact our well-being over and above what we experience. And even if reality could have this impact on our well-being, there is no way to be sure that it actually does because we can't be sure we're not dreaming. Do die-hard fans of reality really want Cobb to sacrifice a guarantee of more enjoyment and a greater sense of meaning in life for such uncertainties? Betting on reality is a bad bet.

The irony is that the more die-hard a fan of reality someone is, the more reason they have to choose the life in Limbo. This is because a die-hard fan of reality who chooses *the real world* might not get the reality he or she is looking for. In fact, the only reality they will get is a reality of which they can never be certain. The more die-hard of a fan they are, the more the thought of forgoing enjoyment and meaning for a nonexistent reality should scare them.

Some "super advanced die-hard fans of reality" (or SADFORs) might think that reality is still worth the risk; they might think that Cobb should take a chance on *the real world* being reality because a chance of reality trumps a guarantee of no reality. These SADFORs presumably think that the mere fact of living in reality is valuable, despite the fact that it can't affect our experiences, because it somehow makes life *meaningful*. There's more than one kind of meaning, though. There is objective meaning (the kind of meaning the SADFORs are talking about), and there is also subjective meaning—the kind of meaning a person finds in something. Cobb's life in Limbo would be subjectively meaningful because he would feel like he is succeeding at his important life plans. So his life would still have meaning—just meaning of a different kind. It's unclear which kind of meaning is more important. Sure, objective meaning *sounds* more important, but even if Cobb lives in reality, the objective meaning of doing so will never be experienced by him—his consciousness is never affected by it. So why care about it? I know which kind of meaning I value more. If only SADFORs could convince themselves to value subjective meaning, they could worry less and enjoy life more.

Why Reality Doesn't Matter

As we were sitting on the edge of our seats, watching Cobb's totem spin smoothly at the end of *Inception*, our minds were racing. When Cobb's spinning top jolted, as though kicked out of a relaxing dream, we heard the sharp intake of breath around us and we felt it in our own throats, too. But Cobb's totem kept spinning until the screen faded to black and the credits rolled. It's only natural that we wanted to know if Cobb's spinning top was going to fall—we are curious creatures who compulsively seek the truth. Now, though, you should realize that it doesn't really matter what happened to that spinning top. Christopher Nolan, who has been notoriously tight-lipped about what really happens in *Inception*, has even said that Cobb doesn't care if his spinning top falls at the end: "The real point of the scene . . . is that Cobb isn't looking at the top. He's looking at his kids. He's left it behind. That's the emotional significance of the thing."[8]

We were caught in the grip of some assumptions that we had good reason to think of as true. But now that we have had the chance to think about *Inception* for a while, we should question those assumptions.

Since things that don't affect our consciousness can't affect how our life goes for us, reality doesn't really matter. We think that reality matters to us, but it's really familiarity that most of us desire more. As long as we experience life as if we are living in familiar surroundings that seem real, it doesn't matter if we are living in reality or in Limbo. In fact, living in Limbo could allow for us to lead lives that we find more enjoyable and meaningful.

Die-hard fans of reality might try to convince you that reality should matter to you, even when it will not affect your consciousness in any way. If this happens, you should point out to them that they are probably being blinded by a couple of assumptions. You should encourage them to watch *Inception* and reevaluate whether they can be sure if they are dreaming or not. Most important, get them to question their assumption that they are currently living in reality. They'll realize that they can't ever be sure that they're not dreaming. And because the cost of more enjoyment and sense of meaning is too high for the mere chance of living in reality, they too will understand that it doesn't matter if Cobb's spinning top falls or not. In fact, they'll probably wish that Cobb would just throw his totem away and focus on finding enjoyment and meaning in his life because they, too, will realize that it's our experiences that really matter, not whether we are living in reality.

NOTES

1. Robert Nozick, *Anarchy, State, and Utopia* (New York: Basic Books, 1974), pp. 42–45.

2. Richard L. Moreland and Scott R. Beach, "Exposure Effects in the Classroom: The Development of Affinity among Students," *Journal of Experimental Social Psychology* 28 (1992): 255–276. Melissa Peskin and Fiona N. Newellô, "Familiarity Breeds Attraction: Effects of Exposure on the Attractiveness of Typical and Distinctive Faces," *Perception* 33 (2004): 147–157.

3. Jack L. Knetsch, "The Endowment Effect and Evidence of Nonreversible Indifference Curves," *The American Economic Review* 79 (1989): 1277–1284.

4. Felipe de Brigard, "If You Like It, Does It Matter If It's Real?" *Philosophical Psychology* 23 (2010): 43–57.

5. Christopher Nolan, *Inception: The Shooting Script* (San Rafael, CA: Insight Editions, 2010): 140.

6. As is pointed out in "The Editor's Totem" and in chapters in this volume by various authors, there are even more reasons that the reliability of Cobb's totem is limited. For one, it's Mal's, not his. So the top falling doesn't tell him he is not in Mal's dream. Second, he told Ariadne how it works, so the top would fall if he were in one of her dreams as well. Third—who doesn't know that tops fall? If Cobb spun a top in your dream, wouldn't you dream that it fell? While the top's perpetual spin tells Cobb he is in a dream, the top falling doesn't tell him much.

7. For more on how to deal with the epistemic angst raised by the lack of certainty that we are not dreaming, see Katherine Tullman's chapter in this volume.

8. Nolan made these comments to *Entertainment Weekly*. See Jeff Jensen, "Christopher Nolan on His 'Last' Batman Movie, an 'Inception' Video Game, and That Spinning Top," *Entertainment Weekly*, http://insidemovies.ew.com/2010/11/30/christopher-nolan-batman-inception/. Retrieved November 30, 2010.

WHY CARE WHETHER THE TOP KEEPS SPINNING?

Bart Engelen

We had our time together. But I have to let you go.

—Dom Cobb

Inception's seemingly happy ending shows Cobb being reunited with his children. To find out whether he is in *the real world* or in a dream, Cobb takes out his totem. We see his top spinning until Christopher Nolan cuts to the ending credits. The open ending inevitably leaves us wondering. Does the top keep spinning or does its slight wobble indicate that it will fall? Such questions drive some of us to Internet forums to discuss whether the ending is indeed a happy one or whether we are being tricked into believing it is. Why do we care so much about whether or not the top keeps spinning? Does it matter whether or not Cobb *really* managed to get out of Limbo? Wouldn't he be as happy if he were dreaming the final scenes?

Others have argued that reality doesn't matter. I will argue that it does.

Epistemology, Descartes, and Skepticism

As other authors in this volume have pointed out, *Inception* makes us think about the possibility of human knowledge as well as its scope and limits. We leave the movie theater not just wondering about Cobb's situation but also whether our own beliefs and experiences are as truthful and authentic as they seem. Can we ever know what the real world is like? Is it possible that the things and people we think we know are figments of our imagination? Here we enter what philosophers call epistemology, the branch of philosophy that studies knowledge. As Nolan shows, the fact that our ideas and beliefs about the world are the result of input processed by our brains raises the possibility of people hacking into our minds and making us believe whatever they want us to believe. If some highly skilled and equipped "dream team" were to kidnap you and hook you up to a machine that registers and stimulates your brain, they could make you see, hear, feel, and think things you would swear were real. From inside this dream, could you possibly discover its illusory nature? What way is there for you to know what situation you are in?

Inception provides a fantastic—in all the senses of the word—version of this problem. It's a problem that has troubled philosophers at least since René Descartes (1596–1650) considered the possibility that he might be living inside a dream. While you might think you are reading a philosophy book about *Inception* right now, Descartes reminds you that you can have exactly the same experience when dreaming. In fact, you can't exclude this possibility altogether: "When I think about this more carefully, I see so clearly that I can never distinguish, by reliable signs, being awake from being asleep."[1] Descartes goes even further and imagines being deluded by "some evil mind, who is all powerful and cunning" so "that the sky, air, earth, colors, shapes, sounds and everything external to me are nothing more than the creatures of dreams by means of which an evil spirit entraps my credulity."[2] It is as if he is imagining an omnipotent but evil dream architect.

Imagine you are Robert Fischer, who ends up in the backseat of a cab with two strangers, getting shot at. Just as we initially can't know that *Inception*'s first scenes of Cobb washing up onshore are set in Limbo, Fischer can't know that he is inside someone's (very wet) dream. Philosophers known as skeptics argue that the very possibility that we are being tricked can never be ruled out completely. After reading Descartes or watching *Inception*, how can you ever be sure that your beliefs are really your own and not the product of someone having performed inception on you? If a single idea can be planted in your mind, how can you be sure that your other ideas are genuinely yours? ("Inception can't really happen," you say to yourself. But how do you know that this very belief is not the result of an act of inception?) Unlike ordinary doubt about a specific belief, which occurs against a background of undisputed beliefs, this skeptical doubt is global, confirming Socrates' insight that the only real wisdom lies in knowing that you know nothing.

If you are reading all the chapters of this book in order, you've heard this before. You know that from an epistemological point of view, *Inception* centers around the question of whether we can ever tell the real world from the dream world. Just like we can't rule out Descartes' evil spirit, it is perfectly possible that every single scene in *Inception* is part of one big dream. The skeptical problem raises another question, however. If you can't know whether or not you are living a real life, why go on living it?

Or, let me put the question another way. If a machine existed that could make you dream of a perfect life, why not plug into it? When Ariadne wonders who would ever want to be "stuck in a dream," Yusuf rightly replies that it "depends on the dream." Some dreams can indeed be much nicer than real life. When given the chance to choose, would you prefer the harsh reality over the perfect dream? This question, which defined the lives of Cobb and Mal, is not an epistemological but an ethical one. It concerns not what we can know but what we should do.

Ethics, Nozick, and Hedonism

Imagine you are Ariadne, sitting outside a Paris café and listening to Cobb's job description of a dream architect: "You create the world of the dream." If you accept his job offer, you will learn to build dreams as you please. Everything will spring from your very own mind. You can draw on your memories (such as the last time you saw your children) or simply use your imagination. It would be "pure creation." Now imagine that you could choose to live your whole life inside those dreams. This possibility resembles a thought experiment from American philosopher Robert Nozick (1938–2002).

> Suppose there were an experience machine that would give you any experience you desired. Superduper neuropsychologists could stimulate your brain so that you would think and feel you were writing a great novel, or making a friend, or reading an interesting book.[3]

To see the genius of this experience machine, try to be like Eames, who tells Arthur not to "be afraid to dream a little bigger, darling." If you like guns, why not go for a grenade launcher? After all, in the world you create, the sky is the limit. To imagine what life would be like inside Nozick's experience machine, think of Mal in Limbo. She and Cobb together could make everything as they wanted it to be, from the shores and the city to the house they lived in. As Cobb explains to Ariadne, they were "feeling like gods." For Cobb, "the problem was knowing that none of it was real." While he held onto that unsettling thought, Mal chose to forget the truth. In the end, "Limbo became her reality." Not only did she live a wonderful life, she also grew blissfully ignorant about its illusory nature. Similarly, Nozick's experience machine can create any experience you might want, including the accompanying sense that all these experiences are genuinely and authentically yours. Nozick stresses that people inside the experience machine don't know that they are dreaming: "While in the tank you won't know that you're there; you'll think it's all actually happening."[4] Similarly, while in Limbo Mal didn't know that she was there; she thought it was all actually happening.

Now think of a machine so powerful that it creates all the dreams you want it to, including the illusion that they are true. Would you plug in? If you feel sad for Mal when she takes Limbo for reality, then you probably think there is more to (a good) life than having (pleasurable) experiences. According to Nozick, you would belong to the majority of people who wouldn't plug into the experience machine. When offered the option to enter the perfect dream, you realize that this is not how you want to live your life. You, too, "want to *do* certain things, and not just have the experience of doing them."[5]

If Nozick is right, most of us are concerned with living not only a happy but also a real life. While this shows that people *want* their experiences to track reality, it does not show that they actually *do* track reality. Nozick's thought experiment reveals that most people *do not want* to live a lie; it does not show that we are not living a lie, or that we know that we aren't. As such, Nozick's arguments are directed not against the epistemological theory of skepticism, but against the ethical theory of hedonism. According to hedonism, a good life simply consists in having pleasurable experiences. But Nozick believes that the value of one's life also depends on the extent to which these experiences are authentic and real. That we want Cobb to really see his children again—we want the top to topple—and that we pity Mal for mistaking Limbo for reality and wishing to stay there seem to vindicate Nozick. Apparently, living a perfect dream does not constitute what most of us would call a good life. As Ariadne knows all along, living a lie is always less valuable than living a life.

Totems as Elegant Solutions to Skepticism?

In the movie, the dream team seems to have found a solution to the skeptical problem. Each of them carries a personal totem, which, as Ariadne puts it, serves as "an elegant solution for keeping track of reality." Cobb's top is so important to him because it allows him to dismiss the skeptical possibility and find out whether or not the sky, air, earth, colors, shapes, and sounds he sees and hears are part of a dream. His faith in the trustworthiness of his totem serves as the basis upon which all his other beliefs rest. It is what epistemological foundationalists call a basic or foundational belief that grounds and gives support to other, derivative beliefs. For Cobb's basic belief in the reliability of his top to serve as a foundation stone, it has to be self-evident. As Arthur explains, the totem has a particular *feel* to it that only its owner is familiar with. When asked how he knows that this particular die is his totem, he can only say that it feels right. This basic belief can no longer be justified by other beliefs.

Upon closer inspection, however, we see that totems don't make for infallible evidence upon which all other beliefs can be grounded. Again, Arthur puts it well: "When you look at your totem, you know beyond a doubt you're not in someone else's dream." While the totem's particular feel makes it nearly impossible for dream architects to re-create it, it does not rule out the possibility that you are inside your own dream (or inside the dream of an architect or dreamer who has touched your totem, or knows how it works).[6] The fact that totems are not foolproof solutions for keeping track of reality illustrates the skeptical doubt. Skeptics ultimately deny the possibility of finding rock-hard evidence to discriminate between what is real and what only seems real.[7] Just as Cobb can't rely on his top to rule out the possibility of being inside his own dream, we can never know for sure that we are not living inside a dream right here, right now.

Because the search for unshakable basic beliefs is fruitless, foundationalism has been challenged by a rival theory: coherentism. According to coherentism, beliefs are justified if they cohere with one another, which means that they do not contradict and can be mutually derived from one another. No belief is more basic than another; they all form parts of a coherent web. Think of inception. If you could install in my mind the belief that I was as handsome, rich, and famous as Leonardo DiCaprio, it would not cohere with my other beliefs. Only if you could change or eliminate most of my other beliefs could this work. Because, as Arthur explains to Saito, "the subject's mind can always trace the genesis of the idea," the subject of inception should not only form the idea but also endorse it, which implies erasing all memories of its origin. On the Fischer job, the dream team has to go through several dream layers to make sure that Fischer will wake up believing that the idea planted there is actually his own.

Consider also Cobb's failed attempts to convince Mal of what he thought was true. Only through inception did Cobb manage to implant "this simple little idea that would change everything." He used Mal's totem—which she locked up in the safe of her subconscious during their stay in Limbo—to make her believe that the world she believed to be real was in fact not. He opened her safe, spun her top (since it was a dream, it never stopped spinning), and then closed it again. But the idea that was true in Limbo—"that her world wasn't real"—lingered on into *the real world*. Once Mal became convinced that her world wasn't real, Cobb couldn't convince her otherwise. He could provide no unshakable evidence for his view that their previous lives in Limbo were part of a dream and that their lives in *the real world* weren't. So Cobb's first successful act of inception worked to get Mal out of Limbo but also led to her suicide in *the real world*. Whereas most skeptics preach radical doubt and ignorance (we can never know for sure whether our world is real), Mal remained suicidal because she took the skeptical dream scenario not as a possibility but as the truth (she thought she knew her world wasn't real). While foundationalists would say that Cobb's inception eroded the pillars of her belief system, coherentists would say that the resulting idea contaminated the other parts of her web of beliefs. As a result, her beliefs were coherent. So there was, in a way, a method to her madness.

Why Care whether the Top Keeps Spinning?

In the end, Nolan himself seems to have performed inception on us, the audience. Through his ingenious storytelling and his focus on totems as truth-telling devices, he has planted a seed in our minds, which in most cases grows into a full-blown conviction that the top will reveal whether Cobb in the end really rejoins his children or whether it is all a dream. The fact that fans go through a lot of trouble to argue why the top will or will not keep spinning shows that Nolan has tricked them into believing that the top is indeed the key to deciphering the ending. They believe that if only they could look past the ending credits and see it topple (or not), they would *know* whether the ending is a happy one.

Besides the fact that the top isn't as reliable as it seems, the crucial thing is that we simply can't tell whether or not it keeps spinning. At best, one can argue why one scenario is more likely than another. Take, for example, the argument that the emotional weight and the narrative force of the story are lost in the "Full Dream" interpretation. Only if Cobb really has to pull off the Fischer job to be reunited with his children, the argument goes, can we get carried away by the plot. Would Nolan really make us watch a movie about a character who is never onscreen?[8] While this is a strong argument, it does not entirely rule out the "Full Dream" interpretation. No totem, scene, clue, or argument can, in fact, ever knock the skeptics down completely.

Even though we can never find out whether the faces we see in the final scene belong to Cobb's real children, it matters to us—and to Cobb—whether they do. Most of us would feel sad for Cobb if the children were mere projections of his subconscious. Does this mean hedonism is refuted? Or are most of us wrong in caring about the veracity of our beliefs and experiences? Aren't hedonists right in arguing that Cobb's well-being depends solely on his experiences, regardless of how they are produced and how they relate to reality? Nozick himself alludes to the intuitive attractiveness of hedonism: *"What else can matter to us, other than how our lives feel from the inside?"*[9]

Maybe this is how we should interpret the final scene. After all, Cobb goes to see his children before he finds out whether his top keeps spinning. Maybe this signals that Cobb is ultimately a hedonist who does not care whether his kids are real. Maybe his preference for illusory feelings of satisfaction— which drove him to the dream machine before—ultimately prevails. Maybe Cobb is happy to live a perfect dream and indulge himself in the illusion that it is real. Recall that the perfect experience machine can generate happy thoughts and the accompanying feeling that they are true. Nolan himself seems to support this interpretation: "Sometimes I think people lose the importance of the way the thing is staged with the spinning top at the end. Because the most important emotional thing is that Cobb's not looking at it. He doesn't care."[10] Realizing that he can never find out what is real and what is not, Cobb dismisses his totem and starts living his life from the inside. In this interpretation, the final scene is part of a dream that effectively has become Cobb's reality. If correct, it would vindicate hedonism against Nozick's criticism.

The basic idea behind this interpretation seems plausible. Once you realize that you can never verify the authenticity of your experiences, why continue caring about that very authenticity? Still, it makes perfect sense to care about something you might never be certain of. You hope your parents, partner, and children love you, even though you can never be certain that they do. You want to live a real life, even though you can never be sure that you are living a real life. Cobb turning away from his totem, therefore, doesn't reveal that he no longer cares about the authenticity of his experiences. All it reveals is that he no longer cares about his totem. While he still wants his children to be real, he no longer wants to prove that they are. Realizing that all attempts to this effect are futile, Cobb turns to what matters to him most: his children.

While hedonists rightly argue that people's subjective well-being depends entirely on their experiences, it doesn't follow that people shouldn't care about their truth or authenticity. The goodness of a life doesn't depend on just the subjective well-being of the person living it; the fact that one feels great inside the experience machine doesn't make it a life worth living. While a slave might enjoy himself perfectly well, his lack of basic liberties makes his life less worthwhile. While Mal is having a ball in Limbo, her life isn't improving, since she is asleep all the time.

While the fact that most people wouldn't plug into the experience machine can't be taken as proof that their beliefs are true, it does show that they hope them to be. Like most people, you probably don't want to become the victim of people penetrating your dreams or bringing you into theirs, even if you're sure that life in these dreams would be perfect. If we think of Cobb's and Mal's lives in reality and in Limbo, we can say two things. First, Cobb seems to lead better lives than Mal does, because he has true beliefs about his condition in both cases.[11] In contrast, we pity Mal for not seeing her situation for what it is. Second, Cobb and Mal live more valuable lives in reality than in Limbo. This is what Nozick was after. We want not only to enjoy ourselves but also "to live (an active verb) ourselves, in contact with reality."[12] While we might agree with Mal that Limbo is more fun than reality, most of us follow Cobb in preferring a real but less-than-perfect life over a perfect but illusory life. Even Mal's suicide was motivated by her desire to lead (what she thought to be) a real life.

Hedonists rightly stress that having pleasurable experiences is an important element of a good life, but they wrongly take this to be the only element. Mal's condition reveals that having false beliefs detracts from the good life. Like deception, inception is bad, partly because it makes people believe things that are completely false. In addition, Nozick rightly argues that a dream life, even if it has "become your reality," is impoverished when compared to a real life. In contrast with what hedonists imply, we are not here merely to enjoy ourselves. Truth and reality are intrinsically valuable. We don't value them because of, or as a means to, something else. They are important for their own sake. This is why people can reasonably choose uncomfortable truth over blissful ignorance. Hedonism's claim that pleasure is the be-all and end-all of life implies an all-too-narrow view of the goodness of a human life. Cobb cares about his children, but not because of the pleasures and profits they might bring him. Even though their being together definitely makes him happy, what ultimately matters to him is that they are *his* children and that he can look after them, in good times and bad.

What Matters in Life

Even though we can't prove that we are living real lives in truth, we shouldn't deny that these things matter. The fact that we can't know anything for sure does not mean that we can or should simply believe whatever we want to believe. What it does mean, though, is that we shouldn't waste our time trying to prove that the world is real. Since no foolproof totems exist, they simply are of no use. Imagine the real-life counterpart to Cobb who continuously aims to find evidence that what he deems real is real (and puts a gun to his head just in case it turns out otherwise). This would be madness. Obsessive attempts to prove that life is real are futile and distract from what matters in life: that we live it. Maybe that is why Cobb leaves his top and goes off to see his children. Instead of trying to remove all doubt and justify his basic belief in reality, Cobb turns away from the top toward his children, revealing that he wants to go on with his life.

As Cobb makes clear to Mal when they meet again in Limbo, he has been racked with guilt after planting the idea in her mind that her world wasn't real. In these crucial scenes, Cobb manages to redeem himself. He understands that his dreams about Mal's projection—who is "just a shade" of his real wife—no longer suffice. Finally, he realizes that he has to move on: "We had our time together. But I have to let you go." What matters in the movie is not so much that the Fischer job succeeds but that Cobb succeeds in getting his life back on track. In the song the dreamers use to signal the end of a dream, Edith Piaf sings: "*Non, rien de rien. Non, je ne regrette rien.*" She regrets nothing. Cobb no longer regrets the things he has done and realizes it is time for him to take up his life again. Nolan has stressed time and again that Cobb coming to terms with his past is the emotional baseline upon which *Inception* is based. It is his redemption, his emotional journey, and his realization that pleasurable dreams don't amount to a life worth living that drive the movie and make us feel for its protagonist.

From Cobb's and Mal's repeated dialogue, which beautifully captures this emotional baseline, it becomes clear that they care more about each other than about epistemological certainty: "You're waiting for a train. A train that will take you far away. You know where you hope this train will take you. But you can't know for sure. Yet it doesn't matter. Because you'll be together." Even though Cobb and Mal "can't know for sure" that their suicide will bring them back to reality, they hope it will. Even though Cobb can't know for sure that the faces he sees are *really* his children's, he sure hopes they are. While he can never completely rule out the possibility that his life is a lie, what matters is that he can live it together with his children.

Instead of asking whether the top keeps spinning, we should wonder why we (or Cobb, for that matter) care about whether it does. The heated debates about the top reveal that we care about the authenticity and veracity of experiences and beliefs. Nobody—not even Mal—wants to live (what is thought to be) a lie. In this sense, we should be glad that the skeptical concern that we develop when watching *Inception* or reading Descartes is not as "resilient" and "contagious" as it would be if it were planted in our minds several dream layers deep. Because we can "trace the genesis of the idea," we never fully endorse the suggestion that our world is some imaginary construction by an evil spirit, a dream team, or ourselves. This is also why it doesn't spur us into action. Fortunately, reading skeptical philosophers typically does not make us lay our heads on a railroad track.

Philosophy and Everyday Life

In a way, *Inception*'s closing image of the spinning top symbolizes the limits of human knowledge. Not only can't we determine

Cobb's fate, we also can't discover the nature of our own predicament. Nolan's cut to the ending credits nicely illustrates the fact that we can never get outside our own mental lives. The point is not that we are living in a dream or that we are living in reality. The point is that we have no reliable way of finding out for sure. And if this is so, what sense is there in endlessly trying to figure it out? We simply have to live with the fact that *Inception's* ending will always remain ambiguous and that our own lives will never be completely free from doubt.

Still, this insight does not drive us into depression or insanity. As hard as it is to philosophically or empirically refute skeptics, it is just as easy to put them aside in the practice of everyday life. In the end, it is real life, not philosophy, that ends the debates between skeptics and its opponents. Rather than trying to justify our basic belief in reality, we should treat it as an unavoidable habit of our minds without which our lives wouldn't make sense. While *Inception's* epistemological puzzles are fascinating and challenging, they can't be solved by philosophers and they should not rule our lives. After entertaining the thought that we are living inside an elaborate dream, we should follow Cobb in moving on with our lives, which are and will always remain our reality. We should, in other words, stop worrying about the spinning top and go watch another Nolan classic.

NOTES

1. René Descartes, *Meditations and Other Metaphysical Writings*, translated with an introduction by Desmond M. Clarke (London: Penguin Classics, 1998), p. 19.

2. Ibid., p. 22.

3. Robert Nozick, *Anarchy, State, and Utopia* (New York: Basic Books, 1974), pp. 42–45. The following quotes all spring from this short but influential passage from Nozick's book.

4. Ibid., p. 43.

5. Ibid.

6. Unfortunately for Cobb, his totem is almost useless because he told Ariadne—who is the architect for the Fischer job—how it works.

7. Peter Klein, "Skepticism," in Edward N. Zalta (ed.), *The Stanford Encyclopedia of Philosophy* (Winter 2010 edition). Online at: http://plato.stanford.edu/archives/win2010/entries/skepticism/.

8. As Dileep Rao, the actor who plays Yusuf, puts it: "To me, it's a far more elegant story if it's a vast job that Leo has to pull off. The threat is real, the growth is real, the adversary is real. The weakness of 'It's all a dream'—why we hate that, why we feel cheated when narratively anything is revealed to be all a dream—is that you've just asked me to spend so much time and emotional capital investing in the stakes of this, and you've now swept it away with the most anti-narrative structuralism that doesn't have anything to substitute in its place." Nick Confalone, "*Inception*'s Dileep Rao Answers All Your Questions About Inception," *New York Magazine*, July 19, 2010. Online at: http://nymag.com/daily/entertainment/2010/07/inceptions_dileep_rao_answers.html. Others have a different take on this interpretation. For a through argument for the "Full Dream" interpretation, see "The Editor's Totem" and the first two chapters of this book. For an argument on specifically why we should still care about *Inception*, even if it is all a dream, see Andrew Terjesen's chapter in this volume.

9. Nozick, p. 43. Italics in original.

10. Robert Capps, "Christopher Nolan on Dreams, Architecture, and Ambiguity," *Wired*, 18(12), pp. 83–87, November 29, 2010.

11. At least, if *the real world* is in fact real.

12. Nozick, p. 45.

PART THREE

IS INCEPTION POSSIBLE?: THE METAPHYSICS, ETHICS, AND MECHANICS OF INCEPTING

HOW TO HIJACK A MIND: *INCEPTION* AND THE ETHICS OF HEIST FILMS

Daniel P. Malloy

An idea is like a virus, resilient, highly contagious.
And the smallest seed of an idea can grow. It can grow
to define or destroy you.

—Dom Cobb

If we strip away all the layers of metaphysical and epistemological issues in *Inception*, what's left is a fairly standard heist film. A job is commissioned, a team is assembled, the job is carried out successfully against nigh-impossible odds and in spite of a team member's failures and betrayals. As such, *Inception* raises the same sorts of questions that accompany almost every depiction of a crime. Is it dangerous? Does watching crime make one more likely to be a criminal? Do violent media make a society violent, or does a violent society make violent media?

Moviemaking as Inception

One might be tempted to brush off such worries, but that would be premature. If inception really were possible, you'd be worried. If there were people who had the ability to implant ideas in a person's mind, without the person knowing, and if the person actually thought they came up with the idea, that would be dangerous. A person with such power could potentially control any person's actions. If inception really were possible, you would really have to worry that someone had done it to you. Yet, isn't inception exactly what media, such as movies, can do?

Inception itself implicitly draws parallels between inception and moviemaking,[1] and Christopher Nolan, *Inception*'s writer and director, explicitly draws the parallels in interviews.[2] Each member of Cobb's team represents a role in the moviemaking process. Cobb is the director. Arthur, who sets everything up, is the producer. Saito? That's easy; he is the bankroller—the Warner Brothers that puts up the money, and stands to make money, from the project. Ariadne, who designs the dreams, is the screenwriter. Yusuf, who produces the sedative that allows them to pull the whole thing off, is special effects. Eames, who is even seen sitting in front of an old-timey vanity mirror as he prepares for a role, is the actor. And Fischer, the mark, is us—the audience—primed, as we watch a movie, to have ideas implanted.

The similarity goes beyond finding parallel roles, however. In constructing the dreams that will serve as the settings for the heist, Cobb and company are really doing what any filmmaker does: establishing a particular story line in a particular place and time. The three levels of the dream are like three acts in a single film: act one establishes the characters and their goals, act two puts them in jeopardy, and act three sees them achieve their goals. The first level of the dream introduces the dream character of Robert Fischer. The second shows Cobb trying to deal with Fischer's subconscious defenses. The third is the scene of successful inception. The difference, of course, is that the dreams designed by Cobb and his companions are intended for an audience of one.

Ultimately, the most important similarity between the story line of *Inception* and filmmaking is inception itself. The goal of inception is to implant an idea in the dreamer's mind. In the film, the implanted idea will lead to the breakup of Fischer-Morrow. The team wants to capitalize on Robert Fischer's poor relationship with his father, but because Cobb thinks "positive emotion trumps negative emotion every time," they don't want the inception to be a negative idea. Eames suggests, "My father accepts that I want to create for myself, and not follow in his footsteps." To incept this idea, on the first level they will suggest, "I will not follow in my father's footsteps," on the second they will feed him, "I will create something for myself," and on the third, "My father doesn't want me to be him." It works. As Fischer says to Eames (as Browning) while sitting on the shore of the river in the first dream layer, "The will means that dad wanted me to be my own man, not just to live for him. That's what I'm going to do."

It's not just Fischer who was incepted, though. You and I were as well. We left the theater debating whether Cobb was still in a dream. That debate led to the debate over whether anything in the film was real, which, followed consistently, led to the question of whether anything outside the film is real. Thanks to *Inception*, a fair number of people were asking these sorts of questions in the summer of 2010. The film itself planted the ideas—*Inception* is itself a kind of inception.

Inception's ability to incept raises concerns about the sorts of ideas we get from films. Some of them are what we might call *overt* ideas, that is, the ideas that are explicit in the film. Before watching *Inception*, you didn't know who Cobb was, what he wanted, or what he was going to do to get it. Afterward, you did. But that's not really inception—you knew that was going to happen, even wanted it to happen. You even paid for the privilege of gaining those ideas. The act of inception is about the ideas you didn't know you were going to get and, indeed, may not have even known you'd gotten. When Saito first asks about the possibility of inception, Arthur compares it to inspiration and claims that that is why it is not possible. But it is possible! Very few people walked out of *Inception* without experiencing at least some doubt about the reality of the world. They may have even thought that the idea to doubt was their own idea. That reality may be a dream is one of the many ideas that Nolan was trying to incept in us. And this idea, in fact, is nearly the same one that Cobb incepted into Mal.

All films do this on some level or another with some idea or another. Indeed, all art could be said to perform this kind of inception. Love songs and romantic comedies, for instance, influence the way we think about our own love lives by creating ideas of what love should be. James Bond films and pornography could influence what we think our sex life should be like. This is why art worries philosophers. Philosophy is concerned with ideas, how we get them, where they come from, and what justification there is for believing them. In implanting ideas, films and other artworks seem to bypass our rational thought processes. There is no chance to critically examine an idea that is slipped in with a lot of other, flashier ideas. As Cobb says: "An idea is like a virus." Once it's in a person's mind, it will grow and replicate and possibly change the very identity of its host. For that reason, we need to be careful when accepting ideas—we need to examine and criticize them rigorously. When an idea is implanted, we are robbed of this chance. It is only once we become aware of the incepted idea that we can examine it, and by then it may already be too late.

Planning the Heist

Okay, so movies can incept ideas into us. But is *Inception* anything to worry about? After all, no one is likely to jump out a window, like Mal, after considering the possibility that reality is a dream. *Inception* does, though, tell the story of a crime, a heist. *Los Angeles Times* blogger Geoff Boucher claimed that it was "Hollywood's first existential heist film," and Christopher Nolan has stated that he originally wrote *Inception* as a heist film.[3] The movie depicts an unusual heist, to be sure, but all heist films tell stories about unusual heists—there isn't much drama to be had from a scenario that begins and ends with someone pulling a gun, getting what he wants, and then walking away. You need some sort of twist to make it exciting.

Some people may cleverly reply that *Inception* is not actually a heist film because Cobb and crew don't steal anything. They attempt to acquire information from Saito and then try to implant an idea in Robert Fischer's mind. Can you have a heist without a theft?

You can. In fact, in the case of Saito, it's not so clear that we don't have a theft. Just because they weren't stealing anything physical doesn't mean they weren't stealing. Couldn't you steal something from someone's online gaming account, by hacking it, yet be taking nothing physical? Likewise, an identity thief doesn't have to take anything physical from his victim. It's just information.

What the dream team does to Fischer is a bit more complex, though. It's one thing to call stealing information a heist; it's quite another to call implanting information a heist. Heist films rarely if ever involve breaking into a place solely to leave something there. Something may be left behind, but that's usually either an accident (as when one of the thieves leaves behind some piece of evidence) or a replica of the object stolen (like Indiana Jones at the beginning of *Raiders of the Lost Ark*). We might see this as a parallel, however, to what happens in *Inception*. On the surface, it seems that Cobb and crew are giving Robert Fischer something outright. In fact, what they are doing is replacing something. They have stolen Fischer's real, albeit dysfunctional, relationship with his father and replaced it with a new one. The new one may be better in some ways, but that does not change the fact that this new relationship is one that Cobb and company created. It is not representative of the actual relationship between Robert Fischer and Maurice Fischer. Thus, peculiar though it is, inception is a kind of heist.

Just including a heist, though, is not enough to make a film a heist film. Plenty of films include heists without being heist films. So, what more do we need to call *Inception* a heist film? Well, contrary to the name and common perception, heist films aren't primarily about the heist itself. The heist is the payoff. The essential action of heist films, including *Inception*, is about the events leading up to the heist—the planning and preparation. The first part of *Inception* is about getting the job set up—Cobb's "audition" for Saito and Saito's subsequent offer. The next part of the film is about assembling the team and making the plan. As in most other heist films, this is the important bit. Each member of the team is brought in for their specific talents. Aside from the Planner (Cobb) and his Enforcer (Arthur), you have the architect (Ariadne), the forger (Eames), and the chemist (Yusuf). Only in the third act do we get to the heist itself.

So the evidence is good that *Inception* is in fact a heist film. The act of inception itself is a kind of heist and the film follows the usual structure of heist films. For that matter, the characters all fill roles typical of heist films—the troubled leader, his loyal right hand, the instigator of the job, the newcomer, and so on. *Inception* does more than simply depict a crime, however. It fosters sympathy for criminals. So now the question is, does *Inception* incept into us the idea to engage in our own criminal behavior?

Homer Hijacks the *Republic*

Long before the first heist film was even scripted, Plato saw this danger coming. Realizing the potential that works of art had to influence our minds and, consequently, our behavior, Plato (428/427–348/347 BCE) offered two arguments in his *Republic* for excluding, or at least highly restricting, the filmmakers of his day—poets and dramatists.

Some context is necessary to understand each of these arguments. Plato's *Republic* is a lengthy dialogue between Plato's mentor, Socrates, and several friends. The topic of the dialogue is justice. Socrates and his friends decide that in order to understand what makes a person just or unjust, they first have to decide what a just city-state would be like. The majority of the book is spent discussing the arrangements for Plato's perfect republic. It's not one that many of us would want to live in, and Plato acknowledges that. The perfect republic would arrange people into classes, but those classes would be determined by people's talents, not their heritage. To determine people's individual talents, Plato has to set up a fairly elaborate educational system for his would-be citizens. At one point he even says that in order to establish this republic at all, his first step would have to be to banish everyone above the age of ten.[4]

The educational system is about more than just ensuring that people's talents are discovered and encouraged, though. It's also about molding people into good citizens. Plato insists on setting up a system of rigid censorship to ensure that the stories children are exposed to send the right kind of message. In particular, Plato is concerned with how gods and heroes are portrayed in the stories of his day. If you're at all familiar with Greek mythology, you can probably guess what Plato objected to. The behavior of Zeus alone in the classic myths would put most of the people on *The Jerry Springer Show* to shame. The gods of the ancient Greek myths are constantly playing tricks on people, feuding with each other, having bastard (in the literal sense) children, lying, cheating, lusting, flying into divine rages at minor offenses, and generally behaving badly. The heroes aren't much better. Odysseus, the wise and cunning hero of the Trojan War, was also a lying, conniving so-and-so. The Trojan

War itself was, of course, set off because of lust and jealousy, and continued largely out of greed for spoils.

So Plato bans the poets from his ideal republic, although he allows that they may return if they compose stories with appropriate messages. The gods must act like gods—divine perfect beings who are above mere human needs and desires—and heroes must act like heroes—exceptional mortals who have raised the bar for honor and moral behavior. Good guys must act like good guys and bad guys must act like bad guys. Why? Because, according to Plato, if we allow people to read the tawdry stories peddled by the likes of Homer and Sophocles, where gods and heroes act like regular people, they'll think that kind of behavior is okay. If Zeus can cheat on Hera with any woman who takes his fancy, they'll think, "Why can't I? Zeus does it."

Now, we have to be careful here. What concerns Plato is not that people will start thinking that because something is good enough for a god to do, it's good enough for any mortal. That would be a bit presumptuous. Rather, the idea is that because Zeus is a god, he can do no wrong. Therefore, whatever Zeus does is right. So, it is right to commit adultery. Thus, without Plato's censorship, Zeus becomes the ultimate bad example.

Applying Plato's theory to the heist film genre is fairly simple: the film follows the adventures of a crew of thieves who become the heroes of the film by default. We sympathize with them; we pull for them. This was not always the case, however. An important change has occurred in the heist film in the last few decades, particularly in its third act, which typically takes place after the heist itself, showing the aftermath. In earlier times, the thieves would have met some form of justice—either the police would have caught them, or their fragile alliance would crumble. This was all in accord with the Hays Code, Hollywood's long-time, self-imposed version of Plato's censorship rules, which called for thieves to be prevented from enjoying their ill-gotten gains. Things have changed recently, but with a caveat. Now, the thieves typically succeed in their crime, but only because the victim of the crime is worse than the thieves themselves. In some ways, Plato's censorship proposals live on, but only because it is difficult to sell a film where the protagonists are unlikable.

In *Inception*, the protagonists are granted redemption, of a sort, not because they are caught or because of the moral decrepitude of their victim—we really don't learn enough about Robert Fischer to judge him—but because of the supposed benefit their crime will bring the victim. It's doubtful that Robert Fischer would see it as a benefit, as Eames claims he would, but regardless, that is how Cobb and company get to remain protagonists and heroes in spite of their crime.

In Plato's eyes, though, that wouldn't be enough. Even showing bad consequences of a crime doesn't justify portraying the crime in the first place—at least, not if the criminals are also the protagonists in the story. An instructive morality play in which the criminal commits a crime and gets caught can actually teach something, an unintended lesson. It can, for instance, teach budding criminals to be smarter than those protagonists, rather than to mend their ways. The danger, according to Plato, lies not in failing to show consequences, but in allowing audiences to identify with and feel sympathy for bad people.

So would Plato allow a showing of *Inception* in his republic? One might still think he would for a couple of reasons, but ultimately, I think he's going to say no.

First, one might think that Plato would sell tickets to a showing of *Inception* because about half of the film is spent showing how tortured Cobb is by his past misdeeds. This goes beyond simply showing the consequences of the action to actually mitigating our identification with him. Unlike many other heist films, which portray their protagonists with a certain degree of glamour, *Inception* shows the mastermind as a broken man. We may pity him, but we never want to be like him. Plato would still be worried, though, because we may be learning the wrong lesson. Cobb isn't tortured because he performed inception or extraction—his actual crimes. Instead he is tortured by the fact that one act of inception may have led to the death of his wife. The lesson is not that we shouldn't commit crimes. The lesson is that we should be smarter about it than Cobb was.

Maybe Plato would be willing to show *Inception* because we will never have the ability to commit crimes like Cobb's. Dream-sharing is not possible now and is not likely to become possible in the near future. Those of us who flocked to the theaters to see the film will probably never have the opportunity to steal information from one another's dreams or to plant ideas there. So why worry about it? Consider Plato's original objection, however. He was worried about the portrayals of gods and heroes. Now, much as I might like to think I could, I can't do most of the stuff gods can do. Nor, I suspect, can you. Nor could the Greeks of Plato's time. He wasn't worried that men might turn themselves into eagles, swans, bulls, or serpents to cheat on their wives; he was simply worried that they would cheat on their wives. In the same way, we shouldn't worry that people might be encouraged to spy on one another's dreams by *Inception*. We should worry that they will be encouraged to violate one another's privacy—a serious concern in the information age.

Dreams within Dreams

Plato's second objection to poets and other artists is particularly relevant to *Inception*. In the opening line of Book X of the *Republic*, Socrates says, "Of the many excellences which I perceive in the order of our State, there is none which upon reflection pleases me better than the rule about poetry."[5] He then proceeds to criticize poetry and imitative art on completely new grounds from the ones offered earlier. An artist, according to Plato, creates a copy of reality. According to Plato, however, our world and the things in it are already mere copies of a higher world, the world of the Forms or Ideas. This world is perfect and eternal, whereas our world is imperfect and ever-changing. The artist creates a copy of this world, thus pulling our attention even further from the truth of things.

There are two ways we can relate this to *Inception*. First, *Inception* is a film—it is an illusion. One of Plato's most famous illustrations is his renowned cave, a darkened hole where shadows are projected on one wall. The people in the cave believe the shadows are real; they are concerned about them, interested in them, and invested in the order and existence of the shadows. Doesn't this sound like a primitive movie theater? Think about how you feel during a movie. You sit, watching a wall on which light is casting images. The images depict a work of fiction that has at most a slight connection to some real event. In *Inception*, you are watching a work of pure fiction, yet you are interested, invested, and concerned. You feel tension and worry about the characters. Once the film ends, you try to figure out what the ending means—did the top fall or not? In so many ways, when sitting in a movie theater, we are like Plato's prisoners in the cave watching the shadows, thinking they are real.

The second connection between Plato's levels of reality and *Inception* has more to do with the content of the film, rather than it simply being a film. *Inception*, like much of Nolan's other work, is about perception and reality. The entire third act, in a sense, never really happens. It's just a bunch of stories being played out in the dreams of various characters, each dream a step further away from reality. So? What's the danger? Just ask Cobb and Mal. It's possible to lose oneself in these various fantasies, to pass further and further away from real life and real concerns.

Plato would be concerned that in becoming more and more enthralled by these illusions, passing into ever deeper levels of the dream, we are not only getting further away from life, we are getting further from truth. Think about the Penrose steps, the never-ending staircase that Arthur uses to teach Ariadne how to build mazes in dreams. In real life, in truth, such a staircase is impossible—it is self-contradictory.[6] But *Inception* makes us believe in its possibility.

It's not the falsehood of art itself that provides the ground for Plato's objection, however. Plato had no qualms about lying per se. He even advocates using lies to help people see the truth—that is, people who aren't smart enough to understand the real truth can be fed dumbed-down versions of it in the form of lies or "myths." Those sorts of lies are fine. The problem with art's falsehood, according to Plato, is that it doesn't get us any closer to the truth. It separates us from the way things really are. For instance, think about war films. With few exceptions, they tend to glorify combat, when the reality is that war is anything but glorious.

Resolving Issues in Dreams

"Look," I can hear someone saying, "aren't you, and Plato, taking this a bit too seriously? It's just a movie. Sure, it's interesting and it's filled with strange ideas, but in the end it's just something to keep us occupied. Harmless escapism."

This response is similar to the one advocated by Plato's most famous student, and most strident critic, Aristotle, who argued that literature and drama that portray bad actions don't necessarily lead us to perform those actions ourselves. In fact, he said, such works of fiction can be cathartic. That is, by watching the characters in a tragedy go through bad times and identifying with them, we can vicariously go through those things ourselves. This vicarious experience would allow us to purge our own minds of those feelings and motives, thus actually decreasing the likelihood that we'd act in similar ways. So a film is not just "harmless escapism." It is a form of therapy.

It's important to avoid a temptation here. We might think that watching a heist film could lessen the likelihood of our committing a heist by demonstrating the potential negative outcome of such an action. Aristotle, however, does not teach us any such thing. According to his theory, the heist film decreases our desire to commit a heist because it allows us to experience the excitement we would in performing a heist without any of the risk. Drama and fiction are not so much about teaching lessons as about releasing emotions.

So what do we purge in *Inception?* A variety of feelings, actually. First, we purge feelings of loss, grief, and guilt in identifying with Cobb's struggles with Mal. More important, though, we get to experience what it's like to invade someone else's mind, to plant ideas there, to fundamentally alter his or her personality. Admittedly, these aren't impulses most of us have. We do, however, have impulses to see how much we can get away with, how far we can push the envelope. And we get to purge these impulses in the course of *Inception.*

In some ways (okay, many ways), Aristotle is more realistic than Plato. A particular virtue of Aristotle's theory is that it recognizes that people don't act because of ideas. Rather, they act out of motives, that is, out of emotions. Plato, by contrast, objects to stories and art based on their epistemic and metaphysical status. He, unlike Aristotle, never considers how people actually interact with works of art. Because stories are works of mimicry and contain certain ideas, Plato presumes that they will have the effects he predicts. Aristotle, to his credit, examines how and why people act in the ways they do.

This is not to imply that there are no objections to Aristotle's theory—far from it. A contemporary variation of Aristotle's catharsis theory is the moral imagination theory. It claims that at least part of the purpose of fiction is to make us better people. By watching movies and reading novels we can exercise our moral imagination, giving us the tools to better sympathize with other people. So, while it has much in common with Aristotle, the moral imagination theory is in some ways opposed to his catharsis theory. Whereas Aristotle holds that narrative art makes us less susceptible to certain emotions, the moral imagination theorist argues that the virtue of films and stories is that they enable us to feel things that we wouldn't otherwise.

Dream Bigger

Most people these days, when confronted with this controversy between Plato and Aristotle, tend to think that neither of them is right. Both have merits, because we can see how both actually do work in our lives. Films and other media do implant ideas in our minds, and plainly many of us mimic things we see in movies—not always, of course, but often enough to make it a concern. At the same time, we do watch movies to escape, to experience things and emotions that we can't or don't want to experience in real life.

The essential difference between Plato and Aristotle really comes down to the mental processes each is concerned with. Plato worries about ideas, whereas Aristotle and the moral imagination theorists are focused on emotions. If we take this distinction seriously, it is possible to argue that the two theories are compatible. It is possible that works of fiction influence us to mimic them while at the same time purging the sorts of emotions and motives that would lead us to actually perform those acts. So, the influence of *Inception* would be mitigated. On the one hand, it gives us a sort of permission to violate the privacy of others. On the other hand, it encourages us not to do so by allowing us to vicariously live the experience instead.

NOTES

1. On this, see, for instance, *AV Club's Inventory* of November 15, 2010, "Lights! Camera! Deconstruction!: 19 Movies That Double as Movie Criticism," www.avclub .com/articles/lights-camera-deconstruction-19-movies-that-double,47629/.

2. "Dreaming/Creating/Perceiving/Filmmaking: An Interview with Writer/Director Christopher Nolan," interviewed by Jonathan Nolan, the preface to *Inception: The Shooting Script* (San Rafael, CA: Insight Editions, 2010), p. 19.

3. Robert Capps, "Q&A: Christopher Nolan on Dreams, Architecture, and Ambiguity," *Wired* 18, no.12 (December 2010): 83–87.

4. Plato, *Republic*, trans. Benjamin Jowett (Mills, MA: Agora, 2001), p. 291.

5. Ibid., p. 365.

6. For more on the possibility of real-world paradoxes, see Tyler Shores's chapter in this volume.

INCEPTION, TEACHING, AND HYPNOSIS: THE ETHICS OF IDEA-GIVING

Adam Barkman

What is the most resilient parasite? A bacteria? A virus? An intestinal worm? An *idea*. Resilient, highly contagious. Once an idea's taken hold in the brain it's almost impossible to eradicate.

—Dom Cobb

Inception is a movie about idea-giving, specifically about "inception" or the act of an "extractor" or dream navigator planting an idea in the mind of his unknowing, dreaming subject. Because idea-giving is a normative act—that is, an act having to do with what's morally right or wrong—inception is also a normative act. As Dom Cobb tells Saito, "You asked me for inception. I do hope you understand the gravity of that request. The seed that we will plant in this man's mind will grow into an idea and this idea will define him. It may come to change everything about him." Large moral issues loom when you tinker with the very fabric of a person's being.

But giving someone an idea—isn't that pretty much what teaching is? If so, then teaching is moral only if inception is. But doesn't it seem that inception is, at least on some level, immoral? And what about giving suggestions under hypnosis? That really looks like inception. Would that be moral? Let's explore the ethics of inception by exploring the ethics of idea-giving in general and specifically talking about teaching and hypnosis—arguably the two most important methods of idea-giving.[1]

Indoctrination and Teaching

Convinced by postmodernist epistemologies, some philosophers of education have argued that *all* forms of teaching—the most typical method of idea-giving—are immoral, since *whatever* is selected to be taught is nothing but the subjective preference of a particular individual or culture. These philosophers would say, for example, that the mere fact that Cobb teaches his young children, James and Phillipa, that "This world is the real world" or even that "Tokyo is a city in Japan" violates their rights to choose to believe whatever they want.

Wisely, few take this view too seriously. The view contradicts itself. It suggests that "All forms of teaching are immoral because everything that is taught is only subjectively true" while asserting that this proposition itself is objectively *true*. In other words, it is objectively true that there are no objective truths. Obviously, this is contradictory nonsense.

As a parent, Cobb can't avoid giving *some* ideas to his children. Moreover, the ideas he gives his children will unavoidably be filtered through his own worldview. For example, if Cobb were a Buddhist, he would believe that the goal of life is to escape the cycle of reincarnation or *samsara*, which can be achieved by adhering to the Noble Eightfold Path, which (in part) states that knowledge of our circumstances is beneficial to such an escape. Consequently, because Cobb, in our example, would be a Buddhist and not, for instance, a Hindu, he would likely think Buddhism to be truer or more correct than Hinduism and would very likely teach this worldview to James and Phillipa.

However, educator I. A. Snook would argue that for Cobb to engage in this form of idea-giving would be immoral. "Teaching for belief in religious propositions is always indoctrination."[2] Snook's comment would suggest that our hypothetical Cobb is immoral for teaching his children particular *content*, namely religious content, because doing so necessarily implies indoctrination and indoctrination is immoral. Yet, one wonders, what exactly is a religious proposition? And why would indoctrination be immoral?

Defining "religion" is difficult. But if a religion is, as one dictionary has it, "a set of beliefs concerning the cause, nature and purpose of the universe, especially when considered as the creation of a superhuman agency or agencies,"[3] then Snook's argument may have a problem. How is metaphysical materialism—presumably Snook's worldview—not a religion? After all, it, just as much as Buddhism, Hinduism, Christianity, and so on, maintains that the world came to be through forces beyond human control and certainly has an account of the cause of the universe (the big bang), the nature of the universe (everything is material), and the purpose of the universe (there is no purpose). Even the agnostic—if Snook happened to be one—could easily be fitted into this definition of religion. So, at least in respect to the definition above, it seems that *every* worldview is a religion. And if so, by the lights of Snook's argument, teaching anything would imply indoctrination, and would thus be immoral. But that just doesn't seem right. Certainly, Snook wouldn't agree.

Maybe it's not religious belief per se that is the problem—but just indoctrination itself. What exactly is indoctrination? Philosopher R. M. Hare (1919–2002) says, "Indoctrination only begins when we are trying to stop the growth in our children of the capacity to think for themselves."[4] According to Hare, an indoctrinated child or person is one who has been given ideas and told to believe them regardless of the evidence—to slavishly accept a proposition or series of propositions in a fashion that disregards his or her autonomy and eliminates critical openness. For Hare, the problem isn't so much the *content* of the teaching, but rather the *method* of the teaching. For example, if Cobb were to teach his children that the Four Noble Truths of Buddhism are beyond question—to teach James and Phillipa that it's unacceptable to reflect critically upon the truth of these claims—then, according to Hare, Cobb would be indoctrinating or engaging in immoral idea-giving.

While Hare certainly seems to be on the right path, he overlooks something that Plato, Aristotle, and modern educational psychologists all insist upon: a child's rationality *develops*. Because a young child like James or Phillipa—let's say a child under or around the age of five—can only reason on a very rudimentary level, the child won't really be able to challenge the beliefs given to him or her. James and Phillipa wouldn't really be able to challenge the Buddhist ideas given to them by their dad, and so they would likely, for a time, make these beliefs their own. There is no avoiding this. Buddhism, then, would become James and Phillipa's "plausibility structure," and this, in itself, would both be moral and, indeed, necessary for healthy growth: a tree can't grow in a vacuum; it needs soil, even, if it were the case, contaminated soil.[5]

What would be immoral, however, is if Cobb failed to encourage rational development in his children—if he failed to give them the tools of logic that would allow them *eventually* to understand the reasons for and against Buddhism and then to accept or reject Buddhism based on their rational autonomy. The word "eventually," of course, neither denotes a set age or time, nor does it indicate a clear, black-and-white argument for-and-against. It is a process. Therefore, if, when James and Phillipa are ready to start school, Cobb were to enroll them in a Buddhist school, he wouldn't necessarily be acting immorally because within the context of the Buddhist school, the children could learn how to reason critically while at the same time learning how a Buddhist might view history, literature, other worldviews, and so on. Secular humanist parents could send their children to secular humanist schools, Christians to Christian schools, Hindus to Hindu schools. And, provided that they were being taught by the schools (and, of course, the parents) to reflect critically on what is being taught and given the freedom to accept or reject what is taught, none of these parents and schools should, in themselves, be seen as indoctrinating.

Nevertheless, if Cobb were a Buddhist, then he might also accept certain Buddhist beliefs that, if *taught*, could easily be seen as immoral. What beliefs? Many interpret certain sayings of the Buddha to entail that the laws of logic are relative and argue that his doctrine of no self—*anatman*—entails that there is no free will.[6] If Cobb passed such beliefs on to his children, he could be seen as discouraging them from thinking for themselves. One cannot reason without the rules of logic and one cannot freely decide what to believe without free will. For teaching to not be indoctrination, some objective truths must be asserted. Without these truths, children won't have the tools necessary to challenge the worldview in which they are raised.

Some philosophers, of course, will argue that to assert any objectivity, much less genuine autonomy, is to assert something that is relative or subjective to a particular worldview. I deny this. While all people work from within a worldview, not all truth claims asserted from within a worldview are relative or dependent on that worldview being true as whole. If nothing is self-evident, nothing can be proven. Some truths such as 1 + 1 = 2, "It's always wrong to torture a child for fun," and the Law of Identity are immediately seen to be self-evident once we understand the terms, and there is no way for these propositions to be false. Even if everyone on the planet thought 1 + 1 = 2 is a social construction, this would not make it so. They would be wrong. Even if some, such as serial killers, thought it okay to torture children for fun, they would be *wrong*—not because most of society agrees, but because it is plainly and simply wrong. We know these truths by what the ancient Egyptians called *Ma'at*; the ancient Iranians, *Asha*; the ancient Hindus, *Rita*; Confucius (551–479 BCE), "the Way of Heaven"; Plato (427–347 BCE), the Form of Goodness; the Stoics, Natural Law; and Protestants, the General Revelation of God. C. S. Lewis (1898–1963) considers educating people in these truths as natural as "grown birds . . . teaching young birds to fly," and surely he is right.[7]

Cobb, then, ought to teach James and Phillipa objective truths, especially the principles of critical reasoning, since either to suppress these or simply to neglect them would be directly or indirectly, through negligence, to indoctrinate. Moreover, if Cobb were to teach his children that free will is an illusion, this would seriously discourage his children from thinking about what they have been taught: If all is illusory or determined, then why bother even trying to change what you've been taught? Indeed, though somewhat more controversial, I tend to side with Descartes and others that the proposition "I have free will" is a truth clearly and distinctly perceived.[8]

What If Cobb Hypnotized Fischer?

Since *critical openness* and *autonomy* are essential in separating teaching from indoctrination, we have nearly all the tools and examples needed to tackle the ethics of inception itself. Nevertheless, one more example, this time from a more extreme idea-giving method—hypnotism[9]—will crystallize what has been argued thus far.

Just as most people have the wrong idea about the connection between indoctrination and religion, so most have the wrong idea about hypnotism and control. Because of popular culture, most imagine the hypnotist to be akin to a magician who through sheer personality or magical ability seizes control of his subject and then force-feeds an idea into him or her. The hypnotist is seen as wholly active; the subject as wholly passive. But this understanding of hypnotism comes from further mis-understanding its origin: exorcism and spirit possession.[10]

In the ancient (and not so ancient) world, people who were thought to be possessed or indwelt by spirits weren't seen as being *forced* against their will to give their bodies and minds over to the more powerful spirit. For example, the shaman *invites* the spirit to take control of him; the witch makes an *agreement* with the demon; the Christian *asks* the Holy Spirit to live in him. Likewise, in hypnotism, the subject must *be open* to the hypnotist: "Without the right attitude—motivation, expectations and willingness—the subject will not experience hypnosis."[11]

Nevertheless, what makes hypnotism a more extreme form of idea-giving than teaching is that once the subject—let's say, Robert Fischer, here—has consented to be hypnotized, many of the suggestions given to the hypnotized subject cannot be critically reflected upon. That is, although the subject, Fischer, is neither asleep nor unconscious when hypnotized, he is in a consented-to state wherein his imagination is active but his experience of the events is felt to be involuntary. If the hyp-notist—let's call him Cobb—suggests that there is a helium balloon in Fischer's hands, then Fischer feels as if there is a balloon in his hands and could not have felt otherwise. Even more remarkable is the phenomenon of post-hypnotic sugges-tion, where the subject will feel the *urge*, for example, to weep every time he sees a picture of his father but will neither *know* why he feels this way nor will he *remember* the suggestion.

The question then becomes whether all hypnotism is immoral, since in the hypnotized state of consciousness the subject—Fischer—isn't free to reflect critically upon what is going on. The Hypnosis Code of Ethics states that hypnotism is immoral if, among other things, the hypnotist places anything above the subject's "welfare, rights, and dignity."[12] This suggests that hypnotism could be seen as moral provided that the subject knows what he's getting into and consents to the general aim of the hypnotist, namely, helping the subject while at all times being, above all, respectful of the subject's right to be treated as an end in himself. If this is so, then Cobb the hypnotist giving Fischer the subject suggestions that are at all times respectful, and for the benefit, of Fischer shouldn't be seen as immoral. Indeed, they should be seen as analogous to a surgeon who, motivated to benefit his patient, respectively tells his patient generally what he is going to do—for example, perform heart surgery—while at the same time feels no need to explain *every* detail to the patient or to get the patient's permission for *each* cut of the knife.

Mal, Fischer, and the Ethics of Inception

Our discussion of the ethics of teaching and hypnosis strongly indicates that the person to whom an idea is being given must at all times be treated with respect as to his or her person. This, however, in no way entails that such a person should never be given ideas that he or she can't *immediately* reflect upon or choose for themselves *at the moment*. The young child will be taught many things that she can process only later, and the hypnotized subject will be given suggestions which he consented to have no power to resist. Given this, how should we view the ethics of inception or the act of an extractor or dream navigator planting an idea in the mind of his unknowing, dreaming subject?

In the movie, we know the details of two cases of inception: the first between Cobb and his wife Mal, and the second between Cobb and Fischer. Both situations are different, but are the ethics different?

In the case of Cobb and Mal, both knew they were sharing a dream. They were there for what felt like fifty years, building their own world, like gods. At first it was fun, but eventually it became impossible for them to "live like that"—knowing it was a dream. Mal responded to this by choosing to forget it wasn't real, locking the totem she used to tell dream from reality in the safe of her mind. But not Cobb. Desperate to escape and wake Mal, he planted the idea in her mind that her world was not real (by spinning her totem, a top that never fell, in the safe of her mind). But he did this with Mal's concession to neither the act of inception nor the content of the act. The idea took hold, and so she agreed to "kill" herself in the dream, under the assumption that this would wake her. However, without Cobb realizing it, this idea had taken root like "a cancer" in Mal's mind, causing her to believe that *the real world* was "not real" and that the only escape was another suicide attempt. She, consequently, threw herself from the window of a hotel that she and Cobb frequented. Ariadne assures Cobb, "You're not responsible for the idea that destroyed her." But it's clear from what we know that he is. Nevertheless, is Cobb *morally* to blame? A bad end caused by an individual isn't the same as the individual being morally to blame for that bad end occurring.

Because Mal didn't consent, as a hypnotized subject does, to being given ideas against her will for her benefit, we can't justify Cobb in this way. However, if Mal was, like a rationally undeveloped child, largely incapable of processing what was true or false, then for Cobb to have treated her in such a manner doesn't seem morally objectionable. Mal clearly wasn't capable of processing what was true or false, and so for Cobb to have incepted her probably wasn't immoral.

But there is more to say about this.

I believe Cobb *is* morally to blame, since he was negligent as to the effects of inception. Yes, it was terrible that Mal was fooling herself into thinking that Limbo was real, but *eventually* they both would have woken up; they couldn't have slept forever. Of course, later Eames worries that a prolonged stay in Limbo might turn one's brain into scrambled eggs. However, it's unclear whether Cobb knew of such risks at the time, so I don't think that was his motivation. What he must have known, though, was that inception was risky—he didn't know what the effects might be. So he should have stayed his hand. He was reckless, and his recklessness led to his wife throwing herself from the hotel window, just as much as if, for example, he neglected to periodically check his natural gas fireplace for leaks and, unchecked, it led to her death by carbon monoxide poisoning. Obviously, he's not as blameworthy as a man who intended to kill his wife, but negligence—failing to think of and perform an act one ought to think of and perform—is still a species of immorality.

The case of Cobb and Fischer is a bit different, but still points to Cobb having acted immorally. To begin with, Cobb and his team were hired by Saito to incept Fischer—to give him the idea "I will break up my father's empire" in order to prevent the birth of an energy monopoly or "superpower." Saito believed the end—preventing "total energy dominance"—justified the means—giving a person an idea against his will. And, just to be clear, inception is against Fischer's will; even though Fischer "gives himself the idea" on the third layer of the dream, it is "obviously an idea that Robert himself would choose to reject" if he were fully aware of what was going on.

Thus, it should be clear that Saito's consequentialist reasoning is incompatible with the ethics of idea-giving I've argued for in this chapter, namely, that a person must never be treated simply as a means to an end. Moreover, since Fischer didn't consent to be incepted (as a hypnotized subject does) and was capable of rationally processing what was going on (unlike Mal and rationally undeveloped children), there is little room to justify what Cobb and his team did. Yes, the world may have been spared an evil, but the cost—treating a person as a mere means—doesn't justify it.

"You Need to Let Them Decide for Themselves"

After Cobb agreed to take the Fischer job, he went to France to visit his father-in-law, who had taught Cobb the ways of dream navigation and who Cobb hoped would introduce him to another skilled dream navigator or "architect." Knowing that Cobb, a fugitive, could only use his skills of dream navigation for illegal ends, the father-in-law plainly stated Cobb's intention: "You're here to corrupt one of my brightest and best." In a flash of moral clarity, Cobb replied, "You have to let them *decide for themselves.*"

Although this statement agrees with what I've argued for in this chapter about the ethics of idea-giving, particularly that a rationally developed person's autonomy must always be respected, Cobb, sadly, didn't heed his own words. In the case of Mal, he didn't let her decide for herself, though this wasn't in itself immoral since she was analogous to a rationally undeveloped child and needed to be forcibly given an idea. Cobb's negligence made him immoral. In the case of Fischer, Cobb again didn't let the other decide for himself since, despite what Fischer in his dream believed, the man didn't consent to being incepted in the first place. Cobb, therefore, acted immorally throughout, though we can soften this by adding that the ethics of idea-giving are often more complex than we imagine.

NOTES

1. One might also wonder about conditioning and brainwashing. But I'll leave out conditioning because it has to do with behavior, not beliefs or ideas, and I won't discuss brainwashing since its immorality is fairly obvious.

2. I. A. Snook, *Indoctrination and Education* (London: Routledge & Kegan Paul, 1972), p. 74.

3. "Religion," Dictionary.com, http://dictionary.reference.com/browse/religion, accessed March 3, 2011.

4. R. M. Hare, "Adolescents into Adults," in *Aims in Education: The Philosophic Approach*, ed. T. H. B. Hollins (Manchester, U.K.: Manchester University Press, 1964), p. 52.

5. Peter Berger and T. Luckmann, *The Social Construction of Reality: A Treatise on the Sociology of Knowledge* (New York: Doubleday, 1966), p. 154.

6. I happen to think this is the correct interpretation. For information on the debate about what the Buddha thinks about the laws of logic, see Mark Siderits, "Buddha," *The Stanford Encyclopedia of Philosophy*, ed. Edward Zalta (Spring 2011 edition), http://plato.stanford .edu/archives/spr2011/entries/buddha. For more on what the teachings of the Buddha entail about free will, see Asaf Federman, "What Kind of Free Will Did the Buddha Teach?" *Philosophy East and West* 60 (1): 1–19.

7. C. S. Lewis, *The Abolition of Man; or, Reflections on Education*, in *C. S. Lewis: Selected Books* [Short Edition] (London: HarperCollins, 2002), p. 407.

8. Of course, people can disagree with *anything*, even propositions that seem clear and distinct. Some, for example, would maintain that even though it seems that we are free, freedom is an illusion. Others will argue that the concept of "personhood" is also an illusion—a mere description that brains apply to themselves to help make sense of the world. Still others would argue that believing philosophically in free will and persons is not required for rational reflection or reasoning. For more on these topics, see Robert Kane, *A Contemporary Introduction to Free Will* (Oxford: Oxford University Press, 2005).

9. Because of popular misconceptions and some bad press, hypnotism is sometimes questioned as a legitimate scientific practice. Despite some people misusing it, it's a legitimate and useful technique. The Harvard Group Scale of Hypnotic Susceptibility and the Stanford Hypnotic Susceptibility Scale, among others, have proven this beyond question. For further evidence, see Amanda Barnier and Michael Nash, *The Oxford Handbook of Hypnosis: Theory, Research and Practice* (Oxford: Oxford University Press, 2008), p. 1.

10. Peter Burkhard, "Gassner's Exorcism—Not Mesmer's Magnetism—Is the Real Predecessor of Modern Hypnosis," in *International Journal of Clinical and Experimental Hypnosis* 53:1–12.

11. Amanda Barnier and Michael Nash, "Introduction," in *The Oxford Handbook of Hypnosis*, p. 10.

12. "The Hypnosis Code of Ethics" (The School of Professional Hypnosis, 2008), http:// hypnosisschool.org/hypnotic/hypnosis-school-code-of-ethics.php, accessed February 28, 2011.

INCEPTION AND FREE WILL: ARE THEY COMPATIBLE?

John R. Fitzpatrick and David Kyle Johnson

The seed that we plant in this man's mind will grow into an idea. This idea will define him. It may come to change—well, it may come to change everything about him.

—Dom Cobb

Cobb and his team successfully implant an idea in Robert Fischer's mind: "My father accepts that I want to create for myself, and not follow in his footsteps." Subsequently (we presume) Fischer chooses to break up his father's empire, the energy conglomerate Fischer Morrow, which would have become a new superpower. The world is saved! To what degree, though, did Cobb and his team *cause* Fischer to break up his father's company? Was it all their doing, or did Fischer play a role? Specifically, was Fischer's choice to break up his father's empire free?

If Fischer's choice is not free, then to what extent are any of us free? After all, as other chapters point out, inception happens to us all the time. Everything from movies to teachers, from politicians to news organizations constantly incept us.[1] Further, many ideas are genetically implanted. Our mind is not a blank slate, as suggested by the philosopher John Locke (1632–1704); we are born with numerous ideas.[2] Many of those ideas are the result of our initial brain structure, which is a direct result of our genetics. Our environment and our genes are natural inceptors. If inception interferes with free will, then it may be that no one is free.

Alternate Wills

When it comes to answering questions, philosophers usually begin by defining terms. In the philosophical debates about free will, however, the correct definition of free will is itself the main issue. Whether or not you can say that you have "free will" in certain circumstances has everything to do with what you mean when you say "free."

Let's begin, though, by articulating what free will is not. We are not talking about political or legal freedom. Whether or not the government should allow you to do what you want, when you want, is not the issue here. That is a philosophical issue, but not the one we are concerned with. We are talking about freedom of the will—your ability to choose to do, or to not do, particular actions. We are talking about the nature of your ability to make decisions.[3] For example, the fact that inception is not "strictly speaking legal" doesn't mean that Cobb can't decide to do it. The question is, regardless of their legality, are such decisions free? Are they "up to you?"

What does it even mean, though, to suggest that Cobb's decision to perform inception is up to him? How could we tell whether it was? What is necessary in order for a decision to be free? One of the most well known statements of the requirements for free will is called the principle of alternate possibilities: A decision to do an action is free if and only if you could have done otherwise.[4] At first this seems right; Cobb doesn't freely choose to leave his children. Mal has "freed [him] from the guilt" of that choice. Either he jumps, he runs, or he's arrested; in any event, he will leave them. Although he can freely choose which option to take, he can't freely choose to leave his children because he can't do otherwise.

One of the most important challenges to this definition[5] comes from John Locke, who asks us to imagine a person placed in a room with someone he wants to talk to. Unbeknownst to the person, the door is locked behind him, so he can't leave— he can't do other than stay. Yet, when he stays in the room to talk to the person, he does so freely. He freely chose to stay even though he was unable to do otherwise.[6]

We might liken this to Cobb's situation with Mal and Ariadne in Limbo at the end of the movie. Cobb is placed in a situation in which he must choose whether to stay with Mal in Limbo or try to return to *the real world*. We might suppose, however, that Ariadne has determined that if Cobb chooses to stay with Mal, she will simply shoot her to prevent Cobb from doing so.[7] Cobb, however, has no desire to stay. He would not be able to stay with Mal (because Ariadne would shoot her), but he freely chooses to leave her. Free will, it seems, does not require alternative possibilities.

Not so fast. What this actually reveals is not that free will does not require alternate possibilities, but that our first definition was not careful enough. After all, both the man in the room and Cobb are able to *choose* otherwise; they would simply find their efforts to perform the action they choose frustrated if they did—one by a locked door, the other by a dead Mal. So the principle should be expressed in terms of choice. In addition, failing to make any choice is also an option.[8] Our original principle didn't account for that, either. It seems, then, that what is necessary for free will is not the ability to *do* otherwise, but the possibility of not *choosing* as you in fact do. If so, Locke's example is not one in which the requirements for free will are not met; it would not serve as a counter example to this definition: *A decision to do an action is free if and only if it is possible for you to not decide to do that action.*

We May Not Be Free

The most popular argument for why we are not free is the argument from determinism. Imagine a billiard table. Once the cue ball is set in motion, where all the balls will end up and the paths that they will take to get there is determined.[9] The table and balls are governed by the laws of physics; nothing but what is determined by those laws can occur once the cue ball is set in motion. The billiard table is a deterministic system.

The argument from determinism against free will suggests that the universe is like a three-dimensional billiard table, where the atoms are the billiard balls and space-time is the table. Everything that happens in the universe is the result of the motions of its atoms, and the motions of those atoms are governed by the laws of physics. Nothing but what is determined by those laws can occur once the universe is set in motion—which it was about 13 billion years ago, when it began with a Big Bang. Since we are a part of the universe—ultimately we are just made of atoms—we can't do anything but what was already determined we would do. Where all atoms will end up, and the paths they would take to get there—including the atoms that make up our bodies—has been set since the beginning of time. So whatever we decide to do, it is not possible for us to not decide to do it. We are not free.

Pierre-Simon Laplace (1749–1827) asks us to imagine a superintelligent demon that knows every fact about the current location and velocity of all particles in the universe, and knows all the laws that govern them. Laplace suggests that his demon could simply *do the math* to figure out what the future holds. Nothing other than what the demon predicted could occur—not because he predicted it, but because the outcome is already determined by the way the universe is.

Laplace's demon is not unlike Cobb and his team. They, of course, are not omniscient (all-knowing), but to them Fischer's brain is like a billiard table. If they just set things up in the right kind of way—cause him to have a certain kind of dream—they can predict exactly how he will react; Fischer will conclude that he should be his own person, and then, in turn, predictably, he will break up his father's empire.

Those who hold that the universe is deterministic and that free will requires the possibility of not choosing as you do are known as hard-determinists. Obviously, they do not believe that we have free will. For those who still want to believe in free will, however, there is an option. If you can't deny that free will requires the possibility of not choosing as you do, then you can deny that the world is deterministic. This is the libertarian view.[10]

The philosopher Jean-Paul Sartre (1905–1980) was an extreme libertarian, arguing that while we don't necessarily choose the situations we find ourselves in, we are free to interpret them any way we choose. He even suggests that we are free to remake our very essence at any moment. Cobb sees himself has a family man, who has to get back to his kids at all costs. When Saito offers him the opportunity, he seemingly can't say no. But Sartre would deny this. Cobb could decide to not be a family man anymore, to not care about his kids, to simply walk away. He doesn't even have to be an extractor anymore. He could become, we don't know, let's say, a postman. No possibility is off limits. We are free to interpret ourselves, and our situations, however we wish.

The biggest problem with Sartre's view, however, is that we don't seem to actually have this kind of free will. Rape victims can't interpret their experience however they want; they can't simply decide to be the kind of person that likes being raped to avoid seeing the event as a misfortune. Likewise, while Cobb could choose to stay in Limbo, it's doubtful that he could choose to believe that Limbo was real.

Perhaps Sigmund Freud (1856–1939) may have been right when he suggested that our sense of free will is merely an illusion. The real decision making is done by the subconscious. The id, the ego, and the superego battle it out for control, and it is the resulting negotiation between these subcons that is ultimately the source of our decisions. Once that decision is made, our brain constructs a pleasing story of "our conscious mind" coming to a decision—but it is only a story. "We" had nothing to do with it.

Although Freudian psychoanalytic thought has gone largely out of style, it seems to be partly right on this point. Most often, we don't choose what we do. We just do it, and then make up reasons and justify the decision after the fact. "I did what I had to, to get back to my children." "I'm doing it for the others, because they have no idea the risk they've taken coming down here with you."

Our ever-expanding knowledge of the brain seems to confirm this. Scans show that unconscious parts of the brain are already in the business of bringing about an action, before the conscious "decision making" parts of the brain are active.[11] Split-brain patients, whose brain hemispheres have been separated, show us justifications for already-made-unconscious-decisions happening in real time. When the nonverbal right hemisphere decides on its own that the body should do something, the left hemisphere will fabricate reasons for why it is being done.[12] The more we study the brain, the more we realize that our conscious mind has very little to do with making decisions.

Recent developments in neuroscience also tell us why it is so difficult to deny that determinism is true. For a long time, it was thought that our free will was the result of our being "ensouled." The reason that it is possible for us to not decide as we do is, supposedly, that our decisions are not a result of a mechanistic physical process, but something that happens in our soul—an immaterial substance, which can reach out from beyond the world and control our body.

Our ever-increasing knowledge of the brain, however, has left nothing for the soul to do.[13] All the things that the soul was supposed to be responsible for—emotions, personality, visual experiences, linguistic ability, you name it—are now known to be a result of brain activity. We even have a pretty good idea where in the brain decisions are made—the right parietal cortex. When certain parts of the brain are damaged, you can actually see specific mental functions diminish or disappear. We do not yet understand everything about the brain, but we do know that all our mental activity is the direct result of its mechanistic physical processes. We, and our decisions, are just a part of the universe; and if the universe is governed by deterministic laws, so are we—so are our decisions.[14]

The last resort of the libertarian is quantum mechanics, which tells us that, at the level of fundamental particles, there are truly random events—events that are, literally, unpredictable and thus undetermined. Even if you knew everything about the universe, you still could not predict a quantum event. Unfortunately for the libertarian, however, quantum mechanics cannot save free will. For one thing, randomness doesn't entail freedom. If Cobb's decision to leave the country before seeing his children one last time is merely the result of a random quantum event in his brain, his decision is not free. Second, the effect of quantum randomness at the microlevel is averaged out on the macrolevel. In other words, even though quantum mechanics is true, and tiny particles sometimes behave randomly, the universe still is deterministically predicable at the scale of large objects like brains and persons.[15]

Compatibilism

Things don't look good for free will. To save it, some philosophers have suggested redefining free will to make it compatible with determinism.[16] Such philosophers are called, not surprisingly, "compatibilists." However, it's hard to call what they are doing "redefinition," since such definitions date all the way back to Aristotle (384–322 BCE).

In Book III of the *Nicomachean Ethics*, Aristotle suggested that actions should be considered free unless they are performed under compulsion or out of ignorance. For example, if the cause of an action is external to the agent, and the agent contributes nothing, then the action is not free. Arguably, inception would be just such an external cause and would invalidate free will. If so, Fischer does not freely choose to break up his father's company. (We'll talk more about that later.) Additionally, if the action is a result of the agent being ignorant—not realizing that his action will have some unintended consequence—then the action is not free. For example, if Cobb had not stopped Eames from shooting Saito in the first layer of the inception dream to "put him out of his misery," Eames's action of sending Saito to Limbo would not have been free. Eames thought that shooting him would wake him up.

There's a problem with this, however, as a compatibilist definition. If determinism is true, it seems our actions are done under compulsion. The ultimate causes of our actions are external to us. They trace all the way back to the Big Bang, and we contribute nothing to those causes. The only contribution we make is being part of the final links in a causal chain that we have no control over. That doesn't seem to be compatible with our actions being "up to us." But Aristotle got the ball rolling, and his ideas were incepted into later philosophers who then developed them.

Locke, inspired by his "locked room" example, suggested that as long as we are acting in accord with our own preferences, we are free. Since we can do this even in the absence of the possibility of not choosing as we do, free will does not require such possibilities. And since we can act in accordance with our own preferences, even if we are determined to have them by causes outside of us, if Locke is right, free will is compatible with determinism. Cobb, for example, freely chooses to not stay with Mal in Limbo because he is acting in line with his own preference to get back to his children. Putting it in terms of choice, if Locke is right, we could say that a choice is free as long as that choice is made in accordance with our own preferences of how to choose.

Contemporary philosopher Harry Frankfurt articulates something very similar to Locke's ideas in terms of first-order and second-order desires and our ability to rank them and act accordingly. You may have a (first-order) desire to eat a whole pizza, but you may also have a (second-order) desire to not have such desires—particularly because you don't want to be sick later or because you want to lose weight. What makes you a free person, says Frankfurt, is your ability to rank these desires and act on them appropriately. If you override first-order desires with second-order desires—say by not eating the whole pizza, but only a slice—then you have produced what Frankfurt calls a "second-order volition." You do so by a deliberation about the kind of person you want to be—namely, thinner or healthier. If you "conform your will" to your second-order volitions, then you act freely.

If this definition is right, then free will is compatible with determinism. We can rank our first-order and second-order desires, override one with the other based on a deliberation of the kind of person we want to be, and thus conform our will to our second-order volitions, even if determinism is true. But is this definition right?

Frankfurt Counter Examples

Frankfurt proposed a thought experiment that attempted to show that his definition was indeed right and that the standard "able to choose otherwise" definition was wrong. It goes something like this. Suppose you were trying to decide whether to take a particular action, and someone planted a device in your brain that would kick in and make you do that action, but only if you were about to decide not to do it. Yet, because you decide to do it on your own, the device never kicks in. Do you not still act freely, even though you could not have decided otherwise? Frankfurt and most other philosophers think the answer is yes.

Inception provides us with the conceptual framework to imagine just such a scenario; inception could be the planted device. Suppose Cobb and his team suspect that Fischer is already considering breaking up his father's company because he wants to be his own person; they just want to make sure he does it. So, they cause Fischer to have a three-layered dream like they do in the film, but they make it a dream that he will forget upon waking—so it does not affect him.[17] However, they leave behind a trace, a trigger, that will make Fischer remember the dream only under certain conditions. (I'm sure you've had the experience of first remembering, in the middle of the day, a dream you had the night before because something reminded you of it.) Perhaps the dream begins with him deciding to keep his father's company together, but that decision is followed by an incepted cathartic realization that his father wanted him to create for himself. So, if Fischer is about to decide to keep the company together, that will trigger Fischer to remember the dream, and the incepted idea will kick in and cause him to break up his father's company. But suppose that Fischer does choose on his own to break up the company—thus he never remembers the dream and the inception never kicks in. Does he not, thus, freely decide to break up his father's company?

It seems so—despite the fact that he was unable to choose otherwise. Further, it seems that his decision was free because he conformed his will to his second-order desire to be his own person (despite, let's say, his first-order desire to be super-duper rich). As Locke would say, he is free because he acted in accordance with his preferences.

Frankfurt's thought experiment does not show what he thinks it does, however. Although it serves as a counter example to many standard able-to-choose-otherwise definitions of free will, it does not do so for ours. Recall, we said that free will requires it to be possible to *not decide* to do the action in question. The placement of the "not" before "decide" makes all the difference. Sure, Fischer can't *decide not* to break up his father's company. If he were about to, he'd remember the dream and the inception would kick in. The inception kicking in, however, is a possibility; and if it did, he would *not decide* to break up his father's company—the inception (ultimately Cobb's team) would decide for him. Since failing to decide to break up his father's company is still a distinct possibility, Frankfurt's thought experiment is not a counter example to our original definition. So it does not invalidate it. Additionally, since *not deciding* to do the actions we do is impossible if determinism is true, Frankfurt's thought experiment doesn't show that free will is compatible with determinism.

This points to another problem with compatibilist definitions of free will. Suppose our preferences, our second-order volitions, are caused by external forces beyond our control. We may act in accordance with such things, but would our actions be free? It seems not, for ultimately our actions would not be up to us.

Aristotle suggested that we form such second-order volitions through long processes of intellectual pursuit (or the lack of it) followed by even longer processes of habituation. This develops our character. But this won't help the compatibilist because if we engage in that intellectual pursuit, and it has the outcome it does because of an external cause (our environment, our genes), then we are not free. If this is right, and the processes that form our character are entirely done for us and never by us, then compatibilism would make no sense.

But John Stuart Mill (1806–1873), in *A System of Logic*, calls such thinking "a grand error." Yes, Mill says, our characters are formed by circumstances, but our desires to mold our characters in a particular way are one of the most influential of those circumstances. In this way, our characters are formed *by us*, and actions informed by such character are free.

This might tempt us to think that inception can't really interfere with free will. Think again about the movie. Cobb and his team might implant the idea "My father accepts that I want to create for myself, and not follow in his footsteps" into Fischer's mind. But they do not implant Fischer's desire for "reconciliation, for catharsis," which ultimately informs the kind of character that Fischer has and thus the way he reacts to the implanted idea. If he didn't care about mending his relationship with his father, that idea might cause him to *not* create for himself, and make the existing company even bigger.

This may not be quite right, though. After all, inception seems to be more than a mere implantation of an idea, because that idea will "define him . . . [and] may come to change everything about him." Cobb and his team seem to be reforming Fischer's character, turning him into someone who creates for himself. And if Fischer had not reacted to the idea in the right kind of way, they simply could have dug deeper, changing his character even further. It's not clear, though, that he could have reacted any other way. As Cobb points out, "We *all* yearn for reconciliation, or catharsis." It's inborn. Cobb and his team don't implant that desire in Fischer, but they don't have to—it was already implanted by nature. But if the way Fischer reacts to the implanted idea is a result of a desire for catharsis that was itself implanted, in what way is his action of breaking up his father's company *up to him*? How is it free?

That Fischer's action of breaking up his empire is not free fits with the intuition that Fischer doesn't deserve any moral credit for saving the world from Fischer Morrow's global domination. The dissolution of the company is caused, ultimately, by Cobb and his team; they deserve credit. If Fischer doesn't get moral credit for the action, though, how can his decision to perform that action be free?

This brings us to where the dispute between compatibilists and non-compatibilists reaches its end. Compatibilists insist that as long as a person's action is in some way brought about by a characteristic of that person—his second-order desires, his habits, his character, or his desire to form his character—then the action is free. Non-compatibilists argue that if the ultimate cause of that person having that characteristic is not the person himself—for example, if it is ultimately a result of his environment or genetics—then how the person acts is not "up to him" and thus the person is not free. Compatibilists, like Mill, suggest that "this feeling, of our being able to modify our own character *if we wish*, is itself the feeling of moral freedom which we are conscious of."[18] Non-compatibilists argue that in order to be free, our actions have to *ultimately* be up to us—we can't be merely a proximate cause.

Should We Worry?

If we are free, then inception is something to worry about. Someone as skilled as Cobb might be able to interfere with something as deep as our desire to have a certain kind of character, and thus hinder our free will. And remember, inception happens in the real world in the form of ideas implanted by teachers, parents, movies, and so on. If we are not free, though, why bother worrying? Inception can't interfere with our free will if we don't have any.

NOTES

1. For more on real-life inception, see Daniel P. Malloy's and Adam Barkman's chapters in this volume.

2. For evidence of this see Stephen Pinker, *The Blank Slate: The Modern Denial of Human Nature* (New York: Penguin, 2003). In the appendix, Pinker offers Donald Brown's list of three hundred human universals found in all cultures. They include magic, luck, incest avoidance, and baby talk.

3. We'll be using the terms "choice" and "decision" interchangeably.

4. To be specific, the principle of alternate possibilities originally referred to the requirements for moral responsibility. But since free will is required for moral responsibility,

if alternate possibilities are required for moral responsibility, they are also required for free will. This has caused the principle to be used in reference to both free will and moral responsibility.

5. Technically speaking, it is not a definition. It is a criterion. It sets forth a necessary condition for free action, but it does not tell us what a free-will decision is. For simplicity, however, we'll refer to such things as "definitions" throughout the chapter.

6. John Locke, *An Essay Concerning Human Understanding* (Oxford: Oxford University Press, 1979), Book 2, Section 21, Part 10.

7. She does actually shoot Mal, when Mal stabs Cobb in the chest. But this is not until after he has chosen not to stay with Mal.

8. Although not always, in the situations above failing to make a choice is effectually equivalent to one choice or other. If Cobb never chooses whether to stay with Mal or not, he will waste away in Limbo, just as he would have had he chose to stay with Mal.

9. This is true, of course, only if there is no interference from external sources.

10. Don't confuse this with political libertarians, who make certain suggestions about what the government can rightfully tell us to do, and not do.

11. See chapter 3, "The Brain Knows before You Do," in Michael Gazzaniga, *The Mind's Past* (Berkeley: University of California Press, 2000).

12. For example, you can communicate the command "walk" to the nonverbal right hemisphere, and the body of the patient will walk away. When patients are asked why they are walking away, their verbal left hemisphere will fabricate a reason. "I wanted to go get a Coke." See chapter 9, "The Believing Brain," in Michael Gazzaniga, *The Ethical Brain* (New York: HarperPerennial, 2006).

13. For one, its explanatory power is quite low—how, for example can an immaterial substance that has no dimension or location affect a material one? And why would one soul move one body's arm and not another's? It can't be because it's closer to one of those bodies. Souls would have no spatial location.

14. For more on these facts about the brain and these points about the soul, see Rita Carter, *Mapping the Mind: Revised and Updated* (Berkeley: University of California Press, 2010), especially chapters 2 and 8.

15. For more on quantum events, and their randomness, see Peter Kosso, *Appearance and Reality: An Introduction to the Philosophy of Physics* (New York: Oxford University Press, 1998).

16. If they are right, free will is also compatible with indeterminism. But we don't want to get bogged down in both issues. We encourage the reader to see if they can figure out why compatibilist definitions of free will also make free will compatible with indeterminism. See, for example, John Martin Fischer's chapter in *Four Views on Free Will* (Oxford, UK: Blackwell, 2007).

17. Inception likely implants the idea into the subconscious so deeply that it doesn't matter if you remember the dream or not. Let's forget about that possibility for the purposes of this example.

18. John Stuart Mill, *A System of Logic, Ratiocinative, and Inductive, Being a Connected View of the Principles of Evidence, and the Methods of Scientific Investigation* (Toronto: University of Toronto Libraries), Book 6, Chapter 2, Part 3.

HONOR AND REDEMPTION IN CORPORATE ESPIONAGE

Albert J. Chan

> I did what I had to do to get back to my children.
> —Dom Cobb

Watching *Inception*, audiences wind up empathizing with an industrial spy. But is this empathy well placed? Is Dom Cobb really a hero? Cobb is a tortured soul who desperately wants to leave his career, clear his name, and return to his family. This modern Machiavellian (1469–1527),[1] while appearing good, is willing to sacrifice everything, including his team members' lives, on his pathway to redemption.

The stage is set for what the philosopher David Hume (1711–1776) describes as an unfair battle between emotion and reason. Why unfair? Because during a short skirmish, emotions knock down logical arguments every time.[2] In today's economic climate, the thief captures more sympathy from the public than the corporate CEO. It's no surprise that film audiences root for Cobb.

In the context of a global economy, the film brings up even larger questions of whether questionable career choices, such as corporate espionage, are inherently unethical. Is redemption possible within these professions? Examining various film sentiments and behaviors regarding work and family provides some answers.

Choosing a Life of Crime

If Cobb has no choice in navigating minds for espionage, then he should not be blamed for his career path. However, there are legitimate ways for Cobb to make the most of his talent, such as searching inside an Alzheimer's patient for critical memories or mining an inmate's inner recesses for evidence to exonerate someone or prevent further crimes. Acceptable paths explicitly mentioned in the film include military combat simulations and "the chance to build cathedrals." Of course, Cobb would certainly point out that he can't choose these particular lines of work because of his murder indictment.

Perhaps Cobb should stop using his talent, as he cannot use his skill honorably. Some might consider withholding his unique skill akin to wasting a precious resource, and thus deem it unethical. Yet it is difficult to imagine theft, much less industrial espionage, as legitimate and virtuous under many circumstances.[3] After all, a professional bank robber is not often looked up to even when exercising great skill during a heist. Cobb's career path wouldn't be blameworthy if he couldn't choose anything else. However, Cobb possesses other gifts and talents to make a living and does not need to steal.

The Hero Is Not a Thief?

If Cobb is not stealing any *thing*—that is, if he is not taking someone's property without permission—then perhaps he should not be blamed for his career path. Especially in the digital age, however, stealing does not require making off with anything tangible. Copyright infringement, identity theft, digital piracy, and computer hacking are all illegal and unethical. Extraction and inception certainly seem analogous to intellectual property theft.[4] Cobb and his team take Robert Fischer's dysfunctional relationship with his father and substitute it with a functional one—much like a thief replaces a stolen diamond necklace with a fake.

So inception seems like dishonorable work, yet the viewing public cheers on Cobb. This sympathy is understandable, given the hero's charm and misfortune. Despite the fact that Cobb chooses to be a thief, there are other ways in which Cobb could still be regarded as honorable.

The Result Should Not Justify the Method

Cobb could be deemed honorable if positive circumstances wind up validating his questionable actions. This notion of good consequences determining the ethical nature of an act fits with the moral theory called utilitarianism. According to this theory, if more good arises from a specific act than other possible options, the act is considered moral. In Fischer's case, inception could be considered ethical because what they are doing to Fischer is beneficial to him. As Eames summarizes, "We repair his relationship with his father whilst exposing his godfather's true nature."

What collective good might result from Cobb's inception of Robert Fischer? Saito's company, Proclus Global, can no longer compete; they represent "the last company standing between [the Fischer Morrow Corporation] and total energy dominance." If Cobb is successful, he prevents Fischer Morrow from becoming a new world superpower, controlling half the world's energy supply and possessing the ability to blackmail governments and dictate policy. As Saito argues, "the world needs Robert Fischer to change his mind," because a virtual corporate monopoly is a threat to economic freedom. Cobb represents a personal antitrust policy that will keep the market free for competition.

If acts like inception are judged solely by whether they are means to good or bad ends, then a case can be made for Cobb being honorable. Utilitarianism is problematic, though, as some things seem wrong regardless of their consequences. For example, torturing a baby shouldn't be done even if a thousand lives could be saved by doing so. In the same way, inception may be wrong, regardless of whether or not Fischer Morrow dominates the world. After all, whatever the motivation, inception violates Fischer's basic rights of privacy, freedom, and property, and the ultimate result of the job will be Fischer breaking up his inheritance against his and his father's will.[5] This makes it, many would argue, inherently wrong.

Moral Hazard

Cobb could be considered honorable because of his professional excellence. He is confident and considers himself "the most skilled extractor" in his line of work. Cobb represents a unique kind of corporate trainer who can protect CEOs from skilled professionals by teaching necessary skills of self-defense. Even when Cobb initially fails to accomplish his objective for the Cobol Corporation, he improvises and rises to Saito's challenge for inception, assembling and leading a team to accomplish the impossible. A survivor of Limbo, he is the only person ever known to implant an idea. Cobb is an intellectual mastermind who can handle military weapons and successfully evade material and subconscious authorities. Thus supporters might believe Cobb is an honorable person because he is one of the best in his profession.

Cobb's gift of navigating minds does not make him honorable, though. Cobb's professional skills are admirable and even enviable, yet his overconfidence in his abilities combined with his obsession with returning home causes him to place his team in jeopardy. Asserting that Cobb is honorable because of his expertise is analogous to claiming that a Nazi officer is honorable because of his efficiency in rounding up Jews for concentration camps.

It's not that a person who is excellent at a craft doesn't deserve praise; the honor associated with developing a talent to its maximum potential is well deserved. Society still needs heroes, role models, and "people to believe in," and we do have a natural tendency to attach noble character to expert qualifications. This does not, however, actually make them noble. Consider athletes and movie stars, who are admired for virtuoso performances but often turn out flawed. Such is the case with Cobb. His professional skills certainly do not make him honorable, and Cobb's expertise contrasts sharply with his reckless behavior on the job.

How exactly is Cobb reckless? What does he do that is so wrong? Economist Paul Krugman describes moral hazard as "a situation in which a person makes the decision about how much risk to take, while someone else bears the cost if things go badly."[6] This describes exactly what Cobb does. Cobb knows that Mal poses a serious threat to anyone who shares a dream with him; yet he does not warn his team members and prevents them from making their own decisions about whether to take on that risk.

Cobb also knows about the consequences of death during the heavy sedation required for inception: the mind can drop into Limbo. Yet he does not tell his colleagues of the threat of a decades-long, possibly infinite existence in "unconstructed dream space." In fact, he gives his entire share of the reward to Yusuf, seemingly as a bribe to keep him quiet. When Arthur admonishes Cobb and points out that he "had no right," Cobb deflects any responsibility for his own actions by blaming Arthur for not knowing about Fischer's subconscious military defenses.

Ironically, he lambasts Arthur for neglecting due diligence even as he himself does not provide informed consent. Cobb justifies his own questionable actions with pragmatic calculations that "there wasn't meant to be any risk."

At a minimum, Cobb has a legal and moral responsibility to protect his co-workers, keep them safe, and not put them in harm's way. So why does he neglect his duty? On four separate occasions (to Arthur, "I did what I had to do to get back to my children"; to Miles, "Those kids are waiting for their father to come back"; to Ariadne, "I need to get home"; and to Saito, "I would need a guarantee"), he directly or indirectly admits that inception is primarily a means to his own end—to return to his children. While any person would strongly identify with Cobb's longing for his children, selfishly hiding these risks as "the only way to do this job" seems negligent, unethical, and dishonorable.

Family Matters

Cobb could still be considered honorable for his uncompromising love of his family. Certainly a case could be made for respectable character traits such as being a devoted father and husband. Phillipa and James are the first and last images on his mind whether he is washing up on the beach, relishing his brief conversations on the phone, sending them stuffed animals, or constantly risking life and imprisonment. Even with Mal's presumed demise, Cobb cannot keep her presence out of his mind, work, and dreams.

The final destination of Cobb's flight from Sydney to Los Angeles—and in fact the entire film—is Cobb's redemption. The "need to get home," a second chance, and release from guilt, becomes his mission, his raison d'être, his obsession—and the only thing he "care[s] about right now." Many people live to work; Cobb works to get back to his family.

Unfortunately, none of this excuses Cobb's behavior. He can be a good family man without deceiving, violating rights, and risking lives. He could stand trial and try to prove his innocence. He could do more to persuade his in-laws to move his kids out of the United States. As dangerous as it is, inception really is an easy way out—not the only way out. Even if it is the only option, it is far from clear that Cobb can ethically risk the lives and well-being of six other people. Cobb's passion for his wife and children is natural and expected, but using his team as a primary means to his own ends is manipulative and irresponsible.

The Oxymoron of Ethical Corporate Espionage

Cobb observes that individuals are often motivated by something other than reason. This is why he doesn't want to simply plant the idea, "I will split up my father's empire" into Fischer's mind—it may not stick. Since the subconscious is motivated by emotion and not reason, the idea must be "translated into an emotional concept" of reconciliation. In fact, the audience also seems to reinforce Cobb's observation by supporting their hero because of their (emotional) empathy[7] for his plight, and not rooting against him because of their (rational) realization that he is a thief.

Of course, if Cobb were stealing from an audience member's own business, there might be a different reaction. Competitive intelligence is the legal, ethical, and useful way of collecting and analyzing critical information to gain an advantage on marketplace rivals. However, many corporations are not satisfied with these legitimate methods of competition. Despite legal prohibitions such as the Uniform Trade Secrets Act and Economic Espionage Act of 1996,[8] companies routinely engage in corporate espionage, using secret agents and surveillance technology to extract information from other businesses. A relative lack of prosecution under such laws disguises the widespread prevalence of underground activity and industrial spying. Business owners, who spend millions of dollars a year trying to prevent corporate espionage, clearly oppose such practices, and so *Inception* fans who also hold executive management positions might judge Cobb and his actions a bit differently.

Of course, even companies that obey the laws walk a fine line between socially acceptable forms of competitive intelligence and intellectual property theft. So Cobb's methods could be excused if they lie in this gray area—something he implies by saying the job "is not, strictly speaking, legal." In truth, though, it's not legal at all, nor is it ethical at all. Cobb's vocation and practice of corporate espionage clearly violate legal and moral norms.

Downward Is the Only Way Forward

For Cobb, the guilt is "always there reminding him of the truth" that the idea that causes Mal to question her reality comes from him. The reason Cobb knows that inception is possible is that he "did it to her first," and he does not want to "become an old man filled with regret waiting to die alone." Cobb needs a new idea, a cathartic prescription to free him from his remorse.

Cobb's initial prescription for himself—not letting Mal go—does not work. He relives memories that he continually regrets. Cobb remains tormented by personified guilt. It's not until he embraces another idea—the truth that Cobb indeed keeps his promise of growing old with Mal (doing so in Limbo)—that Cobb finds freedom. He separates himself from his sinister projections and recognizes that the projection of Mal he has been holding on to is but a shade of his former wife. Only then is he finally able to let her go and realize redemption. Cobb yearns for reconciliation and restoration, and so does the audience.

On Cobb's path to redemption, it ultimately does not matter whether the top stops spinning. Cobb is free from the torment of guilt and forgives himself. He is moving forward, hopeful about his future and ready to dream again with his children. While there may not be intrinsically honorable ways to conduct work as a corporate spy, Cobb shows that reconciliation and restoration can be found . . . in his dreams.[9]

NOTES

1. The term "Machiavellian" is frequently associated with manipulation, deception, and self-serving ambition. Niccolò Machiavelli is famous for the end justifying the means, but it remains an open question whether the historical Machiavelli was truly Machiavellian in the cultural sense. He does seem to lean toward more questionable means if there are clear and justifiable benefits in sight.

2. David Hume famously wrote that "reason is, and ought only to be the slave of the passions." See David Hume, *A Treatise of Human Nature* (1739), ed. L. A. Selby-Bigge, rev. P. H. Nidditch, second edition (Oxford: Clarendon Press, 1978), II.iii.3/415; also watch Cobb conversing with his team during *Inception* at 50:05–51:30.

3. According to Aristotle (384–322 BCE), virtue is found within the means of vice. Too much courage (rashness) and too little courage (timidity) surround the right amount (bravery). Compare the guiding principle of the Neo-Confucian "Doctrine of the Mean" of never acting in excess.

4. For more on this, see Daniel P. Malloy's chapter in this volume.

5. For a discussion of whether or not inception actually does violate a person's free will, see John Fitzpatrick and David Kyle Johnson's chapter in this volume.

6. Paul Krugman, *The Return of Depression Economics and the Crisis of 2008* (New York: W. W. Norton, 2009).

7. Indeed, are we not all morally flawed and in need of redemption?

8. The UTSA is a model law: http://euro.ecom.cmu.edu/program/law/08-732/TradeSecrets/utsa.pdf. The EEA is a public law: www.gpo.gov/fdsys/pkg/PLAW-104publ294/pdf/PLAW-104publ294.pdf.

9. Thanks to the editors for invaluable assistance in focus, clarity, and argument structure; and to *Inception* fans Arin Golestani, Kirstin Hendricks, and Brian "academic Ariadne" Glenney. Cora, Sharla, and Kayden—because of you, I better understand Cobb's motivations for inception!

PART FOUR

WHAT IS DREAMING?: EXPLORING THE NATURE OF (SHARED) DREAMS (UPON DREAMS)

SHARED DREAMING
AND EXTENDED MINDS

Ken Marable

The truth [is] that as we go deeper into Fischer, we're also going deeper into you.

—Ariadne

Inception poses a conundrum: With shared dreaming, where does the dream take place? The obvious answer is that each person has the dream in his or her own mind. Each person has his or her own dream, which, because they are all hooked up to the dream-sharing technology briefcase (the PASIV device), resembles the dream of everyone else. The same basic events take place in each person's dream. Somehow, though, people are able to influence one another's minds and interact within the dream world. This partial blending of minds seems strange at first, but two philosophical notions—extended minds and collective minds—can solve the conundrum.

Extended Minds

Consciousness, or self-awareness, is a fundamental property of the human mind, and it seems clearly limited to the space between our ears and behind our eyes. At most, consciousness goes out to our skin, where we feel sensations. Consciousness isn't all there is to the human mind, however. A mind is actually a loose conglomeration of all kinds of mental and neural processes that we lump together under a single term. Minds have non-conscious processes—processes that, for example, categorize sounds as either mountain winds or slowed-down music. Minds also have subconscious emotional baggage—such as guilt concerning abandoned children and a deceased wife. Still, the mind seems limited to the body.

However, two contemporary philosophers, Andy Clark and David Chalmers, have challenged the bodily limitation with their theory of the extended mind. To see how, consider this example.[1] In *Inception*, we often see Arthur with a notebook. Let's suppose, for the sake of this example, that he has a habit of always keeping it on him, and writing things down in it, because he knows that his memory is not perfectly reliable. After all, how can he ever be sure a memory has not been incepted into him? Furthermore, he knows that human memory is notorious for filling in missing details with what seems plausible.

Let's suppose that Eames, on the other hand, sees Arthur's notebook as remarkably quaint. Having made a living creating false documents, Eames would never rely on such an easily faked physical object. Instead, always self-assured, he relies only upon his own brain for information.

When Cobb arranges a meeting with the group, Arthur writes down the location in his notebook, whereas Eames simply memorizes it. On the day of the meeting, having been busy with other preparations and never trusting his brain anyway, Arthur checks his notebook for the location. Eames, always working another angle somewhere, has been preoccupied as well and has to take a moment to think back and recall the location of the meeting. Common sense would tell us that since Arthur relied on information in his notebook and Eames relied on his brain, they performed very different tasks. But how different are they?

Neither one had the information consciously present. Both had to access that information from somewhere other than conscious thought. Arthur checked his notebook, and Eames dug into his brain. Both had to access a sort of memory storage and recover that information. For Eames, it happened to be "stored" in neural stuff,[2] rather than on simple paper and ink, but in both cases, it had to be stored and retrieved by consciousness. Accessing the storage produced the same thoughts of the proper location for both of them. The difference of where the thoughts were stored (in Arthur's paper and ink or Eames's brain) is irrelevant, according to Clark and Chalmers. In both cases, conscious thought must seek out and find that information, and the end result of the information coming to mind is the same.

According to Clark and Chalmers's theory of extended mind, Arthur's notebook, as long as he uses it reliably, is part of his memory. As long as he keeps it with him, and readily available, most of the time, it works as part of his memory in every way that Eames's more natural memory does. The notebook has the same function as memory, namely a place to store information that can be brought back to mind. Therefore, since it functions in the same way, it is a part of Arthur's memory in every relevant sense. And since memory is part of the mind, his mind is extended to the notebook.

This may not be as strange as it first sounds. After all, even our sense of our own bodies is flexible. Driving a car often leads us to extend our bodily sense to include the car. We stop consciously thinking about *how* to drive the car; we simply *will* it forward (we don't consciously think about putting our foot on the gas pedal) much of the time. So if our bodies can, in a sense, be extended to objects, is it so strange to think our minds can as well?

The brain, though, seems more secure than a notebook. If someone were to take or destroy Arthur's notebook, then that memory would be gone. Even setting aside the possibility of brain injuries, though, people forget information. And grogginess (or the occasional overdose of wine) can make it difficult or impossible to access all memories. Considering the potential problems with relying on our brains, a notebook starts to look like a dependable option.

From simple to-do lists to smartphones providing ever-present schedules and Internet search abilities, our memories and minds are extended far beyond our skulls, even if our consciousness is not. Memory is the clearest example of this, but other mental abilities can be similarly extended, as when we outsource math problems to calculators. According to Clark and Chalmers, differences in the medium (either neuron or device) are irrelevant if they perform the same function with comparable reliability.

Collective Minds

If we follow Clark and Chalmers, our minds, especially our memories, can be extended to notebooks, phones, calculators, and other objects. *Inception* takes us further, challenging us with the question: Can our minds be extended to other people and their minds?

Using the example of memory again, consider Professor Stephen Miles and his wife, Marie. Let's suppose that Professor Miles, whether from being an absent-minded professor or having spent too much time in the dream world, is notorious for forgetting *when* he has to be somewhere. As an experienced dream architect, however, he is excellent at remembering locations and *where* he has to go. Marie has learned to compensate for the professor's failing and is always punctual. Whenever they need to go somewhere, he knows where to go, and she knows when.[3]

So, say the professor and Marie are going to meet Cobb at the airport, as he returns to America at the end of the film. Where is the memory of the appointment? A simple explanation is that he remembers part and she remembers the other. They have their own separate memories, but they have come to rely on each other for important additional information. Just as Arthur's memory is extended to his notebook, the professor's and Marie's memories are extended to each other. Collectively, the couple has reliable complete information on their appointments. The difference is that some of the information is stored in the other person's brain. Again, this goes beyond one happening to remember certain information the other forgot. In this case, they have a reliable system worked out between them for storing and remembering certain kinds of information. These memories are reliably stored and accessible in their collective mind.

Looking beyond memory at another mental function illuminates a more common example of a collective mind. Group decision-making is a form of collective thought. Again, consciousness certainly does not expand beyond individual brains, but our minds are more than just our consciousness. When the team decides how to undertake the Fischer inception, it is debated and discussed as a group, and as a group they are thinking and weighing choices and coming to a conclusion. Cobb and Eames determine the form of the thought to be inserted. Arthur, relying on Yusuf to preserve inner ear function under the heavy sedation, devises the kicks. Ariadne designs the levels (with Eames thankfully adding a shortcut of air ducts to his). Saito, well, Saito decides to buy an airline. This is a prime example of group thought, with everyone contributing to the decisions and overall plan.

Many psychologists have noted that group decision-making can follow the same patterns and carry out similar processes as individual minds. There are certainly differences, but looking at the basic functions, these differences seem to be irrelevant. The group performs the function of deciding just as a single mind would.

In both examples of collective minds, the actions of the group are best explained as collective actions, rather than by trying to reduce everything to each individual decision. Reducibility and the level of best explanation are important concepts in philosophy when dealing with collectives. As an analogy, chemistry may in principle be reducible to physics, meaning all of chemistry could in some complex way be explained by physics, but it seems that the level of best explanation for chemical reactions lies within the laws of chemistry. Even our thoughts and actions might be reducible in principle to neurons spitting chemicals at each other or even to atoms and quarks, but in practice the idea is far more trouble than it is worth. It does not explain anything that is not far more understandably explained by talking about people and minds and thoughts.

Additionally, many philosophers believe that certain actions are irreducible, meaning that even in principle they cannot be explained at lower levels. Consciousness is sometimes said to be irreducible, although that is a point of contention for many philosophers and not often talked about in polite company. On the one hand, the irreducible crowd believes that experiences and waking awareness cannot be entirely explained by mere physics or neuroscience. On the other hand, the reductionist crowd figures that the atoms that make up the neurons that make up their brains made the irreducible crowd say that.

A few philosophers have even argued that group decision-making is also an example of an irreducible action. They say that not only is it easiest and most practical to describe group decision-making as a sort of collective mind, but that certain characteristics can *only* be explained at that level. Anyone observing committees and corporations can attest to the fact that some decisions appear beyond understanding and certainly are not simply a collection of individual opinions. Whether it's irreducible or not, a group making a decision acts as a collective mind.

Blended Minds

The dream worlds of *Inception* take collective minds a step further with minds that are not simply working together, but are to a degree blended. Although the minds continue to have their own separate conscious experiences—each seeing, hearing, and feeling independently of the others—the subconscious level is blended.

Fischer's militarized subconscious follows him through the dreams of Yusuf, Arthur, and Eames. Cobb, against his conscious will, brings Mal and even a train into the dreams. Ariadne, as the architect, reshapes the world of everyone else's dream, and so on. In this mix, it can be unclear just whose mind is responsible for what.

Limbo makes things even murkier. When asked what is in Limbo, Arthur replies, "Just raw, infinite subconscious. Nothing is down there except for whatever might have been left behind by anyone sharing the dream who's been trapped there before, which in our case is just [Cobb]." In Limbo, it seems, the simple notions of architect and dreamer are gone, and we have a hodge-podge of their subconscious minds.

This concept of Limbo somewhat resembles Carl Jung's (1875–1961) notion of the collective unconscious. According to Jungian psychoanalysis, the collective unconscious weaves through all of our minds and can be built up out of shared traditions, archetypes, and other common threads all sitting in the depths of our minds, typically out of the sight of our consciousness, but having a subtle influence.

In the subconscious, each mind appears to have its own influences both on Limbo and on the dream world through projections. As we can see, though, the influences weave together. It's like a rainbow in which red, orange, yellow, and other colors are all very clear and bright, yet the boundaries between colors are ill-defined and impossible to pinpoint.

Returning to the original question, where did the dreams in *Inception* take place? With each mind playing a role in building the dreams, potentially populating them with their own projections, and shaping them with each of their actions, it would seem that the dreams took place in all of their minds collectively. They are group dreams—created by a group, and experienced by a group. They are more than a collection of individual dreams, since separating one from another is impossible. In many important respects, the team is a single collective mind experiencing a single collective dream.

The Movie as Shared Thought

In numerous interviews, Christopher Nolan has discussed the analogy of Cobb's dream team to a film team.[4] Cobb is the director, Arthur the producer, Ariadne the writer, Eames the actor, Saito the studio, and so on. To carry this analogy further, as Cobb's team implants a thought in Robert Fischer, Nolan's team implants a thought in the audience. Indeed, both teams create elaborate stories and hoaxes to implant a thought deep in the minds of their targets.[5]

Think about sitting in the theater, watching *Inception* for the first time. Where did the movie take place? Staring at canisters full of film will not convey any meaning to you about the plot of the film, nor will watching the projector wheels turn. The obvious answer seems to be that the movie took place on the screen. But what's on the screen is just a collection of shapes and colors; without the appropriate sensory mechanisms, it's nonsense. Aliens with senses different from ours would likely not be able to make heads or tails of it. Besides, the sound coming out of the speakers is part of the movie, and it's not on the screen. So where does the movie take place? In *our* heads—the audience's mind.

We experience the movie. In this way, the collective mind of the audience watching the movie is not far from the shared dreaming of the characters. Sitting together watching the story unfold, we all experienced the same movie, albeit from slightly different perspectives and backgrounds, just as the characters all experienced the same shared dreams. We watched Cobb and Fischer wrestle with their inner demons. We saw the folding city. We filled in the details of the worlds, and we were left wondering, as the top wobbled but continued to spin and the screen cut to black, did it fall?

The story, and especially the top itself, was the seed of a thought. Judging from the number of bytes and ink consumed in blogs, magazines, and books such as this one, it is a rich idea (or set of ideas) to contemplate. A collective mind has continued to discuss, study, and debate the movie.

Not only are our thoughts stored in this book, but we are adding to a global discussion on reality, mind, and dreams. Right now you are taking part in it. My consciousness might be stuck in my skull, but in a broader sense, my mind and the thoughts and ideas it contains are going through this book to blend with yours.

The collective mind considering *Inception* (or any film, novel, or common cultural artifact, for that matter) is built from the individual minds adding projections and ideas, blended together to think about the philosophical ideas in *Inception*. Cobb and the team may have had a successful inception into Robert Fischer's mind, but Christopher Nolan's inception into the collective mind of the audience appears equally successful.

The discussion of the film is not simply a group of individual minds, but a group mind with collective memories and distributed thoughts. *Inception* guides us to question reality, but it can also help us to question the nature of our own minds, and realize that the traditional limits of skin and skull are perhaps not as accurate and limiting as we commonly think. Our minds extend into the world and blend with one another.

NOTES

1. This example is repurposed from Andy Clark and David Chalmers, "The Extended Mind," *Analysis* 58 (1998): 7–19. Of the pair, Andy Clark has definitely become the champion of this theory, penning numerous articles and a book on it, *Supersizing the Mind: Embodiment, Action, and Cognitive Extension* (New York: Oxford University Press, 2008).

2. How the brain stores and retrieves memories is not fully understood, but it would be a bit simplistic to think of memories as being stored in specific areas in the brain. We do know that the hippocampus plays a large role in the laying down of memories (if you remove it, you remove a person's ability to lay down new memories). But when retrieving memories, it seems that the brain re-creates the neural firings that were occurring at the time that the memory was laid down. For more on this, see Rita Carter's *Mapping the Mind*, 2nd edition (Berkeley and Los Angeles: University of California Press, 2010).

3. A variation on this example appears in Deborah Tollefson, "From Extended Mind to Collective Mind," *Cognitive Science Research* 7 (2006): 140–150. A nice round-up of the history and variety of arguments for and against extended and collective minds for those wishing to extend their own minds into this area can be found in Robert Wilson, "Collective Memory, Group Minds, and the Extended Mind Thesis," *Cognitive Processing* 6 (2005): 227–236.

4. Among other places, this can be found in the interview with Christopher Nolan contained in *Inception: The Shooting Script* (San Rafael, CA: Insight Editions, 2010). See also Devin Faraci, "Never Wake Up: The Meaning and Secret of Inception," *chud.com*, July 19, 2010, http://www.chud.com/24477/NEVER-WAKE-UP-THE-MEANINGAND-SECRET-OF-INCEPTION/.

5. For more on *Inception* as a film about filmmaking and about how filmmaking itself is a form of inception, see Daniel Malloy's chapter in this volume.

MORALLY RESPONSIBLE DREAMING: YOUR MIND IS THE SCENE OF THE CRIME

Lance Belluomini

> You asked me for inception. I do hope you understand
> the gravity of that request.
>
> —Dom Cobb

Consider what unfolds on the inception job. The dream team kidnaps Fischer's dream self. They manipulate his mind; they coerce him into giving them a combination; they forge identities and emotional concepts to fool him; they fight and kill his threatening projections. In the end, they succeed in fulfilling their mind crime objective. Fischer ends up in *the real world* with a set of false beliefs. If it was all just a dream, though, should Cobb and company be held morally responsible for their misdeeds? This is the "Moral Dream Problem."[1]

Moral Responsibility

For Aristotle (384–322 BCE), voluntary action plays a crucial role in assigning moral blame. Two conditions need to be met to have voluntary action. First, the action must have its origin in the person. That is, the person must be able to control whether to perform an act. Second, the person has to be aware of what she is doing. If these conditions are met, then the person is morally responsible and deserves to receive praise or blame.[2]

Concerning the *Inception* dream team, some of us conclude: "Of course they're responsible. Isn't it obvious? They plan their dream crimes in advance; they have control over what they do in a dream; and they're lucidly aware of what they're doing while in a dream." They certainly meet Aristotle's conditions of voluntariness. For example, the act of coercing Fischer in the warehouse has its origin in both Cobb and Arthur. It's up to them whether to carry out this dream act that they've probably rehearsed in the Paris workshop. So they have control and awareness of what they're doing. Thus, their voluntary dream actions seem to warrant moral blame based on Aristotle's account of moral responsibility.

Cobb's feeling of guilt also comes to mind when considering Aristotle's account, and whether one can be responsible for actions in a dream. One of the driving emotional forces of the movie is Cobb confronting and overcoming his guilt over something he did while dreaming. "Guilt. I feel guilt, Mal. And no matter what I do, no matter how hopeless I am, no matter how confused, that guilt is always there reminding me of the truth." He feels responsible for Mal's death and blames himself for not refraining from the act of inception. If he had refrained, he feels that Mal would still be alive—that his family would still be together. Because he didn't, this guilt continually haunts him both in *the real world* and in his dreams. In an effort to lessen this feeling of guilt, Cobb tries to manipulate his memories during his private dream sessions. In the caged elevator, Cobb tells Ariadne: "You don't understand. These are moments I regret. They're memories that I have to change."

Cobb believes he's responsible for at least one of his past dream acts: planting the idea in Mal that triggers her suicide. But what about the rest of Cobb's dream actions? And what about all the dream violence on the Fischer inception job? Is the dream team blameworthy?

Is Cobb's "Dream Self" Cobb?

The philosopher St. Augustine (354–430) argued that we are responsible for what we do in our dreams because we are responsible for the acts we "intend" to do regardless of whether those acts occur. Contemporary philosopher Gareth B. Matthews (1929–2011), however, nicely captures how one might deny responsibility for one's dreams.[3] One way to deny responsibility is to assert, "My dream self is not really me." In our dreams, we sometimes think of ourselves as characters we are observing in a movie. At other times, we don't see ourselves in a dream. Rather, we think of our dream selves as independent observers of our dream. Because our dream selves are nothing but observed characters or mere observers of our dreams, we can insist that our dream selves are not really us. Thus we are not morally responsible for the acts of our dream selves, since it's not actually "us" who perform those acts.

This is not a solution Augustine would accept, however. He writes: "For in dreams, when we suffer anything harsh and troublesome, we are, of course, still ourselves."[4] Moreover, in Book 10 of his *Confessions*, he admits that he can't distinguish his dream self from his real self. Additionally, Augustine raises a concern about the Moral Dream Problem. He writes in confession to God concerning his unchaste thoughts:

> Indeed the illusion of the deed prevails to such an extent, in both my soul and my flesh, that the illusion persuades me when sleeping to what the reality cannot do

when I am awake. Am I not myself at such a time, Lord my God? And is there so much a difference between myself awake and myself in the moment when I pass from waking to sleeping, or return from sleeping to waking? Where, then, is the power of reason which resists such suggestions when I am awake—for even if the things themselves be forced upon it I remain unmoved? Does reason cease when the eyes close? Is it put to sleep with the bodily senses? But in that case how does it come to pass that even in slumber we often resist, and with our conscious purposes in mind, continue most chastely in them, and yield no assent to such allurements?[5]

Augustine is focused on personal identity in this passage. He voices his conviction that "his dream self is his real self" to God in the question: "Am I not myself at such a time, Lord my God?" Furthermore, he doesn't feel any difference between himself awake and himself asleep, because he recognizes that his reason is often present within his dream, even if it is absent at other times. Augustine's justification is this: because in sleep I often resist pleasures that are suggested to me, my power of reason refuses these temptations. What remains puzzling to him is why his dream self sometimes resists these allurements but at other times consents to them.[6]

Like Augustine, the response "My dream self isn't me" doesn't seem available to Cobb and the team members. The dream team members of *Inception* don't see their dream selves as characters in a movie or as third-party observers; they all identify their dream selves with their real world selves. When they enter a dream, their dream selves are virtually indistinguishable from their real world selves in terms of how they consciously think, talk, reason, behave, and appear—even down to the small projected items they carry such as their wallets and totems. Their mental world while dreaming is no different from their mental world when awake. It seems correct to say, then, that their real selves are committing these dream crimes.

The Dream Is Real

A second way to resolve the Moral Dream Problem is to simply point out that what happens in our dreams is not anything that really happens and insist that we are only responsible for the acts or thoughts that we have in real waking life.[7] This view claims that the dreamer performs no real actions. Rather, the dreamer is a passive participant. Even assuming that one's dream self and real self are identical, still, one's dream self never really acts.

Augustine is not in a position to say that no real action happens when an event takes place in his dreams because he takes an "intentionalist" approach to ethics. For Augustine, one has done something real and wrong by merely consenting to do evil, even if one never carries out the act. When one dreams and receives an evil suggestion, takes pleasure in the thought of performing the act suggested, and consents to performing the act, one does something morally wrong.[8] Thus, Augustine believes that consenting to an evil act in a dream amounts to a mental event happening in oneself—a real action.

Can the characters in *Inception* be absolved of responsibility for what they do in dreams by claiming that they don't "intend" to do what they do, or that there is nothing real about what happens in dreams? Probably not. They even plan their actions out ahead of time, a clear indication that the dream actions are intentional.

In addition, mental states, sensory experiences, and formed images that the dreamers have are real in the world of *Inception*. As Cobb tells his projection of Mal: "Ah, there's no use threatening him in a dream, right, Mal?" Mal replies: "That depends on what you're threatening. Killing him would just wake him up. But pain . . . pain is in the mind." In accord with this, Arthur feels the pain of being shot in the leg even though his actual leg hasn't been shot.

So while the things that are happening in constructed dreams are not actually happening in *the real world*, real mental phenomena are occurring. The thoughts, beliefs, and experiences that each of their dream selves have (including Fischer's) are really happening. So the characters in *Inception* can't use the "it's not real" excuse to avoid moral responsibility for what they do in dreams. Just as Augustine suggested, the intent to do wrong in a dream is in itself wrong in *Inception*.

But They Know It's a Dream

Isn't there an easier way for the characters to be absolved of responsibility for what they do in a dream? Here's an objection some of us have likely formulated at this point: Even if we grant that there are real mental states like intentions taking place while they are dreaming, surely they can't be held responsible for any of their dream actions, since they know they are dreaming. Perhaps if they didn't know they were dreaming and they killed someone, they would have done something immoral. But Cobb and the team realize it's a dream. Thus, they know they are not killing anyone—just like a teenager playing *Call of Duty* knows he is not killing anyone. So when they kill other dreamers or projections, how can this be any more immoral than killing someone in a video game?

One might be tempted to counter this objection by reasserting Augustine's suggestion that the intention to do evil is sufficient to do evil. Doesn't this miss the point, though? After all, if they know it's a dream, and thus that their actions are not really acts of killing, are they really intending to do "something evil"—again, any more than a teenager playing *Call of Duty* intends to do something evil when he "frags" one of his best friends with a grenade launcher?

Perhaps, though, our analogy is off. After all, killing someone in a video game is a bit different from killing someone in a dream; the experience in the dream is almost identical to the real thing. Perhaps a stronger analogy would be with a man who actively fantasizes about having an affair with a co-worker. Isn't the active fantasy immoral? And isn't this more like what the shared dreamers do? Or, to strengthen the analogy, suppose the man is resisting the temptation to have an affair in a dream, until he realizes he is dreaming—and at that point, recognizing that it's not real, he lustfully gives in. Isn't he doing something immoral (albeit not as immoral as having a real affair)? Would his wife not strongly object, on moral grounds, if she knew (especially if she found out because he called out the other woman's name in his sleep)? How is this morally different from when our dreamers willingly (sometimes gladly) kill someone in a lucid dream? Sure, they know it's not real, but it's still immoral on some level.

For those still not convinced, Augustine would take it a step further. He would suggest that even when you know that an imagined immoral action is not real, it is still immoral because it corrupts your character. Augustine believed that there is an important causal connection between habits of thought and one's action. Habits of thought are part of the character of a person, and one's character determines whether one acts morally or immorally. So when Cobb willingly kills someone in a dream, he is developing bad habits of thought. His dream action of killing prevents him from being a virtuous person—negatively impacting his moral character. Thus, the action is immoral.

Alternative Dream Possibilities

Another way to deny responsibility is to assert that one is morally responsible only for what is within one's power to refrain from doing.[9] It seems that a person can't be held responsible for what happens in a dream, since dreams themselves are not voluntary, nor are the actions one performs in a dream.

Philosophers capture this intuition about responsibility in "The Principle of Alternative Possibilities": "A person is morally responsible for what he has done only if he could have done otherwise."[10] In the same way that we cannot be morally obligated to do something that we cannot do, we cannot be morally blamed for something that we could not avoid doing. If it is impossible (for whatever reason) for me to refrain from doing a particular action, how could I be held morally responsible for it?

Augustine would clearly reject this as a possible solution because he says that sometimes it's within his power (with God's grace) to refrain from consenting to and committing immoral acts in his dreams.[11] As for Cobb's dream team, Augustine would rightly point out that it's within their power to refrain from the actions they perform in a dream as well. While the inception job is carefully planned out in the Paris workshop—from the dream narratives to the synchronized "kicks"—there's no guarantee that things will go according to plan. And, we all know, it doesn't. The team often has to improvise. Clearly, they have the freedom to voluntarily choose alternative dream actions. Recall, for instance, when Cobb decides to run with the "Mr. Charles" gambit to turn Fischer against his own subconscious. Surely it's within Cobb's power to refrain from making this decision. He could have freely chosen an alternative strategy to deal with Fischer's security in the hotel. Cobb could have decided not to employ any gambit and just face Fischer's subconscious projections. Their shared lucid dreaming is unlike our normal way of dreaming, where we may have no control over what happens. There are alternative actions available to the dream team, and so they cannot use this excuse to avoid moral responsibility for their actions within shared dreams.

So far we've determined the following: the characters' dream selves are in fact their real selves; what happens in their shared dreams is real in the sense that they involve real mental events; they are acting on their intentions to harm someone even though they know they are dreaming; and they have voluntary lucid control over their dream actions. Of course, we may think that this list settles it. They're morally responsible—case closed. But if there are any creeping doubts, we only need to point out that their immoral dream acts lead to real-world consequences.

Dream Actions That Have Effects in *the Real World*

In the world of *Inception*, dream actions can and do have effects in *the real world* (and if an action has real-world consequences—and let's assume for argument's sake that *the real world* actually is real—then it's a moral action even if it's in a dream). So, what consequences are there when the scene of the crime is in someone's mind? Well, performing dream crimes can change a person or even alter the course of *the real world*. Think of what happens to Mal. The idea that Cobb plants in her mind ultimately leads to her death in *the real world*. The forged emotions created on the inception job have bad effects, as Fischer is led astray, ending up in *the real world* with a set of false beliefs. Cobb explains the kind of effect inception will have on Fischer, telling Saito on the Mombasa rooftop: "Now, the seed that we plant in this man's mind will grow into an idea. This idea will define him. It may come to change . . . well, it may come to change everything about him."

Early on, Cobb tells Ariadne: "It's not, strictly speaking, legal." The obvious reason why is that stealing information from someone's mind or planting an idea there involves taking serious risks that can have damaging consequences in *the real world*. For example, since the inception job involves administering the somnacin drug mixed with a powerful sedative, the dreamers run the risk of ending up trapped in Limbo, where they could lose their minds. Ariadne asks what could happen to Saito if he dies and goes to Limbo. Cobb says: "Worst-case scenario? When he wakes up, his mind is completely gone."

Do all of the immoral dream acts have real-world consequences, however? Perhaps some of the dream actions taken against Fischer—including his projections—do not. How could the dream act of coercing Fischer into giving a combination have an effect in *the real world*? How could Arthur battling Fischer's projections in zero gravity have an effect? It doesn't look like there are real-world consequences to their actions. So doesn't this excuse the team members from responsibility for these actions? No, these dream actions are all collectively playing a part in bringing about real-world consequences. That is, all of the immoral dream actions the team performs against Fischer and his projections play a part in achieving the moment of inception and the real-world outcome they're aiming at—Fischer splitting up his father's empire. So they can't be excused from these actions. And even if their dream actions didn't lead to real-world consequences, intentionalists like Augustine would still say that they are responsible for them since they are being immoral by acting on their intentions to do harm, which, at the least, corrupts their moral character.

"I Need to Get Home. That's All I Care about Right Now"

While Cobb would admit responsibility for what unfortunately happens to Fischer, he would say that it's nevertheless morally justifiable—that what he's doing is not blameworthy, all things considered. Recall what he tells Ariadne in the workshop: "I need to get home. That's all I care about right now." He also tells Arthur: "I did what I had to do to get back to my children." For Cobb, only the results matter, namely, having his charges permanently cleared so he can return back to his children—an outcome that is morally praiseworthy and good in itself. He's only concerned with the immediate welfare of himself and his family. Thus, he's motivated to choose only those actions that produce good consequences for himself and his children. So for Cobb, it's sometimes necessary to commit wrongful acts in order to generate good consequences.

So does Cobb's goal, returning home to be with his children, justify the dream crimes he plans and carries out? The moral problem is that the justification uses a person as a means to an end. Cobb treats Fischer as a means, to be exploited, so that Cobb can return to his children.

We know what Augustine would say in response to Cobb: the "intention" to do wrong in a dream is in itself to do wrong, regardless of the consequences. So while his duty to reunite with his children is his motivation for acting immorally in a dream, that doesn't make Cobb's actions morally acceptable. Augustine would point out that Cobb has a moral duty not to act on his intentions of imaginatively killing, stealing, and manipulating other people while asleep.

Facing the Moral Dream Problem

While dream-sharing technology doesn't exist in our world, people have long debated whether we're responsible for what we do in our dreams. In light of our discussion of *Inception*, do we have any good reasons for denying moral blame for what we do in our dreams? Or are we now convinced, like Augustine, that we're morally responsible for our dream acts?[12]

NOTES

1. For more on the history of "The Moral Dream Problem" and other philosophical dream problems, see Gareth B. Matthews, *Thought's Ego in Augustine and Descartes* (Ithaca, NY: Cornell University Press, 1992).

2. Aristotle, *Nicomachean Ethics*, Book 3, pp. 1–5, trans. Terrence Irwin (Indianapolis: Hackett, 1991).

3. Gareth B. Matthews, "On Being Immoral in a Dream," *Philosophy* 56, no. 215 (January 1981): 47–54.

4. *St. Augustine Anti-Pelagian Writings: Nicene and Post-Nicene Fathers of the Christian Church, Part 5, On the Soul and Its Origins*, 4.17.25 (Whitefish, MT: Kessinger, 2010).

5. Augustine, *Confessions* (New York: Barnes & Nobles Books, 2007), 10.30.41, pp. 168–169.

6. Augustine's own answer to his puzzlement is that he views himself as a flawed human being who, only by God's grace, could consistently refuse to do immoral things in a dream. In a way his dream self makes plain to him, in ways that his waking self does not, his own moral weakness.

7. Matthews, "On Being Immoral in a Dream," pp. 50–51.

8. Ibid.

9. Ibid., pp. 51–53.

10. Harry Frankfurt, "Alternative Possibilities and Moral Responsibility," in *Free Will*, ed. Gary Watson (Oxford: Oxford University Press, 2003), p. 167.

11. His text clearly indicates where he lies on this concern. Augustine writes: "Is not your hand, almighty God, able to heal all the diseases of my soul and, by your abundant grace, to quench even the lascivious motions of my sleep? You will increase your gifts in me more and more, Lord, so that my soul may follow me to you, wrenched free from the sticky glue of lust so that it is no longer in rebellion against itself, even in dreams; so that it neither commits nor consents to these debasing corruptions which come through sensual images and which result in the pollution of the flesh." Augustine clearly thinks that it is within his power (with the grace of God) to refrain from doing lascivious motions in sleep. Augustine, *Confessions*, 10.30.42, p. 169.

12. I would like to thank David Kyle Johnson, Bill Irwin, and Jonathan Evans for their helpful comments.

DREAM TIME: *INCEPTION* AND THE PHILOSOPHY OF TIME

Michael J. Sigrist

I just didn't understand the concept that hours could turn into years down there.

—Dom Cobb

The malleability of time is a fundamental plot device of *Inception*. Because your mind functions more quickly in dreams, time feels slower. Under heavy sedation, ten hours can turn into one week, six months, even ten years. "It could be infinite, I don't know." Since things happen on different dream levels simultaneously, yet at different rates, Cobb and his team not only have to keep track of *where* they are, but *when* they are. "Yusuf's ten seconds from the jump, which gives Arthur three minutes, which gives us . . . sixty minutes." Only such precise calculations can guarantee a consecutive wave of kicks that they can "ride . . . back up the layers."

Cobb and his team are not the only ones with dreams that mess with one's sense of time. Undoubtedly you've woken up from a nap unaware of how long you were asleep or what time it is. You have probably even lost track of time when awake. How do we get lost in time? It's not like getting lost in a maze. So then what could it mean to be lost in time? How do we lose track of time? Does experiencing time as slowing or speeding up—like Cobb and his team seem to experience it—make sense? Is time really malleable, or is it constant? And what is time, anyway?

Trying to Make Sense of Time

Coping with being lost in time does not come easily. We learn this during Ariadne's first lesson in shared dreaming. She and Cobb find themselves sitting at a pleasant Parisian café discussing the basics of dream construction. The dreamer creates the world of the dream, the subject fills it with his or her subconscious; the dreamer need not worry about creating enough detail to make the subject think it's real. "Well, dreams, they feel real while we're in them, right? It's only when we wake up that we realize something was actually strange." When Ariadne eventually realizes she is dreaming, in one of the film's most iconic scenes, the street and café explode. Cobb shields his face from the flying debris, and just as the explosions are about to engulf them both, they awake safe in the warehouse. Arthur, who has been monitoring their session, mentions that they were asleep for only five minutes. "Five minutes?!" Ariadne exclaims. "We were talking for, like, at least an hour!"

Most of *Inception* takes place in a "dream world." A dream world, unlike the real world, exists only in the dreamer's imagination. As Cobb explains, in a dream world, the dreamer's mind creates and perceives their world simultaneously. Not only does the dreamer create the *places* in the dream

(Paris, a rainy city, a snow fortress), he or she creates the *time* in which the dream world unfolds. And when we confuse dream time with real time, we get lost in time.

The most dramatic elements of *Inception* build on this very common form of disorientation. Consider the climactic final moments of the Fischer inception: simultaneously, the van is hitting the water, the elevator is crashing, the snow fortress is collapsing, and Ariadne is free-falling off the Limbo penthouse. The viewer understands that these events must all occur at the same time. The dramatic tension of the final scenes arises from this understanding. If the van hits the water before Arthur has jolted the elevator or before Fischer has accepted the implanted idea, the mission will be a failure and Cobb will never see his children again.

As we're watching, this all seems to make perfect sense. It's like the nearly simultaneous sequence of events orchestrated at the end of *The Godfather: Part III*, when Frederick is smothered with a pillow, Don Altobello is poisoned, the Archbishop is shot, and Don Lucchesi is assassinated in his office. The difference, of course, is that in *Inception*, not only are all of the events fiction, they're all a dream. In a sense, they are not really happening at all, so how can they be simultaneous? Let's use this question to get at the philosophical problem of time perception.

What do we normally mean by "simultaneous"? The reader will be forgiven for perhaps forgetting that on the same day that *Inception* was released (July 16, 2010), *Standing Ovation*, the "musical event of the summer," opened in theaters. These events, we say, were "simultaneous," meaning that they happened *at the same time*. Now, one of the more intriguing features of the world director Christopher Nolan has created is that each dream level runs on *its own time*. If this is right, however, then each of the events happening on different levels is happening *at different times*. If we accept that Yusuf, Arthur, Eames, and Cobb are all on different levels, what could it mean for them to act at *the same time*? For events to be simultaneous, they must share a common temporal frame of reference. Yet if each of these events is happening in different times, what could that common reference be? So when we are led to believe, at the climax of *Inception*, that each of these events is happening simultaneously, something else must be going on other than what we normally mean by "simultaneous." What is it?

The Measure of Movement

It is nearly obligatory for every discussion of time to repeat the famous quote from the philosopher and theologian Saint Augustine (354–430): "What, then, is time? If no one asks me, I know what it is. If I wish to explain it to him who asks me, I do not know."[1] We all have a sense of time. We sense that a little while has gone by—maybe a minute—or that it's been a long time since we ate. How long did it take you to read that last sentence? Our sense of time is responsible for keeping us from getting lost in time. It is this sense that gets confused somehow when we dream. We've all been in Ariadne's position: Have I been asleep for five minutes, or an hour? When we lose our sense of time, what have we lost?

An obvious answer might be that we've lost track of the seconds, or minutes, or hours—but what are these? A second, like an inch, is a measure of something. There are sixty seconds in a minute, sixty minutes in an hour, and twenty-four hours in a day. But this doesn't answer our question. Seconds, minutes, hours, and days—these are themselves units of measurement. There are twelve inches in a foot, but we don't use inches to measure a foot—we use inches to measure the width of a desk or how tall we are. So what do seconds and hours measure? The sort of answer we're looking for might be this: twenty-four hours measure one rotation of Earth around its axis; three hundred and sixty-five and one quarter days measure one revolution of Earth around the Sun.[2]

The Greek philosopher Aristotle (384–322 BCE) gave a similar, but more general, answer to this question: time is the measure of change. Aristotle realized that change could only be explained in reference to time. One type of change is movement, a change of place. Think of Cobb running down the alley in Mombasa. He has moved if at one point in time he is at the start of the alley and at another point in time he is at the end of the alley. Cobb has moved more quickly than his pursuers if he travels farther in the same amount of time. According to Aristotle, a universe without time would be a universe without movement and without change.

If this theory of time makes sense to you, pause and reflect: Is the converse of our last statement true—would an unchanging universe be a timeless universe? If the universe came to a standstill, would time stop? Aristotle's answer is yes. Time is a property of objects. Just as an object might be red or two feet wide, it might also be present or past. Just as an object can change its colors, so too can an object change times, from future to present to past. This view entails that just as there would be no colors or sizes if there were no colored or large objects, so too there would be no time if there were no present, past, or future objects.

Augustine validated Aristotle. Imagine a universe with no objects—no planets, no stars, no light, no sound. Can you imagine time passing in such a universe? It seems so, but only because, Augustine argued, when we try to imagine this sort of nothingness, we are covertly placing *ourselves* in that time-less, motionless nothingness. Even in this timeless, changeless nothingness, *our thoughts* are changing and thus time is passing. Augustine concluded that time exists only in our minds and has no reality besides.

The rise of modern physics in the seventeenth century put this answer out of favor for several centuries, however. For one thing, it was discovered that the rotation of Earth around its axis is not in fact unvarying; it can vary by as much as twenty minutes throughout the year. When it does, we don't conclude that time itself has sped up or slowed down. Isaac Newton (1643–1727) thus theorized that time is "absolute," meaning that it is not relative to anything such as the revolution of the planets or the rotation of Earth. Every event in the universe happens in time, but time itself does not depend upon those events for its reality. Events start and stop, but time itself has no beginning or end. Time passes, regardless of whether there is change.

This "realist theory" of time got a big boost from Albert Einstein's (1879–1955) relativity theory, which treats time as another dimension, along with space, and treats both space and time as substances. Whether the "substantival theory" of space-time is truly entailed by relativity, though, is still a matter of debate.[3] However, it has been argued that a changeless universe in which time passes is, despite Augustine's suggestion, possible. Imagine a universe with three regions that freeze, for a year, at different but regular intervals—every three, four, and five years. When their freeze cycles all align, would we not say that the universe froze (experienced no change) for a year? If so, it would seem that time does not require change, although philosophical intuitions about such a universe vary widely.[4]

Around the same time that Newton was advocating the "absolute" theory of time, the philosopher John Locke (1632–1704) was trying to discover where we learn the idea of time in the first place. And, regardless of whether time is a substance, or a measure of change, our idea of time seems to come from observing change—specifically our own mental changes. Locke's answer echoes Augustine: one does not learn about time by observing the motions of the Sun and the stars, but by observing the changes in one's own mind—specifically, by noticing the succession or flow of one's ideas. Aristotle may have been right that our sense of time measures change, but he was wrong about the change in question. It is not the changing world that our sense of time measures, but the changes occurring in our own mind—the flow of subjective perceptions, ideas, and thoughts. This insight might help us better understand how we retain a sense of time in dreams. The dreams that Cobb infiltrates are, after all, creations of consciousness. Cobb, Arthur, and the others each retain a sense of time throughout the different levels of the dreams because, while oblivious to the world, they remain aware of themselves.

Believing in Time

Time flies when you're having fun. Time also flies, I imagine, when a target's subconscious projections are shooting at you. When we are engrossed in some activity—watching a film, perhaps, or dreaming—we lose track of time. (Ever notice how the second time you watch a movie, it doesn't seem to take as long?) Time also seems to slow down when we are bored or occupied with some unpleasant activity.

When we use expressions like this, we do not mean that events are actually unfolding more rapidly or more slowly. The very premise of this sort of phenomenon belies that interpretation: the reason for our confusion stems from the fact that while time *seems* to be progressing at the normal rate, *in fact* a much longer or much shorter time has passed. It is this confounding discrepancy between what seems to be happening and what in fact is happening that gives rise to temporal confusions. If an hour of time *seemed* to take an hour, even a "faster" or "slower" hour, then time would not surprise us. Recent experiments seem to confirm this explanation. Time does not seem to slow down during exhilarating or harrowing experiences, but when we recall those same experiences afterward, we remember them as taking longer than they in fact did.[5]

So when we say that "time flies," or we feel that some activity is taking *forever*, what we really mean is that our *judgments* about time's passing are mistaken. Our sense of time is not trustworthy in these instances. Yusuf seems to have found a way to reduce this unreliability somewhat. Brand-name Somnacin—the drug responsible for binding dreamers together and allowing dream infiltration—increases brain activity by about ten times. But *Yusuf's* Somnacin compound that he utilizes for the Fischer inception speeds up brain activity by *twenty times*. Within each level of the dream that activity is compounded. Thus the experience of a ten-hour flight to Los Angeles is equal to roughly a week (two hundred hours) in the van level, which is equal to six months (166 days) in the hotel level, and *ten years* on the snow fortress level (111 months). We are not told in detail how Yusuf's serum works, but presumably it is able to increase brain activity to very high rates while keeping the dreamer sedated and maintaining all necessary bodily functions.

The Sense of Time

Our sense of time is just that—a *sense*—and it has to involve more than just our beliefs about time. It's something that we feel or *perceive*. Compare this to the different experiences of reading a comic book and watching a film. A well-drawn and well-composed comic book can sometimes be as engaging—as action packed—as any film. In one panel Batman swats a vile enemy; in the next that same enemy is bloodied and whimpering on the ground. You know well enough what happened. The villain is on the ground because Batman pounded him. All the same, you do not actually *see* this happen. Your knowledge is based on an inference, a judgment. Sometimes this is all we mean by a sense of time. Why does Ariadne, once she gets her bearings, believe that Arthur was telling the truth about her having been asleep for only five minutes? Probably because the sun was still up and nothing much in the room had changed. But knowing that five minutes have passed is very different than *sensing* five minutes pass.

What do we sense with our sense of time? Consider the experience of listening to a melody. A note strikes: say the first note of the song the dreamers use to signal the oncoming end of a dream, Edith Piaf's "Non, Je Ne Regrette Rien." That note is G. Then you hear another, D, followed by F#. You hear each of these notes in succession. But you also hear more than this. You hear G *followed by* D, D *followed by* F#, and F# *coming after* D and G. You are aware, in other words, not just of each successive note, but also of the succession of notes *as* a succession. This is what it means to *hear* a melody, rather than to just know that one has been played.

One of the hardest problems in philosophy is to understand how this is possible—not just in regards to music, but also in our everyday experience. One intuitive principle, proposed by Aristotle (yes, him again), is that conscious experience is confined to the present. We have memories of the past and expectations for the future, but we only ever *experience* the present. This principle is hard to square with the experience of something like a melody. For to hear the melody to "Non, Je Ne Regrette Rien" you must experience not only the third note, F#, but also F# following D following G. Yet by the time F# has struck, D and G are no longer present. How can there be any such "following" experience if Aristotle is correct and experience is confined to the present?

The American philosopher William James (1842–1910) popularized an answer to this puzzle known as the "specious present." According to James, the present "is no knife-edge, but a saddle-back, with a certain breadth of its own on which we sit perched, and from which we look in two directions."[6] James's theory of the specious present purports to explain our sense of time by rejecting Aristotle's principle that experience is confined to the present. At any given moment, we are aware not only of the present but also of the recent past and the near future; we sense not an instant of time, but a durational spread. The sense of time therefore is the sense not only of the present instant, but of the recent past and near future as well. Establishing just how long that spread might be has been a matter of some controversy over the past century. It has been proposed that the specious present might be as long as two to three seconds, but most theorists today acknowledge a much briefer period, between 40 and 200 milliseconds.[7]

The specious-present theory gets something right about time perception but does not explain enough. What it gets right is that, in order to explain our consciousness of temporal phenomena, it must be the case that we actually experience more than just the present instant. The specious-present theory claims, for example, that in listening to the melody you are aware of D and G *at the same time* even though G is no longer present. But if this were all there is to the matter, we would hear a chord, not a melody—and this is not what we hear. When D strikes, you are still sensing G, but you are now sensing G as just-past. You don't hear G and D at the same time. You hear G-followed-by-D. So something has to happen to G between the time it initially registers and when it is experienced as just-past along with D.

The philosopher Edmund Husserl (1859–1938)—the founder of an important school of twentieth-century philosophy known as phenomenology—introduced a new concept in order to make sense of this: retention.[8] In our example from "Non, Je Ne Regrette Rien," when D strikes, you are still aware of G, but that awareness is in the mode of *retention*. A retention is not a memory. While memory is a mode of consciousness by which we are aware of the *past*, *retention* is a feature of our conscious experience of the *present*. You can experience the present moment without memory, but you cannot experience the present moment without retention.

The Speed of Thought

Now let's make things even more complicated. Melodies play more quickly or more slowly according to their tempo. Tempo measures the number of beats played per minute. One of Nolan and music director Hans Zimmer's more clever ideas was to slow down the song "Non, Je Ne Regrette Rien" and use it as the theme for the movie. That low, rumbling horn blast, which has become one of the signature elements of the film, is in fact just the first notes to Edith Piaf's "Non, Je Ne Regrette Rien" played at a much slower tempo.[9] In fact, as Zimmer explained:

> all the music in the score is subdivisions and multiplications of the tempo of the Edith Piaf track. So I could slip into half-time; I could slip into a third of a time. Anything could go anywhere. At any moment I could drop into a different level of time.[10]

Now ask yourself: If the melody has a rate or tempo, does the *experience* of that melody *also* have a rate? If so, and if a melody can be played more quickly or more slowly, can consciousness play more quickly or more slowly? A melody plays more quickly if more beats are packed into a minute. Might consciousness similarly slow down or speed up? Might consciousness play, as it were, to a faster beat? Might those around you experience time differently, so that what you experience as a day seems like a year to them?

Inception suggests that, indeed, conscious experience can speed up or slow down. A week in the van level corresponds to six months on the hotel level, which corresponds to *ten years* on the snow fortress level. Does this mean that dreamers on the snow fortress level *dream faster* than dreamers on the van level?

In order to make sense of time perception, we should distinguish among three things: the objective duration of an event, the subjective impression of that duration, and the objective duration of that perception itself. We might assume that in normal cases these are all roughly equal. A bolt of lightning streaks across the sky in roughly half a second. We also perceive it as lasting half a second. And we can suppose that the duration of that perception itself is one half second. In a dream, these equivalencies break down. To begin with, there is no objective event to be perceived in the first place. More important, while the objective duration of a dream—the measure of how long one was *really* dreaming—might last only five minutes, it can *seem* to one that an hour has gone by.

Let's stick with this distinction between the objective duration of an experience and the subjective impression of duration. What is the relation between these two—between, for instance, how long a dream actually lasts and how long it seems to last? We have two levels to keep track of. On the one hand, we have the experienc*ing* itself, and on the other, what is experienc*ed*. To keep track of times on these different levels, let's refer to the seconds of experienc*ing* as just "seconds" or "minutes," and the experienced seconds as "e-seconds" and "e-minutes." A second is the amount of time that passes in the real world, but an e-second is the amount of time that *seems* to pass. To return to our example from the film: Ariadne and Cobb enjoy five minutes or sixty e-minutes at the café. This distinction might allow us to make sense of the question "What is the speed of thought?" The speed of thought for Ariadne in her first fabricated dream encounter is twelve e-minutes for every minute. During the Fischer inception, in the snow fortress level, the speed of experience is much faster: just over ten e-months per hour. In Limbo, the speed of thought per minute is (perhaps) e-infinite.

The Speed of a Dream

But now we have the further question: How fast is an "e-second" or an "e-minute?" Are e-seconds faster than seconds?[11] There are two difficulties with this sort of question. The first is that we are forced to posit *yet another* level of time units—e*-seconds, perhaps—to measure the first. One e*-second on the hotel level proceeds at the rate of twenty e-seconds on the van level. This does not lead us into any inconsistencies, but it does complicate matters. We should now be comparing seconds, e-seconds (on the van level), e*-seconds (on the hotel level), e**-seconds (on the snow fortress level) *and* e***-seconds in Limbo. This allows us to be precise in our comparisons, but it is not clear exactly *what* we are comparing. The second problem is related to the first: it may make sense to compare e-seconds, e*-seconds, and e**-seconds to seconds, but in the Fischer inception Cobb and his crew must somehow keep track of the relation between e-seconds, e*-seconds, e**-seconds, and even e***-seconds.

To make sense of this I suggest that we give up the notion that experienc*ed* time (for example, e-seconds) has a rate at all. An e-second is how long a second *seems* to pass, but it is not itself a second long. It is a mistake to conflate the properties of an experience with whatever it is an experience *of.* The perception of a red sign is not itself red, and so, too, perhaps with the perception of a minute. Consider our earlier discussion of the specious present. According to the retentional model, we are directly aware not of instants but of durations. At any given moment, I am aware not only of that present instant but also of the just-past and the near future. But now look over that last sentence again: *at any given moment*—is this "moment" a real moment, an e-moment, or something else? Philosophers refer to this idea—the fact that the experience of duration must involve the awareness of several moments simultaneously—as the Principle of Simultaneous Awareness (PSA). PSA suggests that the duration of which we are aware is not the same as the duration of that awareness itself. Recognizing that experiences themselves have a duration—that I can be aware of being aware, and that this second awareness itself has a duration—does not solve the problem but merely pushes it back a step, and another, and another, apparently without end.

The proper way to think about the temporal relation between e-seconds, e*-seconds, and so forth, is to conceive of them as *ratios* rather than absolute measurements. Many philosophers and physicists suggest that we should take this approach to time in the universe; it is one of the ideas behind relativity theory. The ratio approach is one with which Aristotle would have been familiar: instead of asking how fast Earth moves through space, we ask how fast is Earth moving relative to the observer. There is no fixed rate at which time flows, just ratios of velocity among moving objects.

Because of the issue involved with PSA, it does not really make sense to ask how fast an e-second is. But we can ask how fast an e-second is *relative to* an e*-second. Yusuf's serum, in fact, establishes a lawful relation between these: one e*-second (on the hotel level) is equal to twenty e-seconds (on the van level), and one e**-second is equal to twenty e*-seconds but *four hundred* e-seconds. This allows us to understand how a kick is timed: on each level, the person responsible for hitting the kick (Yusuf on the van level, Arthur on the hotel level, and Eames on the snow fortress level) must keep track of e-, e*- and e**-seconds relative to one another, cognizant of the compounding twenty-to-one ratio. In other words, the kicks in each level do not happen, as we initially supposed, *at the same time*, but they do have to happen at the same *adjusted ratio* of time.

Dream Simultaneity

Inception is not only a philosophically rich film, it is a fantastically told story. Like any good story, it needs conflict and drama.

The urgency of the plot arises, especially during the Fischer inception, from our worry that Cobb and his crew will not pull off everything in time, and this means in the dramatic arc of the final act *at the same time*. We have seen that a very curious concept of time must be at work in this dramatically gripping series of events. The time in question is not real time, and even though the characters experience seconds and minutes and even years (in Limbo), these are not *really* seconds, minutes, or years. Despite these complications, Nolan has managed to put together a world in which this all makes sense, and in so doing has proved that philosophy and story can go together in the best of ways.

NOTES

1. Saint Augustine, *Confessions*, trans. Henry Chadwick (New York: Oxford University Press, 1991), p. 230.

2. Some physicists speculate that time measures entropy in the universe.

3. See Peter Kosso, *Appearance and Reality: An Introduction to the Philosophy of Physics* (New York: Oxford University Press, 1997).

4. This thought experiment is based on one proposed by Sydney Shoemaker in "Time without Change," which can be found in William R. Carter, ed., *The Way Things Are: Basic Readings in Metaphysics* (Boston: McGraw-Hill, 1997), chapter 7.

5. See David M. Eagleman, "Human Time Perception and Its Illusions," *Current Opinion in Neurobiology* 18 (2008): 131–136.

6. William James, *The Principles of Psychology, Volume 1* (New York: Henry Holt, 1890), p. 609.

7. See S. Coren, L. Ward, and J. Enns, *Sensation and Perception*, 6th edition (New York: John Wiley & Sons, 2004).

8. See Edmund Husserl, *On the Phenomenology of the Consciousness of Internal Time (1893–1917)*, trans. John Brough (Norwell: Kluwer Academic Publishers, 1991).

9. To be clear, what we hear on the film is not Piaf's song slowed down, but a composition that replicates what Piaf's song sounds like slowed down.

10. For more on how Zimmer used Piaf's song to construct the music for *Inception*, see Dave Itzkoff, "Hans Zimmer Extracts the Secrets of the 'Inception' Score," in the *New York Times*, *Arts Beat*, July 28, 2010. Online, this article includes a video that plays Piaf's song and the *Inception* score side by side. http://artsbeat.blogs.nytimes.com/2010/07/28/hans-zimmer-extracts-the-secrets-of-the-inception-score/.

11. We could also ask about the relation between the time of the experiencing and the time of the event experienced. Again, we can suppose that normally these are roughly the same. If a melody is played for ten seconds, then my experiencing of the melody also lasts ten seconds. In abnormal situations, however, these two durations can themselves be discrepant. For example, the experience of a very brief note might last longer than the note itself (the reader might clap his or her hands very forcefully right now to experience this). In any case, since our concern is with dreams—where there is no objective event—we can set this further complication aside.

DREAMS AND POSSIBLE WORLDS: *INCEPTION* AND THE METAPHYSICS OF MODALITY

Charles Joshua Horn

> It's the chance to build cathedrals, entire cities, things that never existed, things that couldn't exist in the real world . . .
>
> —Dom Cobb

Inception is fundamentally concerned with possibility. Is it possible that we are dreaming? Is it possible that future technology will allow us to share dream states? Is it possible to have a dream within a dream? Although possibility is addressed in several different ways in *Inception*, the underlying feature is always the dream states that Cobb and his team occupy. In other words, one way in which we could interpret the film is that it describes what is possible and impossible *through* the dream states themselves.

A Possible World Primer

Philosophers don't describe possibility through dreams in the way that it is portrayed in *Inception*. Rather, philosophers describe possibility in terms of *possible worlds*. When we say "world," we aren't talking about a planet. A possible world is another way that all of existence could have been.

The actual world is the world that we *really* exist in, whereas possible worlds are worlds that could have existed in a way different from the actual world. To say that some event or thing is *possible* is to suggest that it happens or exists in at least one possible world. For instance, dream-sharing technology is possible if it exists in at least one possible world. To say that a proposition is possible is to suggest that the particular state of affairs described is true in at least one possible world. For instance, the proposition "Cobb and his team failed to plant the idea inside Fischer's mind" is equivalent to saying, "There is some possible world in which Cobb and his team failed to plant the idea inside Fischer's mind." Thus, statements of possibility are claims about the nature of reality. At least one world, either a possible world or the actual world, needs to "exist" in the way described for the state of affairs to be possible. (Although, as we shall see, philosophers disagree about what it means to say that a possible world "exists.")

To say that something is *impossible* is to suggest that there is no possible world in which the thing exists. For instance, a circle composed of straight lines is impossible, since there is no possible world with a circle composed of straight lines. Similarly, to say that a proposition is impossible is to suggest that there is no possible world in which the state of affairs described exists. For example, the proposition "Penrose steps cannot exist" is equivalent to the claim that "There is no possible world in which Penrose steps exist."

To say that something occurs from *necessity* or happens necessarily is to say that in every possible world a particular state of affairs occurs. In other words, there is no world in which a particular state of affairs does not occur. For instance, the claim that "It is necessary that Cobb's children will grow older" is equivalent to saying that "There is no world in which James and Phillipa do not grow older." Hence, a claim about something as necessarily true means that the particular state of affairs exists not only in the actual world, but also in every other possible world.

To say that something is *contingent* is to suggest that a particular state of affairs could happen, but it also could not happen.[1] For instance, it was contingent in the film that Ariadne played the role of the architect for the Fischer inception job. It very well could have been the case that Nash (Cobb's original architect) played the role of the architect instead. (Nash, for example, could have not betrayed Cobb and still been in his circle of trust.) If a particular state of affairs exists in the actual world, we know that it could be true. If it could also be false—that is, if there is some possible world in which it does not occur— then we say that it is contingent. The state of affairs could have been different.

With this modal background in place, we can begin to understand the claim that dreams can be conceived of *as* types of possible worlds. Both dreams and worlds describe a particular state of affairs as possible, that is, something that could happen. As we will see later, even fantastical states of affairs could exist, if and only if certain qualifications are met. To illustrate this point, consider your own most vivid dream. The events that happened in that dream are possible. This does not mean, of course, that the particular state of affairs in your dream is actually going to happen in this, the actual world. (I am in no way suggesting that dreams can predict the future.) Instead, possibility means that the particular state of affairs *could* happen—it is true in some possible world.

For instance, if I dreamed last night that I was fishing at Norris Lake in Tennessee, it would entail that it is possible for me to indeed fish on that particular lake. Even if I do not have the time or resources to go fishing there at this point, the dream would imply its possibility. Notice that even though the dream of fishing is a mundane example, the same principle would apply for any dream. For instance, if I had a dream in which I was actually part of Cobb's team trying to perform inception, then that, too, would satisfy our modal criteria and be possible. Further, the principle would apply not only for my dreams, but for your dreams as well.

Aside from these basic features about modality, it is also important to note what exists *in* these worlds. Although there is wide disagreement on this very question, it would be safe to say that worlds include *almost* anything. There is a possible world with only one tree; another with an infinite number of people; still another with only one tree and an infinite number of people. There is a possible world where the universe contains no life, and there is a possible world where the universe contains only one atom. There is even a possible world with more than one universe.[2] Some possible worlds are very different from our world; some are very similar. There is a possible world in which you exist but are a foot taller, another where you have a different color hair, and another where you chose not to read this chapter—and still another where all three are true.[3] Thus, although worlds can differ dramatically, they can also be incredibly similar to other worlds.[4] It can never be the case, however, that two possible worlds are identical in every single respect. Identical worlds would, in fact, be the same world.

Men Possessed by Radical Notions: Spinoza, Leibniz, and Lewis

Benedict de Spinoza (1632–1677) argued that there is only one possible world, and that it is the actual world. Nature unfolds only one way, and necessarily so. "Things could have been produced by God in no other way, and in no other order than they have been produced."[5] This would imply that it was necessary for Mal to kill herself, for Cobb to flee from the police, and for him and his team to eventually incept an idea into Fischer's mind. Additionally, this would entail that we do not have freedom—at least not in the libertarian sense in which free will requires that it be possible to not do what we in fact choose to do.[6] As Spinoza sees it, one can act freely only if one understands that the universe unfolds one way, and accepts the inevitability of nature. So, although it would have been impossible for Cobb to decline Saito's job offer, Cobb's action still could have been free if he had the proper understanding of nature—one that entails that he could do nothing else but accept the offer.

Gottfried Leibniz (1646–1716) vehemently disagreed with Spinoza's necessitarian understanding of the universe, which suggested that the entire causal structure of the universe is determined—no state of affairs can be any different than it is. Instead, Leibniz thought that there was an infinite set of possible worlds, and that God freely chose to bring into existence the best one. Despite his attempt to preserve human freedom, Leibniz could not reconcile his rationalist commitments with libertarian free will. Even though there are other possible worlds, we would not really have the ability to do any other action, because God created us in *this* world, the actual world. We can do no other action besides the one that God dictated would occur by selecting the possible world he did. We are "locked in," so to speak, by God's choice.

Leibniz's philosophy is critical to understanding the nature of modality because he specifies *compossibility* as a criterion for what allows a possible world to be possible.[7] A possible world is possible because its substances are compossible. Two substances are compossible if and only if there is no contradiction between the properties of the two substances.[8] For example, it would be perfectly consistent for Cobb and Mal to inhabit the world of Limbo because Cobb and Mal do not have contradictory properties. It would be impossible, however, for both Cobb and Mal to be "the tallest person in Limbo." Such a world could not exist because the compossibility criterion is not met. There can only be one *tallest* person. So not even God could create a world with incompossible substances.

Today, philosophers would define Leibniz's idea in terms of "metaphysical possibility." Specifically, something is metaphysically impossible if it is inconsistent given the meaning of the terms or the essence of the things being discussed. There is no metaphysically possible world in which "Cobb is a married bachelor," because the definition of bachelor is "unmarried male." If we plug that definition into the original statement, we get "Cobb is a married unmarried male." And that can't be true; it's nonsense. We might say that "Cobb is a married bachelor" fails to meet the compossibility criterion.

Most philosophers today agree with Leibniz in thinking that there is an infinite set of possible worlds, but when they speak of a possible world "existing," they don't mean it in a literal sense. Most philosophers think of possible worlds as abstract conceptual objects, or coherent and complete descriptions, that help us make sense of modal statements. Most radical among the philosophers, however, who speak about possible worlds is David Lewis (1941–2001), who suggested that each of the infinitely many possible worlds is actual, relative to itself.

In terms of *Inception*, Lewis would argue that the possible world in which Cobb and his team exist (not as characters in a movie, but as real people) is actual—actual relative to itself. It's not our world (what we call "the actual world"), and from the perspective of our world, the world with Cobb and his team is merely possible, not actual. But from the perspective of the world where Cobb's team really exists, their world is actual, and ours merely possible. Key in understanding the boldness of Lewis's claim is understanding that neither we nor they are wrong when we say, "Our world is actual, but theirs is only possible." It's not as if our world is "really actual," but theirs only seems actual to them. No. The existential status of each world is the same—that is, they all equally, objectively exist. They are "on par." Why? Because were Cobb to utter "I exist in this world" in the world where he and his team exist, that statement would be true. Existence, Lewis would say, is an "indexical property." Of course, if you were to say in our world, "I exist in this world," your statement would be true in our world. It's just that no world is privileged over another in terms of existence. Each world is actual, relative to itself.

What this entails is pretty cool, especially since dreams seem to represent possible worlds. There is a world in which Cobb and his team kidnap Fischer in the rain. There is a world in which Cobb and his team are in the hotel with Fischer. There is a world in which Cobb and his team are on the snow-covered mountain. And there is a world in which Cobb lives with Mal in their perfect city. In fact, there is a world in which any dream you have ever had occurs. And although such worlds are merely possible from our world's perspective, objectively they are just as real—they exist—just as much as our world is real. In a way, your dreams really occur . . . at least, if Lewis is right.

But even when we set aside the issue of whether all worlds are existentially on par, the concept of worlds is very useful for exploring some important questions, particularly those related to the very nature of possibility. In particular, some of these questions will be concerned with the ways in which God and the architects within *Inception* are importantly similar and critically different. If dreams are indeed like worlds, then it seems that the architects and God should also be similar in their ability to create. And yet, we will soon find out that the architects within the film are seemingly more powerful than God!

Architects, God, and Evil Worlds

God is similar to the architect of *Inception* in that they both have the ability to construct worlds. The crucial difference between God and an architect is that God seems to be limited in certain ways, whereas an architect is not. Consider this: If God is all-loving, all-knowing, and all-powerful, then he cannot create a world with evil, such as needless suffering. God's creation of such a world would violate his character. If he truly cared about those he created, and had the knowledge and power to stop it, then God would not allow those he cared about to suffer needlessly. He could not do otherwise. Yet an architect could! An architect could create a world with needless suffering, for an architect is not morally perfect, and thus not restricted by his nature to do only that which is good.

That fact that our world contains evil is argued by many to be conclusive evidence that God does not exist; this is called "the problem of evil." But there is another problem here directly related to possibility. If God is all-powerful, how is it that an architect can do something that God can't (namely, create an evil world)? Isn't God supposed to be able to do anything? There seems to be an inconsistency in the very concept of God. God being all-powerful entails that he can create an evil world, but God's being all-loving entails that he can't. So forget wondering whether God exists, and ask yourself, "Is God's existence even possible?"[9]

To avoid this problem, some philosophers have suggested another modality. Leibniz defined it in terms of "moral necessity." He suggested that although it is metaphysically possible for God to create a world with evil (because he is all-powerful), it is morally necessary for him not to (because he is all-loving).[10] Although Cobb *could* create a dream in which his children are tortured, he never *would*. His love for his children would not allow it. In a similar way, God *could* create a world with evil—he simply *won't*. His love for his own creation would not allow it.[11] Thus, God's power is limited by his benevolence, whereas the architect's power is unlimited precisely because she does not have the moral perfection of God.

Today's metaphysicians would object, however, pointing out that given a modern understanding of modality, it is not only morally impossible but metaphysically impossible for God to create an evil world. Recall that something is metaphysically impossible if it is inconsistent, given the meaning of the terms, or the essence of the things being discussed. Let us consider the sentence "God creates an evil world." Creating an evil world would not be loving, so this would entail "God has done something unloving."[12] But what is the definition of "God"? While there is some disagreement on many points, and you can find someone to disagree with any definition you present, it has been widely agreed by the most important theistic scholars for centuries that if God is anything he is a being that is all-powerful, all-knowing, and all-loving. In fact, he has these properties necessarily—in all metaphysically possible worlds. They are a part of his essence. But now, if we plug our definitions into the original statement we were considering, we get "An all-powerful, all-knowing, and *all-loving being has done something unloving*." That can't be true in any metaphysically possible world, any more than "Cobb is a married unmarried male" can be true in any metaphysically possible world. So it seems that God cannot do something unloving.

It is, however, metaphysically possible for Cobb to create a world in which his children are tortured, but this is because "not torturing his children" is not a part of Cobb's definition or essence. If, say, his children really made him mad—so mad that he wanted them tortured—and so Cobb dreamed up a world where they were tortured, Cobb would not cease to be Cobb.[13] If, on the other hand, a being decided to do anything but that which was all-loving, that being could not be God—for God is, by definition, all-loving. Thus it still seems that God has contradictory properties, and that an architect has powers God does not.

Since "an all-powerful being can't do something unloving" is metaphysically impossible, we are still stuck with the problem of divine inconsistency. If God is, by definition, a being that is all-powerful and all-loving, since those two properties are incompatible, it seems that God's existence is metaphysically impossible.

To avoid atheism, many theists have simply clarified what it means to be all-powerful. Being all-powerful isn't being able to do anything, but being able to make any statement that makes logical sense true.[14] So God can make Cobb a bachelor, but he can't make him a married bachelor—that is a contradiction. God can make circles, and he can make squares, but he can't make squared circles—that is a contradiction. Likewise, he can't make it true that he created a world with evil, for the same reason.

This does not, they argue, diminish God's power at all. We don't think any less of God because he can't make "he ba, gee ba, bing bling blah" true—because it's meaningless. It makes no sense. There is nothing it would mean for that statement to be true. But the same thing can be said of "There is a square circle." There is a side-less object with four sides? What does that even mean? Even though each word makes sense by itself, together they make a meaningless statement. The same is true for statements about God creating an evil world. "A loving being does something unloving" makes no sense. Hence God can still be all-powerful, even though he can't create an evil world—even though he can't do something that an architect can.

The Laws of Nature and the Possibility of Miracles

Something else that an architect can do that God cannot is alter the laws of physics. Both worlds and dreams require an environment to inhabit that operates according to certain laws of nature. Although these laws might be very different from the laws of the actual world, it is a necessary feature of any world that it has laws to govern it. That architects can manipulate these laws is made evident in the film. As Ariadne begins her training with Cobb, she realizes that she can change the laws of nature in a particular world. Her belief is justified and verified when she flips the city of Paris on top of itself. Think also of the scene in which Arthur fights Fischer's security in the hotel. Although it is not the work of an architect, as the van flips over and over in the reality one level higher, the laws of nature are affected on the hotel level.[15]

If God were to do this to our world, however, it would seem exceptionally cruel. A world with inconsistent laws of nature would be nearly impossible to live in. The assumption that we all live by, that the future will resemble the past, is necessary to navigate the world. If I press the brake on my car and it stops, the next time I press the brake—it had better stop! If it accelerates forward instead I'll have a bad accident. And if I don't know what it will do next time, then I will be unable to drive my car at all. If the future consistently did not resemble the past, we could not even lead meaningful lives. Further, the very nature of scientific experiments is observing what happens under certain conditions, and then inferring that the same things will happen, in the future, under those same conditions. If the laws of our world were inconsistent, understanding the world would be impossible! So overturning the laws of nature, it would seem, would be exceptionally cruel and something that it would be metaphysically impossible for God to do, because it would be inconsistent with his all-loving nature.

Yet not stepping in once in a while, when the laws are about to cause damage, also seems to be unloving. If Mal is about to fling herself from a window, it would seem exceptionally cruel to not overturn the law of gravity for her specifically, if one could, so that she floats instead of falling to her death. In fact, such violations of natural laws are called "miracles," and many theists not only believe that God could, but that he does, perform them on a regular basis. Whether or not one is ever justified in believing that God performs such violations of the natural law is another issue.[16] Why he doesn't perform miracles more often, if indeed he can, is yet another issue related to the problem of evil. What I am worried about, however, is whether God doing so is even possible. Overturning the natural laws would seem to make the world unnavigable and unknowable, but not doing so at least every once in a while, when it is needed, seems cruel.

So far, it has been demonstrated that God's benevolent nature limits his ability to create an evil world in a way that is not problematic for the architects within *Inception*. But are there any other ways in which the architect can create worlds that God can't?

Dreams and the Possibility of Paradox

Perhaps there is. Yet another thing that architects seem to be able to do, but God cannot, is this: create paradoxes. Take, for example, the Penrose steps—the staircase that Arthur shows Ariadne how to create, and that she designs into Arthur's hotel dream, which enables him to cleverly sneak behind the "subconscious security" he is fighting by running down and away from him, and from above and behind him, at the same time. Although it is possible to draw such a staircase on paper, it is metaphysically impossible to create such a thing in three dimensions. Specifically, the topmost step of a staircase cannot also be the bottommost step. One in the same step cannot be fifteen feet off the ground and also one foot off the ground *at the exact same time*. Given the definitions of the terms, such properties would be inconsistent and therefore metaphysically impossible. And as such, they would be beyond God's power to create. But if *Inception* is right and such paradoxes are dreamable, then architects can once again do something that God cannot.

Does *Inception* describe our dreaming capabilities accurately, though? Can we really dream up metaphysically impossible things? Consider a "square circle." Can you even imagine such a thing? Not a square in a circle, or a circle in a square. But can you imagine an object with four corners and four sides where all points are equidistant from its center? Can you imagine a four-sided object with no sides? Such a description doesn't even make sense! And if we can't imagine it, could we dream it?

If *Inception* describes our dreaming abilities accurately, it reveals something very novel about possibility and possible worlds. If we can dream of Penrose Steps, even though they are metaphysically impossible, then perhaps it makes sense to say that "Penrose Steps are possible," at least in some sense of the word "possible," even though there is no possible world in which they exist. If so, philosophers may have to expand their notion of possibility beyond "possible worlds."

It's Never Just a Dream: Reality in *Inception*

Nolan's masterpiece gives a new insight into the nature of modality by implicitly suggesting that architects not bound by any prior metaphysical commitments to be all-powerful and all-loving have a greater freedom than God to create different worlds. More important, although architects are limited to the film, we are not. Every time we dream, we are constructing *worlds*. As Cobb tells Ariadne, "In a dream . . . we create and perceive our world simultaneously. And our mind does this so well that we don't even know that it's happening." Our dreams *are* worlds. We may not have direct control of our dreams in the way that architects do, but perhaps God does not have that much control over which world to actualize either. After all, if an all-loving, all-knowing, all-powerful God exists, then he would be bound to actualize only one world, namely the *best* possible world. Or perhaps, if God wants us to be truly free, he must let us control our own world, and give up his say about which possible world gets actualized.

Still, why do worlds matter? Why is it necessary to maintain a totem to keep track of reality? What privileges one world over another? A likely response is that we care about the real world. We would not want to live in a possible world that is not actual, no matter how good the world feels while we are there.[17] Yet when Cobb spins the top on the table at the end of the film as he finally makes it home to his children, he does not bother to make sure that it falls. This does not necessarily mean that Cobb does not care if the world in which he resides is the actual world, but instead that there is something more important to him, namely the ability to be with his children, whether it is possible *or* actual. Maybe this is the true lesson that we can draw from *Inception*. Given our analysis of possible and actual worlds, it certainly matters on some level whether the world we are living in is the actual world, but it could be the case that reality has nothing at all to do with the worlds themselves. Perhaps reality is determined by the meaning that we impose on the world around us. This is echoed in the statement by the elderly man in Mombasa when Eames asks, "They come here every day to dream?" and the elderly man responds, "No. They come to be woken up. The dream has become their reality. Who are you to say otherwise, sir?"[18]

NOTES

1. Don't confuse this with saying that it both happened, and didn't happen, in the same way, at the same time. That is impossible; it is a contradiction. It could not happen in any possible world.

2. In fact, some physicists and philosophers say that the actual world may be this way. Our universe may be only one among many universes, in a multiverse.

3. Many philosophers disagree about whether the very same individuals can exist in different worlds. If it is true that you could have been a foot taller, some philosophers wouldn't say that *you* are taller in another world, but that a counterpart of you is taller in another world. The claim that an individual can only exist in one world is a denial of transworld counterfactual identity.

4. When two worlds are similar to one another, philosophers call them "close." Of course, the more similar two words are, the "closer" they are.

5. Benedict de Spinoza, *A Spinoza Reader: The Ethics and Other Works*, ed. and trans. Edwin Curley (Princeton, NJ: Princeton University Press, 1994) Part I, Proposition 33.

6. Please, do not confuse the libertarian notion of free will, which is a philosophical definition of what is metaphysically required for human free will, with "libertarianism." The latter is a political movement that suggests certain boundaries about what the government should and should not restrict citizens from doing. The two are totally different, and unrelated.

7. Certainly it isn't the case that Leibniz's criterion of compossibility is the only measure for whether a world will indeed be possible. Another popular idea is that conceivability entails possibility. If this idea is correct, a world being conceivable by your mind entails that it is possible.

8. There is a great deal of disagreement about what Leibniz means by compossibility. The interpretation offered here follows what is often regarded as the logical or analytic interpretation. Other interpretations include the lawful or synthetic interpretation and the cosmological interpretation, as well as other hybrid views.

9. This was the fundamental mistake that Leibniz thought Descartes made with the ontological argument for God's existence in his Fifth Meditation. Descartes assumed, without argument, that a being having all perfections was possible. Leibniz then went on to argue that a being having all perfections was possible, so that the rest of the ontological argument would follow.

10. The distinction between metaphysical and moral necessity originates in the philosophy of Leibniz. In describing why God must create the best of all possible worlds in his *Theodicy*, Leibniz argues that God is metaphysically free to create any world, but morally bound only to create the best one. He uses an analogy of how a line drawn between two points can be traced in an infinite number of ways, and yet there is only one way in which the two points can be connected in the "best" way, namely, the shortest distance between the points. He writes, "God chose between different courses all possible: thus metaphysically speaking, he could have chosen or done what was not the best; but he could not morally speaking have done so." Gottfried Wilhelm Leibniz, *Theodicy* (Chicago: Open Court, 1998), p. 271. Leibniz is motivated to say this due to Spinoza's conception of God; Leibniz must distinguish between these versions of necessity in order to preserve the freedom of God.

11. One might wonder, of course, how Leibniz reconciled his belief in God with the fact that there in fact is evil in the world. The only book he published during his life was the *Theodicy*; the title is a word he coined to justify God's allowance of evil in the world. In short, he argued that God allows evil because this is the best that he *could* do given the divine properties that he is committed to. Thus, Leibniz reasons that this must be the "best of all possible worlds." Voltaire (1694–1778) notoriously lampooned Leibniz for this belief.

12. Perhaps the creation of some evil world could be an act of love, but I am sure you can imagine a world that is so horrible that in no way could creating it be an act of love. That is all we need for the example to work.

13. Perhaps you think that it is a part of Cobb's essence to not torture his children. If so, then he can't create such a world. If he did, he would not be Cobb. But this does not affect my point, for even if this was a part of Cobb's essence, being all-loving is still a part of God's essence and thus he cannot do anything but that which is loving. Needless to say, there is wide disagreement in metaphysics about what makes someone the same person over time. In this chapter, I am not committed to any particular thesis concerning this issue.

14. Perhaps ironically, some theists have rejected this suggestion. They are called voluntarists. For example, René Descartes (1596–1650), a voluntarist, held that God could make worlds with square circles, rocks that he could not lift, and even worlds in which $2 + 2 = 5$. Given the objections we are considering, however, voluntarism is not a smart move, for it makes unavailable the response I am about to give. It makes other classic theistic moves unavailable as well. For example, many theists have maintained that God created a world with evil in it because it is logically impossible to have a world with free creatures but no evil, and having free-willed creatures would be more important to an all-loving being. If, however, not even logical impossibility is outside God's power, he could have (and should have) created a world with free creatures but no evil.

15. As I pointed out, it was not the architect's or dreamer's doing that the laws of nature change in this example. This instance is merely meant to show what a change of the laws of nature could look like in *Inception* or our own world. In fact, one of the major points that Cobb makes to Ariadne is that the laws of nature *should not* change because that would alert the dreamer to the strangeness of the dream. This would in turn create a risk of the dreamer waking before extraction or inception is possible.

16. For more on this debate, see Part Eight of *Philosophy of Religion: Selected Readings*, ed. Michael Peterson et al. (Oxford, UK: Oxford University Press, 2009).

17. For more on this topic, see Dan Weijers's and Bart Engelen's chapters in this volume.

18. I wish to thank Clint Jones, Kyle Johnson, and Bill Irwin for their extremely helpful comments and contributions with earlier versions of this chapter. This chapter is written for my lovely wife, Katy, who continually reminds me why this must be the best of all possible worlds.

DO OUR DREAMS OCCUR WHILE WE SLEEP?

Keith Dromm

She was possessed by an idea.
　　　　　　　　　—Dom Cobb

We are told in *Inception* that there is no more resilient parasite than an idea. It's highly contagious and almost impossible to eradicate once it's in the mind. One such idea is that our dreams consist of experiences that occur while we sleep. Consider this exchange between Cobb and Ariadne at the Café Debussy:

> Cobb: Where are you right now?
> Ariadne: We're dreaming?
> Cobb: You're actually in the middle of the workshop right now, sleeping.

Cobb is telling Ariadne that the dream they are sharing is taking place *while* they're asleep. They are perceiving the various sights and sounds of a Paris street from their café table, and thinking and talking about the nature of dreams, all while sleeping. Although what they see and hear is not real, they experience it as though it were real. As Cobb further explains to Ariadne, "When you're in [a dream], it feels real." So, according to this view, we can feel the pain of a gunshot, the thrill of being chased by security agents, the sensations of moving weightless through a hotel, and so on, all while we're asleep. We can also fret over the welfare of our children, contend with our feelings for a deceased spouse, or figure out our father's true feelings for us, even though we might be sleeping in an airplane's first-class cabin 30,000 feet in the air. But is this view of dreaming correct?

Norman Malcolm's *Dreaming*

Many others beside the characters in *Inception* hold this idea of dreams. J. Allan Hobson, a prominent dream researcher, wrote that "the most broad, general, and *indisputable* definition of dreaming [is] mental activity occurring in sleep."[1] The philosopher Colin McGinn has written recently: "It appears evident that during sleep we have experiences of specific sensory types."[2] Daniel Dennett, another contemporary philosopher, has labeled this idea the "received view."[3] It is, of course, an idea held by more than just scientists and philosophers. Christopher Nolan, the writer and director of *Inception*, seems to hold this view. In fact, most people are infected by this idea of dreaming.

In a small book with a suitably succinct title, *Dreaming*, published in 1959, the philosopher Norman Malcolm (1911–1990) challenged the received view about dreams. He wrote, "If anyone holds that dreams are identical with, or composed of, thoughts, impressions, feelings, images, and so on . . . occurring in sleep, then his view is false."[4] In other words, our dreams are not experiences that we undergo while asleep. It is not the case that while we sleep we have sensory and other sorts of experiences that, if our memory manages to retain them, we can recall upon waking. Malcolm tries to extract this idea from our minds in the most complete way possible. He doesn't want merely to find and copy it; he wants to remove it entirely from our minds—a kind of anti-inception.

Malcolm doesn't deny that we have dreams, but he believes that scientists, philosophers, and most everyone else goes wrong when they try to explain the basis of dreams, which are the impressions we often have upon waking of having experienced certain events. Malcolm points out that we must infer that those events belong to a dream. We do so either by comparing them to the events of the previous day and concluding that they did not actually occur, or we realize that the events—given our beliefs about, for example, how reality works—simply could not have occurred. (For example, if I wake with the impression that I was flying weightless through the halls and rooms of a hotel, I would infer that it belongs to a dream, because I know I can't really fly.) We can then recount these events in a dream report to others or to ourselves. Malcolm insists, however, that it is a mistake to further infer that we experienced the events of the dream while we slept.

Apart from trying to show that the received view is wrong, Malcolm does not try to explain what dreaming is; as he says, "I do not understand what it would mean to do that."[5] Rather, he is trying to correct some errors people make in their thinking about dreams. For example, there is the "error that philosophers, psychologists, physiologists and everyone who reflects on the nature of dreams tends to commit, namely, of supposing that a dream *must* have a definite location and duration in physical time."[6]

Temporal Location and Duration of Dreams

The dream extractors in *Inception* tell us that dream time does not correspond to sleep time. Cobb explains to Ariadne that "in a dream, your mind functions more quickly, therefore time seems to feel more slow." Arthur adds, "Five minutes in the real world gives you an hour in the dream." With the especially strong sedative that Yusuf develops, brain function is even more accelerated, so that 10 hours of sleep time will "feel" like a week on the first level of the dream, 6 months on the second level, and 10 years(!) on the third. The characters believe that the dream they will share on the plane while under this sedative will all occur—even though it will feel much longer—within those 10 hours, such that it will begin as soon as they fall asleep, end when they wake up, and take place throughout all ten hours that they are asleep.

However, according to Malcolm, "the notions of the location and duration of a dream in physical time . . . have no clear sense."[7] While we typically talk about dreams occurring *in* sleep, Malcolm insists that we should not take this way of talking to indicate temporal location for our dreams. He explains our use of "in sleep" in this way: when we wake up and report our dreams, we are reporting that various events "took" place; that is, we use the past tense to describe them. They are not events that are transpiring as we report them, as in the case of hallucinations. This explains why we favor the locution "in sleep" when talking about our dreams. But this is just how we happen to "label the above facts, which imply nothing about the occurrence of dreams in physical time."[8]

There appear to be at least two different sets of facts that undermine Malcolm's view that dreams do not occur in physical time. First, there was the discovery in 1953 of brain activity during sleep.[9] Malcolm discusses the subsequent interest that dream researchers took in a phase of sleep in which the brain is especially active, known as REM sleep (for rapid eye movement). Researchers concluded that dreams occur during this phase of sleep because subjects were more likely to remember their dreams when they were awoken during REM (though dream researchers today believe that dreams can occur during other phases of sleep as well).[10] Researchers concluded further that the length of dreams matches the length of REM sleep, because subjects' reports about the duration of their dreams tended to correspond to the length of the recorded brain activity.[11]

According to Malcolm, the results of such experiments do not establish either the temporal location of dreams or their duration. When dreamers report their dreams, they often give what seem like locations in time to them. For example, someone might say that he was having a dream "just before" he woke up or that he had a "very long" dream. Malcolm points out, however, that such reports do not give us "a determination that would be satisfactory to physical science."[12] It is not something that would allow us to locate the dream "on the clock," as Malcolm puts it.[13] All that such reports amount to is merely what dreamers are "*inclined to say* on waking up."[14] We have no way of translating these inclinations into specific locations in physical time.

In fact, dream researchers are willing to admit that their methods do not provide direct observations of the temporal characteristics of dreams. For example, Hobson says: "While recording the state of the brain—by means of brain wave, eye movement, or muscle tone—does not reveal the state of the mind, it can predict mental state with high statistical confidence."[15] The only thing that would provide any degree of confidence, however, would be an independent means of confirming such "predictions" about dream length. The reports of dreamers cannot do this. Dreamers are only able to provide their impressions about their dreams' temporal characteristics; these impressions are not measurements of physical time.

The characters in *Inception* clearly understand that these impressions are not reliable indicators of temporal duration. Recall Ariadne's surprise to learn that she had only been asleep for five minutes even though her conversation with Cobb at the Café Debussy seemed to last at least an hour. However, it is never explained in the film how Cobb and the others established the precise rate at which dream activity increases as one moves deeper through the levels of a dream. Malcolm would be equally intolerant regarding claims about dream duration. He insists that dreamers' reports about the length of their dreams "is not duration in physical time. Dream-telling cannot yield *that* concept."[16]

So this research on correlations between brain activity and dream content does not confirm the received view; it presupposes it. It cannot show when and for how long dreaming takes place. Only if we already assume that dreaming occurs while we sleep and for definite periods of time could we accept this research as telling us something about the temporal characteristics of dreams. According to Malcolm, though, there is no way to verify that dreams have these temporal characteristics, so we should abandon this assumption.

The other set of facts that appear to undermine Malcolm's position is anecdotal evidence about the influence of external stimuli on dream content. People sometimes report dreaming of thunder when a thunderstorm occurred while they slept. Yusuf, on the first level of the inception, dreamed of rain because he had too much free first-class wine and had to urinate. In fact, the influence of external stimuli on dream content is important to *Inception*'s plot. Often, "kicks" work when a stimulus on one level is experienced on a lower level. It might seem that the incorporation of "kicks" in a dream can determine a location in physical time for the dream. If the "kick" in waking reality occurs at a particular point in time, we might say that we experienced it in the dream at the same time. For example, if the "kick" occurs at 3:44 A.M., and the dreamer reports the "kick" upon waking, then we might be tempted to say that the dreamer experienced that "kick" in her dream at 3:44 A.M.

Malcolm doesn't deny that the contents of dreams can be causally influenced by external events. However, this correlation in content does not permit us to establish temporal correlation. Even if we entertain the notion that dreams occur during sleep, there is no way to establish that the external stimulus was not incorporated by the dream at a later point during sleep and not when it occurred in physical time. Alternatively, the "kick" might have only causally influenced the impression the dreamer has upon waking and not been experienced by the dreamer at any point while she slept. This, in fact, is what Malcolm would prefer saying. (As we will see, he doesn't think that such "kicks" are ever experienced by the dreamer while asleep.)

Some people, however, might still insist that the events of our dreams have to occur at some time because they are events of a particular sort—mental activities. We dream of seeing, feeling, hearing, thinking, and so on. When we do these things while awake, we do them at particular times and for determinate lengths of time; the same must be true of dreams. Malcolm responds by trying to extract from our minds the idea that we perform mental activities while asleep.

Mental Activity during Sleep

To complete his extraction of the received view of dreams, Malcolm asks us to consider how we could verify that some kind of mental activity occurred while a person slept.[17] Malcolm begins by noting some of the criteria we use in determining whether someone is asleep: "He is recumbent, his eyes are closed, his breathing regular, his body mainly inert, and . . . he does not react to various sounds and movements in his vicinity to which he would normally react if awake."[18] Other criteria include a person's behavior and appearance upon waking. Someone who was just sleeping can *look* as though he or she was asleep. Someone can also simply report that he or she was asleep, and if we can assume he is being sincere, we simply take him at his word.[19] Someone could always feign some of these criteria in order to trick us into thinking that he or she is asleep. Nevertheless, she could probably not feign all of them, and in any case, these are still the criteria we draw upon when determining whether another person is asleep. For someone to be asleep, these things have to be true of him or her. These criteria show that being asleep involves being in a state of unconsciousness, although a state from which someone can be roused. In this respect, sleeping is unlike being in a coma or, of course, being dead.

Now, let's consider a specific mental activity. Think of Fischer forming the judgment: "My father accepts that I want to create for myself, not follow in his footsteps." One thing that could tell Cobb and his team that the inception was successful is Fischer expressing this judgment when he is awake—he opens his eyes and announces, "My father accepts that I want to create for myself, not follow in his footsteps." And if he subsequently broke up his father's company, they'd be sure. But assume they want to know whether he made this judgment while asleep. Eames might see him make the judgment "during" his dream, but whether any dream experiences (including Eames's) actually occur during sleep is part of the question. So that won't help. Could the flight attendant, perhaps, tell by observing him while he slept? No. Any observable thing that Fischer did to confirm that he made this judgment would be inconsistent with him being asleep—for example, asserting this judgment, breaking up his father's company, and so on.[20] As Malcolm puts it, "Whatever in his behavior that showed he was making the judgment would equally show he was not asleep."[21]

Perhaps the flight attendant could observe his brain activity by hooking him up to an EEG. Let's say scientists have established that every time someone consciously makes the judgment, "My father accepts that I want to create for myself, not follow in his footsteps," a certain type of brain activity occurs. Now suppose that the flight attendant observes that same electrical activity occurring in Fischer's brain while he is sleeping. Can she rightfully conclude from this that he made the judgment while he was asleep? No. As Malcolm points out, the correlation found between brain activity and waking conscious states can only tell us about the experience of persons who are awake:

> The attempt to extend the inductive reasoning to the case of sleeping persons would yield a conclusion that was logically incapable of confirmation. It would be impossible to know whether this conclusion was true or false.[22]

If some particular electrical phenomenon occurred in the brain every time a waking subject judged, "My father accepts that I want to create for myself, not follow in his footsteps," finding the same activity *while a subject is asleep* would not entitle us to say that he made that judgment while sleeping. Like the anecdotal evidence for the temporal location of dream events, observations of brain activity cannot establish that a judgment was made while sleeping. They might enable us to predict that he will awake believing this judgment, but that he made this judgment while asleep is not something we are entitled to infer.

So it cannot be observed of Fischer while he is asleep that he is making a judgment. It might, however, be thought that Fischer could report when he wakes up that he made this judgment while asleep. But how could he know this? He couldn't be aware of both being asleep and making this judgment. What would awareness of being asleep consist of? He can know that he *was* asleep, sure. Such knowledge, though, is derived from his waking impressions—he remembers lying down to go to sleep and waking up in roughly the same place. There is not, however, an experience of *being* asleep. When you are asleep, you are unconscious. How could you have a conscious experience of being asleep?[23] A *memory* of being asleep, therefore, would be one without any content: "The memory of my state of sleep turns out to be an unintelligible notion, since nothing can be plausibly suggested as the *content* of the memory."[24] So Fischer cannot remember both that he was asleep and making this judgment.

Perhaps Fischer can *infer* when he awakes that he made the judgment while asleep. For example, he might say that he made it while also perceiving some external stimulus, like the airplane flying through some rough turbulence. But if he perceived the turbulence, then he was not asleep. As Malcolm points out, "Having some conscious experience or other, no matter what, is not what is meant by being asleep."[25] Maybe he could reason that since he did not hold that judgment before going to sleep, but awoke with it, he must have made it while asleep. Malcolm responds, however, that "it would not follow that he *arrived* at it *before* awaking. It would sufficiently describe the facts to say that when he went to sleep he was not of that belief, but that he *awoke* with the belief. . . . The inference to an intervening judgment is not required."[26] It would be similarly impossible for Fischer, or anyone, to confirm that he performed any other mental activity while asleep, such as seeing, hearing, believing, thinking, and so on.

Is Malcolm's Extraction Successful?

Malcolm believes that after considering these challenges to the received view, we should not only believe that the received view is wrong, we should think it's *nonsense*. He doesn't mean, however, that we should say we don't understand the received view. He thinks that the received view "is senseless in the sense that nothing can count in favour of either its truth or its falsity."[27]

To illustrate how this makes the received view nonsensical, let's borrow an example from *Inception* and imagine a safe to which we don't have the combination. Without the combination, we cannot know what is in the safe. This is an obstacle that we could *conceivably* or *theoretically* overcome, however, even though it is practically impossible for us to get into the safe. In the case of dreams, though, it is not even *conceivable* that we could know the location and duration of dreams, or whether they consist of mental activities that occur in our sleep. It is not merely a limit in our perceptual or technological ability that prevents us from knowing these things. As Malcolm explains, these are claims "whose truth or falsity are theoretically unverifiable."[28]

Malcolm believes that the theoretical unverifiability of the received view makes it nonsense. He is more careful when he describes the received view as an "unintelligible hypothesis."[29] By this he means that it is nonsense *as a hypothesis*. A hypothesis is a testable claim that—if it's shown to be true—explains some phenomenon. A theoretically untestable claim, however, like the received view, is not even a hypothesis. The received view attempts to explain the waking impressions that serve as the bases of our dream reports. It says that those impressions are recollections of mental activities that took place during sleep. But since there is nothing that "can count in favour of either its truth or its falsity,"[30] it's incapable of explaining those impressions. It just sort of hangs there, like a sleeping body floating weightless in a hotel room, doing nothing.

We have seen that the received view doesn't play the role of a hypothesis in scientific investigations of dreams. Researchers just presuppose it and then interpret the brain activity they observe in accordance with it. Malcolm believes that they should, instead, abandon the received view. At the very end of his book, Malcolm quotes favorably a psychiatrist who admits that whether our waking impressions correspond to "actual dreams" is an "insoluble problem." And therefore, "one never, under any circumstances, deals directly with dreams."[31] Malcolm would prefer we give up on this notion of an "actual dream." He says: "Dreaming is not to be conceived of as something logically independent of dream reports."[32] This means that there are no dream reports without dreams, and, more interestingly, there are no dreams without dream reports. A person cannot wonder whether they had a dream last night if they have no waking impressions on which to base a dream report. So the only "actual dreams" are those we can recount in our dream reports. Nevertheless, the psychiatrist recognizes that what cannot be observed—mental activity during sleep—should not figure into scientific investigations.

Now, there are lots of claims that are untestable but still intelligible and believable. For example, most of us believe that we are not dreaming right now. However, this belief is much more important than the received view. We have to believe that we are not dreaming right now to carry on our lives, whereas nothing important turns on the truth of the received view. Scientists have to assume that they are not dreaming while they perform their observations or experiments, otherwise they could not believe in the reliability of their results. Belief in the received view does not play such a role in their investigations. Scientists can, and should, stop assuming it.

Some might still insist that there must be an explanation for why we often wake up with impressions of having had all sorts of experiences. There certainly is, but Malcolm doesn't offer one. He's only interested in rejecting one ostensible explanation for those impressions; he doesn't try to fill the gap that appears left behind after the received view is extracted.[33] But a part of his extraction is showing us that the received view is not an explanation: "[A]n 'explanation' explains nothing if it involves an unintelligible hypothesis. Nothing can count for or against the truth of this hypothesis."[34] As an unintelligible hypothesis, the received view doesn't do anything in our minds but take up space. Malcolm quotes the famous philosopher Ludwig Wittgenstein (1889–1951) about such superfluous explanations: "A wheel that can be turned though nothing else moves with it is not part of the mechanism."[35] The mechanism in our case is the concept of dreaming. Since the received view never has been, and never could be, verified, it is not really a part of this concept. We don't need it to talk or think about our dreams.

Like Mal, many people get "possessed by an idea"; they think that dreaming must take place during sleep and involve various mental activities. Once we see that this idea plays no essential role in our concept of dreaming—it is like a wheel that doesn't turn anything—we should no longer be possessed by it. We might still feel irresistibly drawn to the received view, but the recognition that there is nothing holding up the view—that is, that there are no good reasons for believing it—should cure us of our infection by it. Also, unlike the belief that I am not dreaming right now, it is not a belief that we *need* to hold. A belief in the received view doesn't have that importance. As an unintelligible hypothesis, it doesn't even add to our understanding of one small part of our reality, our dreams.

While we lose what seemed like an explanation for our waking impressions, we no longer need to worry about whether we are dreaming right now when we abandon the received view. At least, this is what Malcolm argues toward the end of *Dreaming*. Other chapters in this volume explore this worry, a worry most famously considered by René Descartes (1596–1650).[36] Watching *Inception* might inspire some to ask, "Am I dreaming right now, or am I awake?" But Malcolm points out that the first part of this question doesn't make sense. In the received view, dreaming entails that you are asleep, but as we saw before, you cannot be aware of being asleep. So the question "Am I asleep?" and likewise the question "Am I dreaming?" is not even intelligible.[37] Malcolm also points out that the claim "I am awake" doesn't amount to an interesting piece of information. Since "I am asleep" can never be true, "I am awake" can't really express any knowledge about our condition. The most it can do is demonstrate to someone else that you're awake. For these reasons, Malcolm believes that the efforts by many philosophers to prove that they are awake and not dreaming are misguided.[38] Just as the received view only appears to be an explanation for our waking impression, "Am I awake or dreaming?" only appears to be a sensible question.

Is *Inception* Nonsense?

Does the nonsense of the received view make *Inception* nonsense as well? No, the coherency of its plot does not depend upon the intelligibility of the received view. The characters in *Inception* hold the received view, so they believe a lot of things they shouldn't about their dreams. For example, they believe that they dream while asleep and that their dreams consist of various experiences. In order to accept the film's portrayal of their dreams, though, we don't need to understand them exactly as they do.

Some inventions of the filmmakers, elements unique to the story of *Inception* such as shared dreaming, are also not made less coherent by the falsity of the received view. The film conveniently does not explain the technology that makes shared dreaming possible. If it did, some of that explanation might require the received view. In a way, the vagueness of the film helps preserve its coherency. We can, however, easily view the briefcase as a machine that somehow works directly on our neurology to cause us to have the same, or similar, waking impressions. We don't need to imagine that it causes people to have shared experiences with one another while asleep. So we don't need the received view to make sense of the shared dreaming in *Inception*. There might be other problems with the plot of *Inception*, but none seem to be the result of its acceptance of the received view.

NOTES

1. J. Allan Hobson, *Dreaming: A Very Short Introduction* (Oxford: Oxford University Press, 2005), pp. 6–7; emphasis added.

2. Colin McGinn, *Mindsight: Image, Dream, Meaning* (Cambridge, MA: Harvard University Press, 2004), p. 74.

3. Daniel Dennett, "Are Dreams Experiences?" in *Brainstorms: Philosophical Essays on Mind and Psychology* (Cambridge, MA: MIT Press, 1981), p. 129.

4. Norman Malcolm, *Dreaming* (London: Routledge & Kegan Paul, 1962) p. 52.

5. Ibid., p. 59.

6. Ibid., p. 75.

7. Ibid., p. 70.

8. Ibid., p. 77.

9. Hobson, pp. 38–40.

10. Malcolm, p. 71.

11. Malcolm reports conclusions reached by researchers in one such study that seem to contradict the views about accelerated dreaming in *Inception*: "[Dreams] seemed to progress at a rate comparable to a real experience of the same sort" (W. Dement and N. Kleitman, "The Relation of Eye Movements during Sleep to Dream Activity: An Objective Method for the Study of Dreaming," *Journal of Experimental Psychology* 53 (1957): 339–346, at 346; quoted in Malcolm, p. 73).

12. Malcolm, p. 76.

13. Ibid.

14. Ibid.

15. J. Allan Hobson, *The Dreaming Brain* (New York: Basic Books, 1988), p. 143.

16. Malcolm, p. 77.

17. In his book, Malcolm actually begins with this and then moves on to examine beliefs about the temporal characteristics of dreams. I'm presenting his challenges in reverse order because it just seems a better way to present them. I'm also not presenting his entire book in this chapter. For example, at the end of his book he uses his argument to refute the famous skeptical "dream argument"; I hope that readers will be interested enough to take a look at Malcolm's book.

18. Malcolm, p. 22.

19. Malcolm distinguishes being asleep from cases of sleepwalking, hypnotic trance, and nightmares, which do not satisfy these criteria. He calls them "natural extension[s] of the use of that word ['asleep'] beyond its primary use" (p. 28).

20. He could, of course, talk in his sleep and say this sentence. But for that to be a criterion of his making this judgment, he would have to be awake. Otherwise, we cannot know what—if any—mental activity is accompanying his saying this sentence.

21. Malcolm, p. 36.

22. Ibid., p. 43.

23. In fact, this seems to suggest that there is something a bit oxymoronic in the received view. How can one have conscious experiences while one is asleep—while one is unconscious? For more on this, what might be called the Paradox of Dreaming, see Tyler Shores's chapter in this volume.

24. Malcolm, p. 13.

25. Ibid., p. 12.

26. Ibid., p. 38. This is similar to our conclusion about observation of brain activity; we are not required to infer that the judgment was made while he slept.

27. Ibid., p. 37.

28. Ibid., p. 39.

29. Ibid., p. 86.

30. Ibid., p. 37.

31. Ibid., p. 122.

32. Ibid.

33. In fact, he is content to accept these impressions as a "remarkable human phenomenon" (p. 87). There is probably more that can be said about this phenomenon, including by scientists.

34. Malcolm, p. 86.

35. Ludwig Wittgenstein, *Philosophical Investigations*, G. E. M. Anscombe, P. M. S. Hacker, and Joachim Schulte, trans. (Oxford: Wiley-Blackwell, 2009), §271.

36. See, for example, Katherine Tullman's and James Miller's chapters in this volume.

37. Malcolm says that the statement "I am asleep" is "strictly senseless and does not express a possibility that one can think" (Malcolm, p. 118).

38. For a complete presentation of Malcolm's very interesting, but complex, arguments, see chapters 16 through18 in *Dreaming*.

PART FIVE

SHOULD I TAKE A LEAP OF FAITH?: RELIGIOUS THEMES IN *INCEPTION*

TAKING A LEAP OF FAITH: A HOW-TO GUIDE

David Kyle Johnson

> I'm going to jump, and you're coming with me . . .
> I'm asking you to take a leap of faith.
>
> —Mal

Faith is often described as a virtue, although clearly it is not always so. It's not even always a good idea. I doubt that many *Inception* fans thought it a good idea for Cobb to take Mal up on her offer. On the other hand, a leap of faith is exactly what Cobb asked Saito for in Limbo at the end of the film.

> Cobb: I've come back for you, to remind you of something—something you once knew. That this world is not real.
> Saito: To convince me to honor our arrangement.
> Cobb: To take a leap of faith, yes.

To oblige, Saito would have had to take Cobb's gun and shoot himself in the head. Ironically, most hoped he would—in fact, they thought he should. So when, exactly, should one take a leap of faith? It supposedly would have been a bad idea for Cobb to take the leap of faith Mal suggested, because they were not (one presumes) dreaming. It supposedly was a good idea for Saito to take the leap of faith Cobb suggested because they were dreaming. But how do we know? If we could tell what was true and what was false, we wouldn't need faith. So how can you ever tell whether taking a leap of faith is the rational thing to do?

What Is Faith?

Let's begin by avoiding a common confusion. When philosophers talk about "faith," they don't mean what people usually do when they talk about having *faith in a person*. Faith is belief that something is true without sufficient evidence or reason to think that it is true. Faith in a person, however, is having confidence in that person. That confidence is still belief that something is true; you might believe, for example, that it is true that they can do what they have set out to do. But usually you believe this with sufficient evidence; although you may not be sure, most often you have a pretty good indication that they will succeed. Cobb's team, for example, has faith in him—confidence that he can pull off inception. But this is not belief without sufficient evidence. They've had experiences with Cobb that demonstrated his extraction and dream-sharing skills. They don't have proof that he can perform inception, but they have enough evidence to justify their belief. So it's not "faith" in the philosophic sense.

Likewise, consider the belief that your significant other loves you. You can't know for sure (they could be faking it), but you probably have pretty good indicators. This is not really faith—that is, belief without sufficient evidence. If there is a situation, however, where you really don't have sufficient evidence—for example, you might have *faith in your favorite sports team* despite the fact that they have sucked all year—that would require faith, in the philosophic sense. You might believe, without sufficient evidence, that they can win the game. So sometimes *faith in* (confidence in) something can require faith (belief without sufficient evidence).

You might be wondering, however, what counts as sufficient evidence. Just how much evidence is enough to make a belief justifiably held, instead of merely held by faith? It's a matter of degree ("sufficient" is a vague notion), and I don't think anyone can draw that line. Yet some things clearly are matters of faith, whereas others are not. And there are some important distinctions to draw along that continuum that will help us understand what faith is.

Rarely, we face situations in which there is no evidence or reasons either way, or where the evidence and reasons perfectly balance out—like it did for Mal and Cobb's after exiting Limbo. They try to figure out if they are still dreaming, but since their vivid dreams are indistinguishable from the real world (and they both know how Mal's totem works), they can't have any evidence either way. No observation they could make would support either theory over the other. They have to take a leap of faith. Cobb has faith that the world is real; Mal takes her leap of faith that it is not, right out the window.

There are also spots along the continuum where we have reason to think a belief is true—just not very much reason. Yet even when the evidence (overall) is in favor of some belief, if the amount of evidence that favors the belief is small we might still say that to believe it requires faith. (After all, one could remain agnostic, and not believe one way or the other, given that there is so little reason to prefer one belief over the other.) For example, perhaps Cobb didn't know for sure whether his father-in-law, Miles, was going to be able to supply him with another architect. Sure he had some idea; given his father-in-law's line of work and history, it was somewhat more likely than not that he knew someone (like Ariadne) who would make an exceptional architect. If Cobb believed, based on such a small probability, that his father had an architect in waiting, we might say Cobb took a leap of faith by coming to Paris.[1]

In another possible scenario, a person has reason to think a belief is false and yet still thinks it is true. Such a person believes despite some evidence to the contrary; this definitely qualifies as faith. Ariadne does this when she returns to be Cobb's architect. She believes that everything will work out fine despite the fact that she has evidence that it will end disastrously: Cobb's serious subconscious problems. She even tells us why: "It's just pure creation." She ignores her mild reasons for doubt, and believes anyway, because of her fascination with lucid dreaming. She takes a leap of faith.

In the examples we have considered so far, it's not clear whether the person is being rational or not. So, to get a handle on the question of when it is rational to have faith, let's look at some examples where very clearly it is not rational.

The Pitfalls of Blind Faith

Some people tout the "right to their opinion" despite overwhelming counterevidence and arguments against their beliefs. This is most definitely irrational faith. Suppose, for example, your friend believes that Matt Damon played the part of Dom Cobb. You point out that it was, in fact, Leonardo DiCaprio. You show him *Inception* movie posters, the IMDB cast listing, the film's credits, interviews with the cast and crew, all showing DiCaprio played the role. "Nope," he says. "It was Matt Damon. I have a right to my opinion. I just have faith."

Your friend is wrong on many counts. He doesn't have a right to his opinion, at least in an epistemic sense. You certainly have no duty to just let him believe whatever he wants. He is also, of course, wrong about who played Cobb. Since he does believe something without sufficient evidence, however, he is right about the fact that he has faith—he just is not rational for doing so. Instead, he is stubborn and ignorant. He reveals that he has no concern for believing what is true, but is only concerned with protecting his belief and not admitting he is wrong.[2] This is "blind faith." He turns a blind eye to the evidence.

Another kind of blind faith is belief in absurdities, things that common sense or common knowledge shows to be false. Some people use *the possibility* that our common sense or knowledge is wrong as a reason to believe that an absurdity is true. But the fact that our common sense might be wrong—and of course it might be—is no reason to think it is wrong, and thus that the opposite of what it tells us is true. The fact that something is possible does not make it so.

Take, for example, the dream-sharing technology in *Inception*. Not only is it unexplained, but it is absurd. Controlling dreams with a tube hooked up to your arm? An IV can be used to knock someone out, but to control brain patterns so they can be synchronized with the brain patterns of others and thus share a dream would require direct manipulation of the brain—neural firing patterns would have to be controlled in very specific ways. You could send signals to the brain along nerves in the arm, but grandiose neural manipulation though nerves in the arm would be like trying to reprogram a computer with only a shift key. It can't be done.

Don't get me wrong. Understanding the dream technology is not important for the movie, and the film would not be better if it was explained. And maybe one day we will have the ability to alter brain states through the arm. If you said, "It probably won't ever exist, but I wouldn't say it definitely won't"—sure, I could agree with that. But to believe that such dream-sharing technology *actually exists*, or that it *will exist*, is not rational. It requires us to ignore the overwhelming evidence of common sense, as well as scientific knowledge of how the brain works. It would be irrational faith.

On a related note, consider the case of someone who commits the fallacy of "appeal to ignorance," believing something is true simply because it can't be 100 percent disproved. The fact that something cannot be proven false is no reason to think it's true. Why? Because practically nothing can be proven 100 percent true or false. For example, I can't even 100 percent prove that DiCaprio played Cobb. Any evidence I produce could be faked. Perhaps there is a grand conspiracy by DiCaprio fans to make it seem as though he played Cobb in the wake of the movie's success. Maybe DiCaprio and Damon were secretly switched at birth. As long as one is willing to change one's background assumptions (about, for example, the reliability of the evidence given), one can dismiss any evidence in order to protect a cherished hypothesis.

This is what keeps conspiracy theories alive. Any lack of evidence for the conspiracy is said to be the result of a cover-up, and any evidence against the theory is believed to have been planted. This is why you can never convince a conspiracy theorist they are wrong and one reason why belief in any conspiracy theory is fundamentally irrational.

Although I can't prove that DiCaprio played Cobb, what I can do is what I could do with any conspiracy theory—present a wealth of evidence and point out that the conspiracy theory is completely inadequate compared to another theory. My theory that DiCaprio played Cobb, for example, is simpler, explains more, makes no unjustified assumptions, and does not have to excuse away evidence. In other words, I can prove it beyond a reasonable doubt. Someone who continues to have faith despite sufficient evidence to the contrary is clearly acting irrationally. When sufficient evidence is available, we should follow where it leads, at least if we want to be rational.

Existential Matters

Belief in ghosts is irrational. Of course, I can't "prove 100 percent" that ghosts don't exist. I can, though, demonstrate that most ghost reports are bogus (as are ghostly pictures and videos) and that the ones that aren't bogus are easily explained away as hallucinations, "waking dreams," or other trickeries of memory and perception. In addition, the idea of visible disembodied spirits conflicts with scientific knowledge that is as certain as anything can get.[3] If you continued to believe in ghosts after considering such evidence, you could only do so by blind faith, and would thus not be acting rationally.

Suppose, instead, you believed in "Dream Ghosts"— mysterious beings that appear and share the dreams (and only the dreams) you can't remember. It is impossible for us to have evidence of their existence, and impossible for us to gather evidence against their existence. You can't examine a dream you can't remember to see if they are there or not. Obviously, belief in Dream Ghosts could only be had by faith. But equally obvious is that belief in Dream Ghosts would be irrational. When dealing with existential matters—that is, matters regarding existence— the rational default position lies in disbelief. The "burden of proof," we might say, lies on the person who wants to believe in Dream Ghosts. Without evidence for their existence, we should not think they exist.[4]

Along these lines, consider a thought experiment from Bertrand Russell (1872–1970). Suppose someone suggested that orbiting the sun, between Earth and Mars, there was a teapot so small that no telescope could ever see it. Looking for the teapot but not finding it could never be evidence that it does not exist because the teapot hypothesis predicts you could never see it. So, there is no evidence either way regarding the teapot's existence. Is faith in the teapot's existence rational? Obviously not, says Russell. If you want to rationally believe that the teapot exists, it's up to you to provide evidence for it. Since we are dealing with an existential matter, the burden of proof is upon you.[5]

This seems right. I can't 100 percent prove that unicorns, fairies, or leprechauns don't exist. I can't look everywhere in the universe to verify that one isn't hanging around somewhere. But that doesn't make belief in such things rational. Unless I have sufficient evidence or good reason to think such things exist, it is irrational to believe they do. Faith—belief without sufficient evidence—in the existence of something is irrational.

Additionally, if I realize that the origin of my belief in the existence of something is not rooted in the existence of that thing, this would demote such a belief further, to the level of blind faith. For example, when a child realizes that belief in Santa is not rooted in the existence of an actual jolly fat man but in a story told by parents, continued belief in Santa would be a matter of irrational, blind faith. Likewise, realizing that someone's belief in the actual existence of dream-sharing technology simply traces back to that person watching *Inception* is reason enough to dismiss the idea that such technology actually exists.

Some might object, however, because of "the genetic fallacy," which is commonly understood as suggesting that the origins of an idea can't count as evidence for or against the idea. Such an understanding of this fallacy, however, is too simplistic. For example, the fact that the ring structure of benzene came to Friedrich August Kekulé (1829–1896) *Inception* style—that is, in a dream (he dreamed of a snake eating itself)—does not disprove the idea. This, however, is because his suspicion has been confirmed numerous times since he proposed it. The genetic fallacy is only committed when we ignore or dismiss the evidence for a belief by simply pointing to its origins. If we had absolutely no evidence for the ring structure of benzene, the fact that the origin of the idea tracked back to a dream would be good reason to doubt it. Indeed, Kekulé's contemporaries would not have been justified in believing him, until his idea was shown to be scientifically sound, because the idea merely came to him in a dream.

Belief in the existence of something by faith is irrational—even more so if a faulty origin of the belief can be identified. You might be wondering, then, can faith ever be rational?

An Example of Rational Faith

Inspired by science, some people claim that faith is always irrational. In response, however, it is pointed out that it seems impossible to do science without faith—specifically, faith in *induction*, the notion that the future will resemble the past. If sodium and chloride have combined together and produced salt before, we can infer that anytime anyone anywhere puts sodium and chloride together, they will get salt. If certain symptoms have been correlated to a specific disease in the past, and someone displays that set of symptoms, we can conclude they probably have that disease.

Why does belief in induction require faith? Because there is no way to gather evidence or argue for it without assuming it. We might present an argument like this:

Induction has been reliable in the past.
Therefore, induction will be reliable in the future.

Notice, though, that this argument is an inductive argument; it infers what the future will be like based on our experience of the past. To even make the argument, you have to already assume the truth of the conclusion—that induction is reliable. This makes the argument circular, and no circular argument can provide sufficient evidence for its conclusion. Circular arguments don't work for the same reason that Penrose steps are impossible—your first step can't also be your last.[6]

This *problem of induction* was most famously raised by the philosopher David Hume (1711–1776), and is indicative of many similar problems. When we make arguments, we make all kinds of assumptions. We assume *modus ponens*—that if a conditional (If P then Q) is true, and the antecedent of that conditional is also true (P), then the consequent (Q) must follow. We assume *noncontradiction*—that nothing can be both true and false at the same time. In short, to make arguments, we have to assume that the basic rules of argumentation are valid. But how could you present an argument for such rules without assuming them? You can't present an argument for the reliability of arguments without (once again) making a circular argument.[7]

In general, we might say that anyone who says that "evidence is reliable and it's never rational to believe anything without it" is stuck between a rock and a hard place. Where is their evidence for their claim that evidence is reliable? If they have none, then they merely assume that evidence is reliable and thus believe it by faith (that is, without evidence) and break their own rule. If they try to provide evidence, they argue in a circle and thus fail to meet their own criteria for believing their own claim. To reason and argue at all, we have to have faith in argument and evidence.

However, there doesn't seem to be anything irrational about doing so. In fact, if you rejected such things (and I'm not even sure you could), there would seem to be something seriously wrong with you. Einstein suggested that the definition of insanity is "doing the same thing over and over again and expecting different results." Induction suggests that doing the same thing gets the same results; to not have faith in induction would be insane! If you truly think that the fact that the hot stove burned you last time is not reason to think it will burn you next time, there is something wrong with your head (and very shortly your hand). The same holds for all the rules we have been talking about: modus ponens, noncontradiction. Try to live your life without these rules. Try to find someone who doesn't.[8] Even primitive societies, which may not even have language to articulate such rules, assume them in their everyday life. Not even the most uncivilized tribesmen would come to the edge of a cliff and think, "Everything else fell, but I won't." Everyone believes, in general, in the reliability of evidence and the basic rules of argumentation.[9]

Although belief in the reliability of argument and evidence in general must be taken on faith, that faith is universal. No one disagrees. We couldn't get along without it. It seems to be hard-wired into us—probably because it has worked so well in the past. So, it seems, there is nothing irrational about faith in argument and evidence itself.[10] But, of course, this does not mean that faith in anything and everything is rational. Contrary to the desires of those who want to believe in Dream Ghosts, regular ghosts, unicorns, and the like, the fact that faith in the reliability of evidence and argumentation is rational does not open up the flood gates and make faith in anything and everything rational. After all, belief in the reliability of evidence and argumentation is hard-wired, uncontroversial, and universally asserted. If a belief is not these things, without evidence one will have a difficult time showing that belief to be rational.

Faith That We Are Not Dreaming

As many chapters in this book have pointed out, *Inception* raises the classic philosophical question: Can you know that you are not dreaming right now? Many have argued that we can't. In fact, since the experiences of a vivid lifelike dream are indistinguishable from the experiences of a waking life, we can't have any evidence either way. Any experience you had would be predicted by both the waking and the dream hypothesis. Again, this seems to be just the situation that Cobb and Mal are in upon exiting Limbo. If so, doesn't this mean that if we are to believe that the world exists (that we are not dreaming), we would have to do so by faith? And since that is belief in the existence of a thing, wouldn't that be irrational—at least, if what I have said so far is right?

The answer is no because there is a way to settle the dream question. Although I can't gather any evidence, per se, to show that I am not dreaming, I can compare the dream and real-world hypotheses to see which one is better—which one is more adequate. The real-world hypothesis, as it turns out, is simpler (it makes fewer assumptions), explains more, leaves fewer questions unanswered, and is certainly more conservative. Although I might think differently if, like Cobb, my profession required me to continually enter vivid dreams, in my current profession the adequacy of the real-world hypothesis presents good enough reason to favor it, and removes the need for faith.

In addition, even if belief in the real world did require faith, what I have said so far does not make it irrational. One of the key components that made belief in induction and the rules of argumentation rational was the fact that they are universally shared, and that to reject them would seem to make one insane. The same seems to be true regarding belief in the real world. No one really thinks the world doesn't exist, and if they did we would lock them away. So belief that the real world exists does not require irrational faith.

A Rule to Follow

We have concluded that it is not rational to hold a belief without sufficient evidence (by faith), especially on existential matters, unless that belief is uncontroversial and universally shared or the rejection of that belief would indicate insanity. This is our criterion for judging the rationality of belief by faith. By this criterion, however, we would label the examples from the first section irrational. If Cobb believes that Miles will have an architect for him, he's being irrational. When Ariadne believes that everything will be fine despite Cobb's dangerous subconscious, she is being irrational. What is nice, however, is that since both rationality and sufficiency are a matter of degree, we can rate these actions accordingly. Sure, it might be irrational to believe that something is true when you have very little evidence for it, but it is not as irrational as believing something is true when you have evidence against it. And it certainly isn't as irrational as continuing to believe that Matt Damon played Cobb.

Unavoidable Irrationality?

Our criterion may render irrationality unavoidable in some circumstances. Think again of the situation that Cobb and Mal are in after exiting Limbo. There is no evidence to prove who is right. And since they continually enter vivid dreams, the belief that the world is real is not universally held or uncontroversial, and rejecting it would not make one insane. (Mal, in fact, had herself declared sane by three psychiatrists.) Last, in the movie, both notions seem to be equally adequate; they both, for example, leave no questions unanswered. So whether Mal or Cobb believe the world is real or that it is a dream, they will have to do so by faith—the kind of faith that our criterion says is irrational.

If the criterion implies that sometimes there is no rational choice, must the criterion be wrong? No, even when we set our criterion aside, it's clear that sometimes there is no rational choice. Consider one of my favorite thought experiments. You're in hell, and God makes you a deal. For every day you spend in hell, he'll grant you exponentially more time in heaven. So, one day in hell earns one day in heaven, two earns two. Three, however, gets you four. Four days in hell gets you eight days in heaven, five gets you sixteen, six gets you thirty-two, and so on. When do you cash in? When you have earned a thousand years of heaven time? A million? Maybe a billion? But if you just stay one more day—only one more!—you would double your time, earning just as much time in one day as you have earned all previous days. It doesn't seem that it would ever be rational to cash in your earned heaven time; staying one more day would always be too valuable—even more valuable than the last time you did it. Yet, clearly, never cashing in your earned heaven time is equally irrational. Thus we seem to have a situation where there is no rational option.

This doesn't mean that you can choose irrationality whenever it suits you. Clearly, if there is a rational option, it's the one to take. What it does mean is the fact that our criterion entails that sometimes there is no rational option is no reason to reject the criterion. Sometimes, there just is no rational option.

There is still a problem, however. What should we do in circumstances when there isn't enough evidence to decide the matter—when there is no rational choice? Our criterion doesn't tell us.

The Ethics of Belief

Blaise Pascal (1623–1662) considered us to be in just such a situation when it came to belief in God, and argued that one should choose belief because it is the better bet. If you believe, you stand to gain everything (heaven) but lose nothing, whereas if you don't, you stand to lose everything (hell) and gain nothing.[11] His "wager," however, is one of the most contested arguments in all of philosophy. For one, his payoff matrix is off. Belief in God is not without risk; you might waste your life worshiping a nonexistent god, or end up in the hell of another deity you didn't worship, or worshiped incorrectly. (After all, if we have no evidence as Pascal suggests, we have no way of knowing that God wouldn't prefer and reward disbelief. Maybe that is why he gave us no evidence.) Disbelief is not without reward, either; you will more fully appreciate this life if you think it is the only one you have. But Pascal is right about this: if you are in a situation where evidence cannot decide anything—thus, there is no rational thing to do—it can still be *reasonable* to choose what is in your best interests.

We could liken this to when Saito asks Cobb to take a leap of faith and believe that he can deliver on his promise to get the charges against Cobb dismissed, if Cobb successfully performs inception on Fischer. I don't think that Cobb has sufficient evidence to believe that Saito can deliver, but given the potential payoffs, it's worth the risk. It's not rational, but it's reasonable for Cobb to attempt inception.[12] It's even, perhaps, something he should do.

But now we are delving into the ethics of belief. What is morally acceptable to believe or disbelieve? William Clifford (1845–1879) argued that it is always morally wrong to have faith, because doing so always risks harm to others (and even yourself).[13] Clifford, I think, overstates his case a bit; certainly my faith in induction harms no one. And faith can't be morally wrong when it's unavoidable. What he gets right, however, is that we can't merely concern ourselves with how our beliefs affect us. Belief is not a private matter. Our beliefs drive our actions and our actions affect others. Most certainly, we should believe what is rational when we can; but we must ask ourselves whether our beliefs will risk harm to others before we decide to believe them by faith.

This is perhaps why Cobb should not have believed that Saito could deliver on his promise. Sure, it's worth the risk to Cobb, but this belief informed his decision to perform inception, and that decision put Saito, Arthur, Eames, Ariadne, and Yusuf in danger—not to mention Fischer himself. In fact, Cobb violated Fischer's rights extensively, for his own gain.[14] Cobb's faith that Saito can deliver is not virtuous, intellectually or ethically. It puts others at risk.

So the next time you are wondering whether to take a leap of faith, ask yourself: Am I risking harm to others? Remember, beliefs are not private matters. They affect your actions and your actions affect others. Your faith might even encourage others to believe, and though you would never harm someone because of your belief, can you guarantee others won't? Have they done so in the past? Faith, like inception, is a risky business. On the other hand, no one ever harmed anyone by proportioning their belief to the evidence.

NOTES

1. If, however, Cobb didn't truly believe that Miles would have an architect, but was merely taking a chance that he did, we wouldn't call that faith. Why? Because he didn't believe anything; he was simply taking a risk. When I pick lotto numbers, I don't have faith that I'll win, because I don't believe that I'll win.

2. The conclusion that persons who claim to have a right to their opinion most often lack it and simply reveal their lack of concern for true belief is defended by James White in the first chapter of his book *Crimes Against Logic* (New York: McGraw-Hill, 2004). I highly encourage you to check out this wonderful little book.

3. For just such an argument, see Theodore Schick and Lewis Vaughn's *How to Think About Weird Things: Critical Thinking for a New Age*, 6th edition (New York: McGraw Hill, 2010), chapter 7.

4. Another great example comes from science history. When Einstein realized his theory of relativity entailed the possibility of black holes, we had no evidence they actually existed. As such, belief in black holes was unwarranted, even though they were known to be possible. Belief in them became rational when their existence was confirmed by evidence.

5. Russell made this argument in a article that was commissioned, but never published, by *Illustrated* magazine in 1952.

6. The argument is not circular in the same way most others are; its conclusion is not one of its premises. That such arguments are still circular was brilliantly demonstrated by Peter Achinstein in "The Circularity of Self-Supporting Inductive Arguments," *Analysis* 22(6) (1962): 138–141.

7. Of course, you could argue that since these rules have worked in the past, they will be reliable in the future. But then we are back to the problem of induction. Indeed, all argumentation may be rooted in the assumption that induction is reliable.

8. The only time you might succeed is when you find someone who realizes that they have to give one up, when dealing with a certain topic, because that is the only way they can hold on to some cherished belief. You will notice, however, that as they go about their daily life, they will retain belief in the rules. They only say that they reject them when they are forced to do so to avoid the consequences of giving up their cherished belief.

9. And if you reject these rules, you can never argue or even communicate meaningfully again. To even make sense of what you say, I have to assume that when you say something is true, you necessarily believe the opposite of that thing is false. I can't do this, if you reject non-contradiction.

10. Some philosophers might disagree and argue that the unavoidability and uncontroversial nature of belief in induction and argumentation indicates that it is not faith. Such a disagreement, however, is merely semantic; such philosophers simply have a different definition of faith—something along the line of "avoidable belief without sufficient evidence." There is no real difference in our positions. I tend to think, however, that they might choose this definition so that they can assert that all faith is irrational. I am comfortable distinguishing between rational, and irrational, faith.

11. Blaise Pascal, *Pensées*, translated by A. J. Kailsheimer (New York: Penguin Books, 2011), p. 122.

12. One may wonder whether Cobb can avoid irrationality by truly remaining agnostic—not assenting to either believing or disbelieving that Saito can deliver, but simply acting as if Saito can, because of the potential benefits. Not only can he do this, I think he should. It avoids irrationality, but still gets him what he wants. But, for simplicity's sake, let's assume that if Cobb takes the risk, he believes.

13. William K. Clifford, *The Ethics of Belief and Other Essays* (Amherst, New York: Prometheus Books, 1999).

14. For more on why Cobb's actions are not virtuous, see Albert Chan's chapter in this volume.

LIMBO, UTOPIA, AND THE PARADOX OF IDYLLIC HOPE

Clint Jones

You're waiting for a train, a train that will take you far away. You know where you hope this train will take you. But you can't know for sure. But it doesn't matter—how can it not matter?

—Mal's riddle

In the opening sequence of *Inception*, we see Cobb awash on a nameless beach adjacent to a Japanese mansion. Later, we learn that this beachhead was once the entry point to a majestic urban landscape that, in its original state, was Mal and Cobb's rendering of an ideal world. Cobb describes building the world with Mal as a time spent living like gods, creating and destroying according to their whims, having what they wanted without having to compromise their tastes. They built their perfect ideal world together—a utopia. In fact, the Japanese mansion was apparently Saito's version of utopia, where he could live out his days in pure comfort. Everyone, it seems, longs to live in a utopia. But could they? Should they?

On the Shores of Utopia

Every culture throughout history has produced a vision of an ideal society. Whether it's an ancient idealization (like Plato's Republic), a medieval jest (like Thomas More's [1478–1535] *Utopia*),[1] a modern flight of fancy (such as Samuel Butler's [1835–1902] *Erehwon*),[2] a contemporary intentional community (like Twin Oaks), or an enduring belief (like heaven), such "idyllic hope" helps us define what we should be striving for socially. As Max Weber (1864–1920) says, "[Humans] would not have attained the possible unless time and again [they] had reached out for the impossible."[3]

The recurring theme of the idealized utopian future is a consequence of our continuing desire to improve our lives. Its flip side is dystopia, the need to envision the worst possible future as a way to express the dominant fears of the day or dissatisfaction with the status quo.

Utopias are places where all is well. Depending, primarily, on who is dreaming up the utopia in question, *all being well* might encompass some extravagant notions like "you never have to change your socks / and little streams of alcohol come trickling down the rocks."[4] Other utopian models merely strive to ensure that everyone's basic needs are met. Dystopias, however, are not merely the opposite of utopias. They are more like attempted utopias gone bad; they can share many facets of a utopian worldview but simply emphasize the negative aspects of such a world.

Often, when people talk of dystopian futures they confuse the idea with something far more terrible. Take, for instance, Cormac McCarthy's novel *The Road* (2006). Some would describe it as dystopian, but it isn't. It's post-apocalyptic.[5]

The key difference between McCarthy's future and, say, a real dystopia like Aldous Huxley's (1894–1963) *Brave New World*, is that in a dystopia, like Huxley's, there is a small class of people (usually the powerful) for whom the society is one they would gladly live in. No such class exists in *The Road*. We might say that a post-apocalyptic world is one we can't change—it's already doomed—whereas a dystopian state could be improved.

Our stories about utopia and dystopia can tell us a lot about ourselves, and *Inception* is no exception. Such stories, or narratives, tell us about what kind of world we really want—our idyllic hope. They also function as a social critique, telling us what we see as wrong with our current world. By looking at what motivates the team to incept Fischer and avoid falling into Limbo in the process, we can examine the difficulties of utopian narratives. We can also look specifically at the paradox of Utopia—the fact we strive for the perfect world, but we would never really want to live there.

Nolan's Dystopian Future and the Emergence of a New Global Superpower

Limbo is an obvious example of a utopia in *Inception*, but where might one find a dystopia in *Inception*? After all, with the exception of mind invasion technologies, the world of *Inception* is readily recognizable. There is, however, one seemingly innocuous difference: corporations are beginning to dominate the world. Like its predecessors, *Inception* deals with questions surrounding the best possible future by playing on current social fears of a corporate state. It presents a glimpse into a harrowing future where our energy supply, and the corporations that control it, are redefining the social and political landscape by jockeying for control of energy resources and influencing government policy. Saito's promise to eliminate the charges against Cobb with a single phone call is a testimony to the power of such companies. To get Cobb pulled from a most wanted list, he can't just call some lackey at the State Department; he's pulling the strings of someone in the uppermost echelons of government.

The future *Inception* depicts is quite bleak. Saito's company is the last one that stands between the Fischer-Morrow energy conglomerate and "total energy dominance," but Saito's company can no longer compete. If Robert Fischer does not break up his father's company, he will soon be in possession of his own corporate global superpower—one that controls the world's energy supply. The implications of such a possibility are precisely what make the setting of the movie seem dystopic.

The dystopian elements are clearer in the graphic novel.[6] Cobol Engineering (along with Saito's own company, Proclus Global, and presumably Fischer-Morrow) wields considerable power and political influence using tactics that are not, as Cobb later tells Ariadne, "strictly speaking, legal." They answer to their own authority.

"Downwards Is the Only Way Forwards"

The most utopian element of the movie is Limbo—"unconstructed dream space." In this lowest level of subconscious dream space, one can create for oneself an ideal world, or, like Dom and Mal, share the dream and create an ideal world together. Living in such a world would seem desirable. In fact, the theme of desire for a utopia, or at least a better world, runs throughout the film.

Recall the team's first meeting with the chemist Yusuf. In the basement of his apothecary shop, a group of people gathers every day to share a dream. In *the real world* they sleep for four hours, but Yusuf's compound provides them with forty hours of dream time. So they spend twice as much time dreaming as they do awake.[7] This is why Yusuf's assistant claims, "They do not come to sleep, but to be woken up." What, other than an idyllic existence, could compel people to do such a thing? The dream they share must be better than the reality they actually inhabit. In fact, "The dream has become their reality." They have not opted for an altered reality, but rather an alternative, more utopian, reality.

Now think about when Ariadne storms off, after being "killed" by Cobb's projection of Mal in the training dream. Cobb confidently tells Arthur that "she'll be back—reality won't be enough for her anymore." Apparently, even the most basic level of dreaming can become preferable to reality. Ariadne's reasons are very different from those of the people sleeping in the chemist's basement yet both cases reveal why idyllic hope is valuable to us. For Ariadne it's the pure creativity and god-like powers; for Yusuf's customers it's the ability to escape the drudgery of their lives. Once we have a vision of a better world, we can't help but prefer it.

Yet, during the Fischer inception, the prospect of finding themselves in Limbo leads to a heated quarrel among key members of the inception team. Dying on any level will, thanks to Yusuf's sedative, automatically land them in Limbo.[8] Echoing Virgil's directions to Dante at the beginning of the *Divine Comedy*, Cobb says that "downwards is the only way forwards," strengthening the resolve of the group. But why are they so terrified of living in a utopia? Eames suggests that it's because they don't want scrambled eggs for brains. Limbo is undesirable for a few more reasons than that, though.

The first reason is simple. One can get lost in Limbo; it's a bit like prison in that it is a place from which it is difficult to escape. When the characters speak of Limbo, they talk about being "trapped" or "lost," and Ariadne argues with Cobb about the "risk the others have taken" just by joining him in the dream state. Cobb warns Saito that if he is killed and drops into Limbo, he will get stuck down there, lost, because he will forget *the real world*. Clearly, the prospect of getting trapped in a fake world, believing it is real, and thus never even trying to get out, is horrifying. Of course, as Yusuf says, "it depends on the dream." So if Limbo is a utopia, maybe you would trade in its fake perfection for a real world of imperfection.[9]

Ultimately, the most frightening thing about Limbo is that it's a shared state. This might work out well for a married couple, like Mal and Cobb, who can come to an agreement about what an ideal existence is like. But if you shared Limbo and tried to make an ideal world with someone whose vision of an ideal world was radically different from yours, Limbo might turn out to be hell. In fact, inhabiting someone else's utopia is a prospect our characters worry about. "What the hell is down there?" Ariadne asks. "Nothing is down there," Arthur replies, "except for whatever might have been left behind by anyone sharing the dream who's been trapped there before. Which, in our case, is just [Cobb]." So, in many ways, the most utopian element of the story is also dystopic. We ourselves may, ultimately, want to avoid utopia for similar reasons.

Think about your ideal world; what would it take to make it truly perfect? You might start simply enough, but the more you think about it, the more details you will add, and the more you will realize how much utopia requires. The problem is that as we develop those ideas, just like multilayered dreams, their complexity makes them unstable. The more complex the utopian vision, the less likely it is to stand up to criticism or be appealing to others. As one adds details specific to one's own vision of utopia, one creates space for others to find fault.

In George Orwell's *1984*, the protagonist, Winston Smith, is quite unhappy with society, and yet the society itself is meant to be a utopia. The same is true of More's *Utopia*, where everything is taken care of for the inhabitants—they are provided all of their food and clothing, have a reasonably short work day, and so on. All of these utopian perks come at great cost to the citizens themselves in terms of personal freedom. So one reason we may not truly desire utopia is that we are afraid that it won't be our ideal, and may in fact be our own personal hell. The cost of "perfection" may actually make a world that is perfect for everyone impossible.

Who Wants to Be Stuck in a Dream?

Though we might be inclined to give up on utopias at this point, *Inception* gives us a reason to continue dreaming. The characters work to prevent their dystopic reality from getting worse while simultaneously striving to avoid being trapped in a utopic Limbo. Utopian and dystopian ideas are often the product of augmenting the extremes of what is desirable and undesirable in society. So idyllic hope reminds us that by approaching the extremes of the best and worst imaginable, we can achieve social change. Staying where we are accomplishes nothing. Taking the risk of being stuck in Limbo means at least having a chance at changing the dystopic reality of *the real world*. Likewise, our driving toward a utopia, which we don't even want to fully reach, helps us improve our world for the better.

As he and Ariadne search for Mal, Cobb indicates that he knows where she'll be. When they arrive at the building, he explains to a befuddled Ariadne that he and Mal had always wanted a house, but they loved that particular type of building. In the real world they would have to choose one or the other, but not in Limbo, where the imagination is the limit. The same is true of utopian thinking in our society. We are only limited by what we can dream, and dreaming about a better society or about how to avoid a disastrous dystopic future motivates us to make relevant changes.

Social change is slow to occur, though, because it takes a lot of time and energy to create a communicable utopian vision that others won't reject. On the one hand, a simple version of an idyllic future is often unappealing because it is too bland or too vague to convince people to think of the possibilities it affords them. On the other hand, a complex version of an idyllic future has many potential problems and will not appeal to everyone. What is perfect for one person is imperfect for another.

This leaves us with a challenging question: If complexity means that people are less likely to share your vision of the future and simplicity isn't compelling, then what are we to make of the most pervasive utopian vision of all—heaven?

Does It Depend on the Dream?

When Ariadne poses the question "Who'd want to be stuck in a dream for ten years?" Yusuf immediately replies that "it depends on the dream." Like Yusuf, most people could think of a dream state they wouldn't mind being stuck in for years, but that's not the issue when it comes to utopias. Consider heaven. If heaven lasts forever, one eventually would become bored, tired of living an idyllic existence, and would want to opt out. Without the ability to opt out, however, heaven would become hell.

This is exactly the problem that Julian Barnes deals with in his most popular novel, *A History of the World in 10½ Chapters*. In the final chapter, aptly titled "The Dream," the unnamed dreamer wakes to find himself in heaven. The place is decked out with everything he desires, tailored specifically to his tastes. He enjoys his favorite breakfast perfectly prepared for every meal. He plays his ideal golf course so often that eventually he can get through in eighteen strokes. He meets all the famous people he's ever been interested in and some others just for fun. He eats, drinks, shops, copulates, learns every new activity he can think of (after golf becomes a bore), and finds that every whim is catered to, immediately, without question or fail. He eventually realizes that "they even make the bad things good," so that no experience is unpleasant.[10] This is especially true of hell, which is a theme park of sorts that heaveners can visit; it provides a "good scare . . . as opposed to a bad scare."[11]

After a considerable amount of time (the dreamer loses track fairly quickly), perfection becomes routine and boring. The things he didn't enjoy in life, like reading, bring little or no pleasure in heaven, and his attempts to pursue those things do nothing to alleviate his boredom. This is the problem of heaven—eventually we would want out. And this fits with Ariadne's horror at being stuck in a dream.

When we talk about heaven, it is always its simplest form, never with specificity, somehow always vague—the land of milk and honey,[12] the pearly gates and golden streets. It's idyllic and can be whatever you want. But the *idea* of heaven is not simple; no idea is, as Cobb is quick to inform Saito during their exchange in the helicopter. It requires a lot of faith and a lot of work to maintain a belief in heaven. Once someone starts to put details in place beyond the basic features, people start to disagree about what ought to be included. This, then, is the paradox of idyllic hope. On the one hand, any particular utopia is only going to appeal to a small group of people (perhaps only one person), and though we continually strive for it, no amount of work is going to bring it into existence. On the other hand, if, like heaven in Barnes's story, utopia could be what each person wanted, given enough time everyone would opt out because heaven would become hell.

If Ariadne is correct that it would be difficult to spend even ten years of accelerated time in a dream, then how could we ever spend an eternity in such a place? The land of milk and honey is appealing precisely because that's where the description stops; everyone is allowed to fill in the gaps for themselves. That's the appeal. We are under no obligation to tell people how we fill in the gaps—even Barnes's dreamer discovers that there is a confidentiality rule that prevents him from finding out what others do in heaven. As soon as we start to share our utopian vision, disagreements become apparent. Even Yusuf's basement-dwellers need to be woken up from their dreaming (or put to sleep, depending on how you look at things). If you could not be woken up, if you could not escape the perfection of the ideal, you might, like Cobb, start to feel cooped up. Your brain might even turn to scrabbled eggs, as Eames suggests.

Why Is Dreaming So Important?

Idyllic hope allows us to challenge entrenched notions of how the world is and how it could be. Without hope, expressed in the form of utopian visions, human society would stagnate. We need to imagine tomorrow because that is how we learn what we want to change about the present. Understood in this way, Limbo becomes more than just another level of subconscious dreaming; it is the perfect *temporary* escape from an increasingly dystopic reality. Contemplating Limbo provides the best method for understanding the complex and slippery nature of idyllic hope and the human relationship to the ideal world. It also allows us to provide a better answer to Mal's riddle. Cobb's answer to "how can it not matter?" is that "we'll be together." But we already know this isn't true. The better answer is because wherever the train takes us, eventually we'll want to leave.[13]

NOTES

1. Thomas More used the term to play on the Greek word *utopia*, meaning "no place," and its Greek homophone *eutopia*, meaning "good place."

2. Like Thomas More before him, Butler's utopia's name is a play on words—it is "nowhere" spelled backward.

3. Max Weber, "Politics as a Vocation," in *Max Weber: Essays in Sociology*, trans. and ed. H. H. Gerth and C. Wright Mills (New York: Oxford University Press, 1958), pp. 77–128.

4. This is a sampling of the lyrics from Burl Ives's version of the classic country song "Big Rock Candy Mountain." These lyrics parallel nicely with "Cockaigne," a utopian poem popular among medieval peasants that includes depictions of geese flying around on spits and larks cooked and covered in stew that fly right into your mouth. For more, see Gregory Claeys and Lyman T. Sargent, *The Utopia Reader* (New York: New York University Press, 1999).

5. We might think of the post-apocalyptic as being what follows a dystopian future but not the necessary outcome of a dystopian future. An example would be the now-classic 1980s trilogy *Mad Max* starring Mel Gibson, which is also post-apocalyptic following a nuclear war. Presumably nuclear war could have been prevented, but any future where a nuclear holocaust is a genuine possibility is dystopian.

6. The graphic novel, one of several features included in the Blu-ray deluxe edition, tells the story of how Cobb and his team find themselves in the position of having to perform extraction on Saito.

7. While it is tempting to ask here why 4 hours = 40 hours in the basement, but 10 hours = a week, or 168 hours, at the first level of the attempted inception of Fischer, it is important to remember that Yusuf blends a special compound for the inception of Fischer that accelerates brain function to twenty times normal. Still, the people in the basement are spending most of their conscious existence in a dream world.

8. Cobb also uses the fear of Limbo, albeit implicitly, to prevent Fischer from committing suicide in the hotel bathroom to wake up.

9. For more on whether one should make such a trade, see the chapters by Dan Weijers and Bart Engelen in this book.

10. Julian Barnes, *A History of the World in 10½ Chapters* (New York: Vintage Books, 1989), p. 289.

11. Ibid., p. 299.

12. Although this phrase originally described the Jewish promised land (and actual physical place on Earth), it now is often used by Christians to describe heaven.

13. I would like to thank the editors of this book for their helpful suggestions and additions to this chapter, as well as Josh Horn for reading several drafts and my wife and family for their unflagging support.

UNLOCKING THE VAULT OF THE MIND: *INCEPTION* AND ASIAN PHILOSOPHY

Scott Daniel Dunbar

> We'd become lost in here. Living in a world of infinite possibilities. A world where we were gods. I realized we needed to escape, but she'd locked away her knowledge of the unreality of this world.
>
> —Dom Cobb, *Inception: The Shooting Script*[1]

Inception takes its viewers on a reconnaissance mission into the philosophy of mind. It suggests that the mind is like a fortress, which may be deceptively penetrated, as well as like a womb, wherein ideas can be planted to germinate as seemingly innate thoughts. Additionally, the film deploys metaphors that portray the mind as a vault, an ocean, and a maze of mystery. Curiously, these metaphors are often embedded in Asian contexts, which may hint at a deeper level of Asian ideas underlying the film. Although Christopher Nolan may not have had Asian philosophy in mind when he created *Inception*, the philosophical insights of Asia can be useful in interpreting the film and enriching our understanding of it.

Wake Up and Smell the Wasabi: Dreams in Asian Philosophy

Asian philosophy rings like a Zen temple bell alerting us to the possibility that sleeping and dreaming could be valuable opportunities for personal growth and spiritual awakening. Once we start to look at dreams as occasions for deeper understanding of the world and ourselves, sleeping and dreaming become arenas for serious contemplation and spiritual work, triggering a paradigm shift in our thinking about dreams. Kelly Bulkeley suggests that when we acknowledge sleeping and dreaming as times of "virtuous spiritual practice [then] the whole realm of sleep and dreaming becomes the subject of tremendous spiritual interest."[2] We may even have discovered a respectable reason to sleep in late! After all, our dreams could be authentic efforts at hard spiritual work.

Thus Asian philosophy teaches that dreams are not just wasted moments of dormant life: dreams bestow beneficial mindscapes for philosophical insight by opening us up to lateral thinking, allowing us to see the world in ways that are unconstrained by ordinary expectations. Dreams help us to think outside the mental boxes that we use to construct and filter everyday reality; they have the power to free us from our imprisoning habits of thought and behavior.

Consequently, Asian philosophy is receptive to the possibility of lucid philosophical insights arising from lucid dreaming—being aware in a dream that you are dreaming. As a case in point, Buddhist monks deliberately practice watchful meditation exercises not only during the day but also at night (as a type of sleep yoga) to aid their mindfulness training. Indeed, the fourteenth

Dalai Lama encourages "the continuation of meditation practice in sleep 'otherwise at least a few hours each night will be just a waste.'"[3] Likewise, Asian philosophers, from Zhuangzi (c. 369–286 BCE) to Śaṅkara (788–820), claim that dreams provide fertile moments for spiritual practice that may even lead to a type of profound spiritual "awakening."

It was the Buddha (c. sixth–fourth century BCE) who famously described everyday reality as a dreamlike illusion from which he woke up. In fact, the title "Buddha" literally means "Awakened One." And Buddhist teachings suggest that each one of us can, like the Buddha, wake up from our everyday dream worlds to see things as they really are—which is not as we typically think they are. Buddhist meditation helps us to look beyond everyday appearances to discover what is found within and how it connects to the rest. It takes us on a ride through the waves of everyday turbulence into the calm ocean of compassion and wisdom.

Christopher Nolan's *Inception* also takes us on a journey through mind-bending cityscapes, which evoke the awe-inspiring possibilities of the creative mind. His levitating buildings raise our expectations for lofty philosophical insights, and he delivers by contrasting the mind's creative freedom with the gravitas of its characters' heavy emotional attachments and protected secrets.

Mind as Fortress and Vault: The Paradox of Accessing the Inaccessible

The mind is like a powerful fortress that must be assailed, and a vault that must be penetrated, if inception is to succeed. Infecting someone's subconscious with an idea is analogous to a covert military operation to break into a defended compound. In the real world, dreams have actually been employed in Asian cultures as a type of weapon in this fashion.[4] Likewise, in a symbolic manner, the film's picturesque scene of the mountain fortress in a snowy landscape goes beyond eye-catching imagery; the fortress represents not only a place to hide our secrets but also the defenses we build against new threatening ideas.

What does this "fortress mind" teach us from the perspectives of Asian philosophy? Nolan's metaphor offers an apt representation of what Buddhists call "the ego"—the notion of an independent "self"—which is the erection of mental defenses against perceived threats to the "I." The ego is a fortress of self-deception and delusion because, according to Buddhism, a separate "self" does not exist. Thus, the fortress can be interpreted as a manifestation of human attachments to the idea of a "self."

The film's image of the fortress also adeptly conveys the Buddhist notion of being a prisoner of one's own fortified psychological attachments. The theme of struggling with emotional ties to family members runs throughout the film—especially in Cobb's relationships with his family and Fischer's love-hate relationship with his father. The guilt Cobb feels that stems from his belief that he caused his wife's suicide causes him to suffer from ongoing delusions in which his wife appears in his dreams. Fischer's strained paternal relationship is exploited as the gateway to performing inception. From a Buddhist angle, these characters' "strong personal attachments in the waking world . . . carry into [their] dreaming world."[5] Their clinging manifests itself as deluded dream states.

When we consider Cobb's strong desire to see his children again through a Buddhist philosophy of attachment, we learn that it is this desire that lies at the heart of his suffering and is his motive for inception. It is only after Cobb eventually discovers the truth of impermanence and the need for detachment that he seems to eventually find peace. "We had our time together. . . . I have to let you go." In these lines, Cobb echoes the Buddhist principle of detachment; he releases Mal from his emotional grasping, and abandons his feelings of guilt for her death. Thus freed, he is liberated from his deluded mind cages. Such emancipation is reinforced by the scene of Arthur cutting the elevator cables, since the elevator also affords an excellent symbol of the mind as a trapped cage moving between different levels of perceived reality.

Even though Cobb's dream worlds are mesmerizing and captivating, he comes to realize their illusionary nature, and he does not allow himself to get caught up and entrapped inside these dream "realities" like Mal.[6] Cobb recognizes that the fortress is unreal, the skyscrapers are unreal, even his thoughts are unreal, and as such the illusionary dream worlds collapse (or explode) in his mind.

Asian philosophical works such as the *Tripurā Rahasya* likewise equate the world to a fortress of illusion that one needs to overcome: "O valiant hero, batter down this impregnable fortress of illusion and conquer your misery."[7] Paradoxically, the fortress being assailed does not exist. One wonders how it's possible to conquer an illusion, to penetrate something that doesn't exist. Trying to explain the riddle of awakening from something that is not "real," and contemplating the illusionary nature of dreams and life itself, is something over which generations of Asian philosophers themselves lost quite a bit of sleep.

Mind as Mirror: Just What Exactly Is Being Reflected, and Who Reflects?

Another salient metaphor in *Inception* is the notion of mind as a mirror. Consider Ariadne's first attempt at designing dream architecture. She and Cobb come across two large mirrors that Ariadne positions to produce paradoxical perceptions of *confined infinity* (imprisoned infinity) in the mirrors' refractions. When she touches her reflection, the mirror suddenly shatters, representing the falsity of the dream world. Yet, still captivated by the illusion of infinite creative power, Ariadne boldly steps into the mental space beyond. Likewise, both Hindu and Buddhist philosophers use mirrors as educational tools to teach lessons about the dreamlike status of the world.

The "mirror mind" is a common motif in Buddhist philosophy. The *Hua-yan* ("Flower Ornament") and *Wei-shi* ("Consciousness Only") schools of Chinese Buddhism, for instance, both espouse a form of *philosophical idealism*, claiming that the world is just a fabrication of the mind, like a dream or a reflection in a mirror.[8] The *Wei-shi* school praises "The Great Mirror Wisdom" (*da yuan jing zhi*)[9] as an esteemed "mental state in which all discriminations are terminated. [Mind] is likened to a perfectly clean mirror, which contains no impurity and hence reflects the true nature of everything."[10]

From another angle, Chan Buddhism "deconstructs the mind, showing us the futility in trying to grasp its nature through philosophical reflection—since there is nothing there to know."[11] Steven Laycock's book *Mind as Mirror and the Mirroring of Mind* provides an especially good discussion of Chan's "mirrorless mirror" in which the views of two Chan masters—Shenxiu (c. 606–706 CE) and Huineng (638–713 CE)—are juxtaposed.[12] Whereas Shenxiu suggested that the mind is originally like a clean mirror but becomes covered by hate, greed, and ignorance, Huineng argued that there is no mind and thus no defilements.[13] He rejected Shenxiu's assumption of an ontological essence called *mind* that needed to be cleaned. In other words, no one reflects and nothing is reflected.

In India, the polysemic Hindu tradition likens a mirror's reflection to one's innate spiritual identity as well as a perceptual fallacy: the reflection can be illusionary, such as mistaking a snake for a rope. The mystic Śrī Ramaṇa Māhṛṣhi (1879–1950) thus said: "The mirror reflects objects; yet they are not real because they cannot remain apart from the mirror. Similarly, the world is said to be a reflection in the mind as it does not remain in the absence of mind."[14] Yet the "mind" is not always viewed as a reliable source of knowledge. Hence, the motif of the mirror mind creates a paradox: "Ordinarily we say that what exists is real. But we do not say that what exists merely as a construction in the mind is real. Thus, though we admit that various objects exist in our dreams, we deny that they are real."[15]

Asian thought therefore encompasses two opposing views on the mind: one in which everything could be considered to be a manifestation of "absolute mind" or "pure consciousness," and another in which mind does not actually exist ("no mind"). This is where the mirror becomes a useful metaphor but also a double-edged sword. On the one hand, the reflection of a mirror is an illusion and a shattered mirror represents the fragmentation of reality. On the other hand, a clear blank mirror can also symbolize the deeper truths within one's mind that are beyond the level of fleeting thoughts. Given these ambiguous messages, Asian philosophy suggests a rather startling twist on *Inception*'s use of mirrors: *the truth has no reflection.*

Mind as Womb: The Ethics of Insemination

The image of the broken mirror is not the only sharp idea in the movie. *Inception* also suggests that penetrating someone's mind is like inseminating a womb with a foreign idea that can gestate to become a self-referential thought. Associating the mind with a womb invites further comparison of the mind with a garden of prodigious potency, a veritable "mind-field" in which thoughts are planted and enabled to grow. The mind is thus seen as a receptacle for inception. The mind, however, can also be a generator of thoughts—a proverbial "sperm bank" of ideas. The symbiosis of these two dimensions of the mind has intrigued Asian philosophers in their efforts to account for the possibility of conceptual self-generation.

The Buddhist school of *Yogācāra* (also known as *Vijñānavāda*) likens the mind to a womb that gives birth to the universe, which arises out of a core storehouse consciousness (*ālaya-vijñāna*).

Yogācāra claims that everything in the universe consists of mind only (*chitta mātra*), and that things can only exist in the *process* of knowing, not as objects of knowing. Outside of the process of knowing, things have no independent reality. Consequently, there is no subject to experience anything, and the universe is pure *chitta* (mind). All of us participate in a social network of interconnected consciousness.

Yogācāra has some common ground with Carl Jung's (1875–1961) concept of a collective unconscious but Asian philosophers beat both *Inception* and Jung to the punch since they recognized types of dream incubation practices that supposedly lead to successful shared dreaming.[16] Dreams were visualized as vehicles that could connect consciousness on a different level—a level sometimes transcending even death. Asian cultures value ancestor veneration; rituals and dream-incubation practices are believed to induce a type of spiritual "social network" that straddles a subliminal space between living and dying. The appearances of dead relatives in dreams are often deemed to be moments of genuine contact with the deceased. Compare this to the scene in Yusuf's basement when we see comatose patrons who have renounced *the real world* in favor of a catatonic social dream world.

This metaphor of mind as womb, however, raises some disturbing ethical issues. Couldn't minds be raped and infected with unwanted ideas? How, then, is Cobb's act of inception to be morally evaluated? Moreover, does morality apply within dreams? Is it ethically acceptable to rape, kill, steal, or perform inception in dreams if dreams aren't real? Such questions deserve their own separate treatment.[17] I raise them merely to suggest that deploying the metaphor of the "womb mind" leads to the question of unwanted conceptual pregnancies and mental STDs—unwholesome mind-states such as Mal's deluded sense of reality that led to her "suicide." Mind wombs are not only gardens, but also potential mind-fields with latent seeds of delusion and destruction. Such ambivalence sets the stage for the "battlefield for mindfulness," which is found as a frequent motif in Asian thought.

Cobb's Wet Dream: The Ocean as a Consummate Metaphysical Metaphor

If you are looking for a film with sexual content, you might want to watch another movie—unless you interpret Cobb's dreamy skyscrapers as Freudian phallic symbolism. Nevertheless, the role of Cobb's "wet dream," his awakening on the seashore soaked by the ocean's waves, offers seminal insights into *Inception*.

In the Hindu philosophical tradition of *Advaita Vedānta*, the ocean is a metaphysical metaphor for the ontological ground of Being. Advaita argues that the nature of Reality is ineffable (beyond language) because it transcends subject-object thinking altogether. Reality is affirmed as undifferentiated consciousness, which is why the name of this school literally means "non-duality." Nevertheless, for the benefit of preliminary understanding, the ontological ground of Being is called *Brahman*, which is tentatively described as immensely deep and unfathomable, akin to an ocean of absolute truth, consciousness, and bliss. Enlightenment occurs when one acquires the proper experiential wisdom (*jñāna*) of this non-dual Reality and loses all egotistical sense of self. Then the notion of individual identity vanishes to reveal a spiritually awakened Monism (non-dual consciousness).

Intriguingly, the stages of Cobb's journey in *Inception* echo the levels of consciousness found in the Advaitin philosophical journey to spiritual awakening. According to its primary exponent, Śaṅkara (c. 8th century CE), there are four levels of consciousness in the quest for metaphysical certitude: (1) the waking state (*jāgrat*); (2) the dream state (*svapna*); (3) deep sleep (*suṣupti*); and (4) self-realization (*turīya*).[18] Our everyday life is characterized by the state of waking consciousness, which perceives objects through the senses. Conversely, when we dream, internal objects are constructed in our dream consciousness.

In deep sleep, no objects appear, and there is an experience of what could be described as "nothingness." According to Śaṅkara, this level of deep sleep is very close to the ontological truth, because it represents a non-dual form of consciousness where there are no distinctions in the mind. It is at the fourth level (*turīya*) where one is said to become enlightened beyond all ordinary understanding. It is a state that is impossible to describe because it surpasses dichotomous language.

Turning back to the film, Cobb planned to perform inception on Fischer by way of a three-stage process, a dream within a dream within a dream. However, when things went wrong— Mal sabotaged their plans by shooting Fischer—Ariadne and Cobb improvised by "adding" another level. It was on this level, in the period of blackness prior to waking up on the seashore, that Cobb arguably entered into the "deep sleep" of Indian philosophy.[19] After awakening, he finds his dream world collapsing around him. To the Advaitin Hindus, "the total collapse of such distinctions in sleep reveals a fundamental truth (non-duality), not a lessened grasp on reality."[20] Thus, Cobb's sojourn into "deep sleep" becomes a metaphor for Vedāntic spiritual realization where the imposing structures of ideas that form the conceptual architecture of his mind collapse into the experience of pure Being.

Mind as Emptiness: What Happens When the Spinning Top Stops Spinning?

Much of Asian philosophy speaks of life as a cycle of suffering, a cycle characterized by instability and unsatisfactoriness, impermanence and entropy, like a wobbly spinning top. Yet, this painful and poignant cycle can be overcome and escaped by recognizing that the world is unreal, like a dream, and the key to ending the cycle is held in your own mind.

The symbol of Cobb's totem (a spinning top) offers a clever allusion to this perennial cycle of *samsaric life* (the rebirth-life-death cycle). The spinning top ensnares us all until we reach a profound spiritual awakening. True freedom comes from letting go, and such spiritual release allows one to become devoid of illusion. But all words fail to express the moment of spiritual awakening, and silence becomes the best way to describe the ineffable.[21]

Indeed, silence remains a highly respected modus operandi in Asian thought, which may be especially pertinent to contemplating dreams. After all, if dreams are not necessarily verbal, linear, or logical, then why must we always try to understand dreams using language, rationality, and linear thinking? Asian philosophy is frequently suspicious of binary, dualistic approaches to understanding, and, like Cobb, it jumps into the void of emptiness.

In some ways, *Inception* provides a cinematic *koan* (a Zen tool of awakening), since its complex story line sometimes defies logical explanation. But like a Zen master, it proverbially asks its viewers to contemplate the question: What is the sight of no eyes? The film pushes us to *in-sight* through *dream-sight* to gain meaning from *non-sight*. Zen *koans* and dreams, like floating clouds in the sky, make us aware of the vast emptiness that lies beyond the realm of everyday fleeting thoughts. Zen earthquakes of ideas deliberately shake our worldviews. Dream worlds fall apart and rise again like the tides of consciousness. Everything sounds like riddles, but nothing is as it seems.

Is Saito an Old Man Dreaming That He Is Flying?

After performing inception, the main characters wake up together on an airplane in a state of shock and bewilderment from the realization of having successfully carried out their mission. Their stunned appearances also suggest a sense of profound confusion about what is real. Are they still dreaming, or have they woken up to reality? Saito, who seems to have been rescued by Cobb after an entire lifetime, is especially stunned. He is immobile, caught in the headlights of a new reality, before recognizing his youthful rebirth.

This scene from *Inception* brings to mind parallel episodes of disorienting dreams in Asian philosophy.[22] The most famous example comes from the Daoist tradition of China, attributed to the master Zhuangzi, in a story about a butterfly.[23] In this episode, Zhuangzi dreams of flying as a butterfly and experiences complete freedom from ordinary human constraints. Suddenly he awakens to discover that he is not a butterfly, and he begins to wonder whether he is really a man, or merely a butterfly dreaming that he is a man. The story captures the ambiguity of the boundaries between the dream state and wakefulness—between what is real and what is illusory—and suggests that the boundary may be artificial and overstated.[24]

In the film, Saito becomes the metaphorical butterfly of his deep-level dream. He identifies himself so completely with his dream reality (when he was old) that he had forgotten what *the real world* was, that it even existed. As Saito stares at the spinning top, he says:

> I know what this is. I've seen one before. Many, many years ago. It belonged to a man I met in a half-remembered dream. A man possessed of some radical notions.

Saito's dream of old age had become so realistic that when he awoke, he wasn't sure if he was actually awake or still dreaming. *The real world* (in which Saito hired Cobb to perform inception) had become a "half-remembered dream." As Bulkeley explains:

> [V]ivid yet confusing experiences like these grab our attention because they disrupt ordinary assumptions about the line that separates dreams from the waking world. Many people think of waking and dreaming as polar opposites as synonymous with real and unreal,

objective truth versus subjective fantasy. But this kind
of sharp distinction is not a psychological [or spiritual]
given.[25]

These examples of disorienting dreams suggest that meditations on dreaming can be simultaneously destabilizing and
liberating: like a bird that suddenly finds itself freed from a cage
and flies, vast new worlds open up to the dream investigator.
The inception team's successful mission also alters more than
just their target for they are all profoundly affected as well.

Lucid Ambiguity: Paradoxically Obscuring and Clarifying Dreams

Inception's multiple layers of dreams raise a profound philosophical question: How do we know when we're dreaming and
when we're awake? Unnervingly, the film never answers this
question and suggests that we simply cannot know for certain
whether we are currently dreaming. Such lucid ambiguity
remains part of the plot right to the very end: the film cuts to
black before seeing whether Cobb's totem falls so we wonder:
Is he still dreaming? Has he awakened? Or are the final images
we see the neurological spasms of a dying mind?

Viewed through the lenses of Asian philosophy, *Inception*'s
metaphors of the mind as a fortress, womb, mirror, and ocean
resemble Eastern teachings because they suggest "the possible illusoriness of the experience of the waking state which we
take for granted as real,"[26] and they reflect notions of a collective mind, where the world itself becomes a figment of a shared
imagination or common participation in cosmic consciousness.
Inception's metaphors suggest that dreams, and especially deep
sleep, also reveal metaphysical insights into the possible nature
of reality, since everything in dreams has a shared ontological
status, thereby conveying a message of non-duality—a key
theme in Asian philosophy.

Nevertheless, dreams remain an ambiguous vault of ideas in Eastern thought. They simultaneously offer opportunities for interconnected understandings of the cosmos (thereby facilitating spiritual awakening), but also present occasions to exacerbate states of attachment, clinging, delusion, and fear (thereby entrenching ignorance and suffering). After glancing into this dream vault of Asian philosophy, we may find that the vault itself is ultimately empty. To put a Zen spin on things, if there is "no-mind," then there is no fortress-mind to assail, no mind-cage to release, no mirror-mind to clean, and no key to unlocking the vault of the mind. True "awakening" may come from discarding these illusory concepts, including the very notion of inception itself . . . unless, of course, this very thought is the result of an inception?

NOTES

1. Christopher Nolan, *Inception: The Shooting Script* (San Rafael, CA: Insight Editions, 2010), p. 191.

2. Kelly Bulkeley, *Dreaming in the World's Religions—A Comparative History* (New York: New York University Press, 2008), p. 32.

3. Dalai Lama, *Sleeping, Dreaming and Dying: An Exploration of Consciousness* (Somerville, MA: Wisdom Publications, 1997), p. 124; cited in Bulkeley, p. 108.

4. The recorded use of dreams as weapons in Asian thought can be traced back to ancient India in the writings of the *Atharva-Veda* (chapter 6: line 46). Likewise, the *Zuo-zhuan* (Zuo Commentary Tradition) of ancient China contains stories of dreams used to gain victory in military contexts.

5. Bulkeley, pp. 95–98.

6. This point alludes to the process of metaphysical entanglement between *Puruṣa* (spirit) and *Prakṛti* (matter), described by the Sāmkhya school of Hindu philosophy, whereby the original dualistic basis of ontology becomes muddled due to intoxicating captivation of the spirit by the dance of the *guṇas* (strands).

7. Swami Sri Ramanananda Saraswathi (trans.), *Tripura Rahasya: The Secret of the Supreme Goddess* (Bloomington, IN: World Wisdom, 2002), p. 82 (chapter 13: lines 53–55).

8. JeeLoo Liu, *An Introduction to Chinese Philosophy: From Ancient Philosophy to Chinese Buddhism* (Oxford: Blackwell Publishing, 2006), p. 250.

9. See Xuan-zang's (602–664 CE) text, *Cheng We-Shi Lun* ("A Treatise on the Establishment of Consciousness Only"), cited in Liu, p. 231.

10. Liu, p. 231.

11. John Schroeder, review of Steven W. Laycock's "Mind as Mirror and the Mirroring of Mind: Buddhist Reflections on Western Phenomenology," *Philosophy East and West* 47 (1) (Jan. 1997): 91–95.

12. Steven W. Laycock, *Mind as Mirror and the Mirroring of Mind: Buddhist Reflections on Western Phenomenology* (Albany: State University of New York Press, 1994).

13. Liu, p. 308.

14. *Talks with Śrī Ramaṇa Maharṣi* (Tiruvannamalai, India: Sri Ramanasramam, 1984), pp. 412–413, cited in Arvind Sharma, *The World as Dream* (New Delhi: D. K. Printworld (P) Ltd., 2006), p. 48.

15. John M. Koller, *Asian Philosophies*, 4th edition (Upper Saddle River, NJ: Prentice Hall, 2002), p. 87.

16. In China, dream incubation rituals "to fend off bad dreams were called *rang-meng*, and praying for good dreams was called *qi-meng*." Bulkeley, p. 73.

17. For just such a treatment, see Adam Barkman's, Albert Chan's, and Lance Belluomini's chapters in this volume. Barkman discusses the morality of real world inception, Chan discusses whether Cobb can be considered a moral virtuous person, and Belluomini discusses whether moral rules apply to our actions in dreams.

18. Sharma, p. 198.

19. Vedāntic teachings about undifferentiated consciousness are echoed in the Buddhist text *Milinda-panha* (Questions of King Milinda), where an Indo-Greek ruler engages in philosophical discourse with a Buddhist monk. Among other things, the monk's explication of deep sleep resembles Hindu notions discussed here.

20. Arvind Sharma, *Sleep as a State of Consciousness in Advaita Vedanta* (Albany: State University of New York Press, 2004), ix.

21. Even the Buddha chose to remain silent about certain types of metaphysical questions when pressed by his students. For further insight into this topic, see Troy Wilson Organ, "The Silence of the Buddha," *Philosophy East and West* 4 (2) (July 1954): 125–140.

22. Disorienting dream stories are found in several Asian religious traditions. For instance, the Hindu King Janaka is said to have had a dream upon waking from which he asked his guru: "Am I a king dreaming of being a beggar or a beggar dreaming of being a king?" (Sharma, 2006, p. 2). Likewise, the Hindu drama text the *Yogavāsiṣṭha* involves characters experiencing "sleeping, dreaming, and then waking into a new identity" (e.g., a Brahmin priest who dreams of being an "untouchable" peasant who dreams of being a powerful king). The bizarre narrative complexity of the *Yogavāsiṣṭha* had the effect of decentering its audience, intentionally frustrating people's ordinary assumptions about the ontological boundaries between waking and dreaming in order to provoke a more enlightened spiritual perspective. See Bulkeley, p. 39.

23. See Brook Ziporyn's (trans) *Zhuangzi: The Essential Writings with Selections from Traditoinal Commentaries* (Indianapolis, IN: Hackett, 2009) p. 21 (chapter 2: line 61).

24. Hans-Georg Möller challenges this common interpretation of Zhuangzi's butterfly story; his translation of the story goes like this:

Once, Zhuang Zhou [Zhuangzi] fell into a dream—and then there was a butterfly, a fluttering butterfly, self-content in accord with its intentions.

It did not know about a Zhou. With a sudden awakening there was, fully and completely, a Zhou.

One does not know whether a Zhou dreams and then there is a butterfly, or whether a butterfly dreams and then there is a Zhou. When there is a Zhou and a butterfly, there has to be a distinction (between them). This is called the changing of things.

See Hans-Georg Möller, "Zhuangzi's 'Dream of the Butterfly'—A Daoist Interpretation," *Philosophy East and West* 49(4) (Oct. 1999): 446–47.

25. Bulkeley, p. 20.

26. Sharma, 2006, p. 64.

PART SIX

WHAT DOES IT ALL MEAN?: FINDING THE HIDDEN LESSONS OF *INCEPTION*

MAL-PLACED REGRET

Kimberly Blessing

Cobb: You're going to be an old man . . .

Saito: Filled with regret.

Dom Cobb is an international fugitive—a sophisticated criminal who can steal others' ideas by infiltrating their dreams. Living on the run for allegedly killing his wife, all he wants is to return home to his children. Cobb's former adversary Saito offers Cobb a ticket home, promising to pull some strings that will allow him to return to America. But only if Cobb can do the impossible: plant an idea in someone else's mind. Inception.

As other chapters in this book make clear, for a philosopher, *Inception* naturally calls to mind the famous dream argument developed by French philosopher René Descartes (1596–1650). Descartes wrote about more than dreams, though. He also wrote about regret, an important theme in *Inception*. Cobb's painful feelings of regret stand in the way of seeing his children, James and Phillipa. Cobb thinks that he is responsible for the death of his beloved yet twisted wife, Mal (French for "bad" or "evil"), and he deeply regrets his decision to walk away from his adorable son and daughter to avoid facing murder charges. These powerful feelings of regret play on Cobb's subconscious and creep up on him when he is infiltrating others' dreams. Wise-beyond-her-years Ariadne knows that if Cobb doesn't exorcise his demons once and for all, they will sabotage the job that is supposed to buy back his freedom and reunite him with his children. Ariadne tries to assuage his guilt, but Cobb can't let go of the regret. Is Cobb, however, regretting the right things for the right reasons?

Hell Hath No Fury Like a Woman Scorned

Dom (from the Latin *Dominic*, meaning "of our Lord" or "belonging to God") feels that he is responsible for Mal's suicide because he changed her vision of reality.[1] Cobb explains to Ariadne how their exploration of dreams within dreams eventually drove Mal and him to Limbo, a deep level of the subconscious where people risk losing their grip on reality. There they spent what seemed like fifty years building a lover's paradise. "It wasn't so bad at first, feeling like gods," Cobb explains. "The problem was knowing that none of it was real. Eventually it just became impossible for me to live like that." Mal, however, chose to forget it wasn't real so she could stay indefinitely. Limbo became her reality. So in order for them to leave Limbo together, Cobb had to undo that choice by getting Mal to believe "one very simple idea that changed everything. That our world wasn't real. That she needed to wake up to come back to reality. That in order to get back home, we had to kill ourselves." It worked, but when they returned to *the real world*, Mal was never the same. Not only was she an "old soul living in a young body," but the idea Cobb incepted persisted into *the real world*. Mal believed that she was still dreaming, became convinced that their kids were projections, that their real kids were waiting for them on the other side of the dream, and that suicide was the only way to reach them.

In a memorable scene, director Christopher Nolan takes us to the hotel room in which Mal is trying to convince her husband to jump off the ledge, begging him to take "a leap of faith" to get back to "reality." Cobb refuses—he can't leave their kids. Mal attempts to persuade him by saying, "I filed a letter with our attorney explaining how I'm fearful for my safety, how you've threatened to kill me." Having framed him for her murder, Mal insists she has actually done him a favor. "I love you, Dom. I've freed you from the guilt of choosing to leave them. We're going home to our real children." Cobb explains to Ariadne that Mal went to the trouble of having three psychiatrists declare her sane, which made it impossible for him to try to explain "the nature of her madness." He confesses that instead of staying to fight the murder rap, he fled. "I ran. . . . I left my children behind and I've been trying to buy my way back ever since." Ariadne (in Greek mythology Ariadne—the holy maid—helped Theseus slay the Minotaur)[2] encourages Cobb to let go of this guilt.

> Your guilt defines her. It's what powers her. But you're not responsible for the idea that destroyed her. If we're going to succeed in this, you're going to have to forgive yourself, and you're going to have to confront her. But you don't have to do that alone. I'm doing it for the others because they have no idea the risk they've taken coming down here with you.

Of course, Ariadne doesn't yet know why Cobb feels so deeply responsible for Mal's state of mind, but she knows what he does to deal with this regret. Instead of asking for forgiveness for his trespasses, he tries to reengineer his memories, which are the only places where he can find his beloved wife. Ariadne's curiosity gets the better of her, and she taps into one of Cobb's self-therapy sessions:

> Ariadne: These aren't just dreams. These are memories. And you said never to use memories.
> Cobb: I know I did.
> Ariadne: You're trying to keep her alive. You can't let her go.
> Cobb: You don't understand. These are moments that I regret. They're memories that I have to change.

Ariadne knows that inception is a cakewalk compared to what Cobb is trying to do. "Do you think you can just build a prison of memories to lock her in? Do you really think that is going to contain her?" Cobb was quick to warn his protégée that building dreams out of your own memories is the surest way to lose your grip on what's real. Cobb does not obey his own rules, however. His efforts to change his memories are unsuccessful, and his subconscious—the lockbox that contains his painful moments of regret—continually haunts him. The more Cobb tries to run or hide from his regrets, the more quickly they find him. Ariadne-as-psychologist doesn't ever come out and say to Cobb, "Denial ain't just a river in Egypt," but she does tell Cobb that if he wants to move forward he is going to have to let go of these painful memories of his wife. If he is going to successfully complete the Fischer inception, he needs to stop regretting what he has done.

"One Simple Idea Could Change Everything"

While concern with regret is implicit throughout *Inception*, three scenes explicitly mention the issue. First, Saito asks Cobb if he wants to be an old man filled with regret for not taking the job that will buy Cobb his ticket home. Second, in the first level of Fischer's dream, after Saito has been shot, Cobb tells him that he's not going to die: "You're gonna become an old man," Cobb says, and Saito replies, "Filled with regret." Third, in Limbo, when Cobb finds the aging Saito, Saito declares that he is "an old man," to which Cobb replies, "filled with regret." Throughout the movie, Nolan uses an elevator to take us through various levels of Cobb's subconscious and back to specific moments that Cobb regrets. In addition, the song the dreamers use to signal the onset of a kick ("that feeling of falling that jolts you awake and returns you to reality") and to synchronize their trip back up the layers of the Fischer inception is about regret. In the slowed-down dream world, the song's first notes give the movie its signature ominous base tones—dun duh, dun duh! But in *the real world*, those notes quickly give way to the sound of a woman singing beautifully in French. We hear Edith Piaf's signature song "Non, Je Ne Regrette Rien."[3] Translated, the title is "No, I Do Not Regret Anything," with a long, repeated emphasis on the *"non."*

The audience was still applauding half an hour after the performance when Edith Piaf first sang this song in 1960 at the Paris Olympia Theater, just three years before her death. The next morning, December 30, newspaper headlines proclaimed: "Piaf Resuscitated by Love." "To her contemporaries, it was a triumph for the French spirit, embodied in the Little Sparrow's revival [her nickname was *La Môme*] and her resolve to save the Olympia."[4] Many years later, Joni Mitchell declared, "Edith Piaf knocked my socks off although I didn't know what she was singing about."[5] You might wonder what a famous French singer has to regret, especially after such a well-received performance, but what not even her fans knew at the time was "that same little disjointed doll who had torn their hearts out with her songs . . . was taken backstage and stuffed with vitamins and injected with drugs to keep her going."[6] Piaf's life was genuinely tragic. Born into abject poverty, with an absent father, she was abandoned by her morphine-addicted mother (who literally died in the gutter). As a girl, Piaf prostituted herself to buy food. While Piaf's childhood was unhappy, her adult life was equally filled with pain and suffering, marked by a series of tragic love affairs.

In contrast to Cobb, though, Piaf regrets nothing. Her song can be understood as an anthem that reinforces a particular philosophy of life: "Regret nothing. Good or bad, it makes no difference." We often hear this kind of idea espoused by celebrities and athletes baring their souls to Oprah. "Sure I've made mistakes. But they made me who I am today. I don't regret any of it. They made me stronger. And whatever doesn't kill you makes you stronger. Blah, blah, blah." In response we tend to think, "What conceit. What hubris. What a jackass!" Coming from Piaf it's different, though, because she is not one of the unrelenting and self-indulgent celebrities who fill our airwaves and monopolize our culture today. It's different because if ever a life were regrettable, it would be hers. That's why when we hear this tiny woman with the big voice belt out this song, we are moved. We believe her, and we applaud her defiance because we realize it's remarkable that she was able to survive such a life. This song—Nolan's kick back to reality—affirms an entire life: the good, bad, and especially the ugly. While Cobb is consumed by regret, this Little Sparrow resolutely affirms her life, warts and all.

Regret and Guilt

Although guilt and regret involve recognizing responsibility for doing something wrong, they are not the same thing. Guilt, often a more intense emotion, tends to have a more negative connotation than regret, which is a broader notion. People may regret things for which they do not feel guilt. I might, for example, regret my decision not to attend Syracuse University for graduate school or my decision not to break up with my boyfriend *before* leaving to spend a year in France, but I don't feel guilty about these decisions or actions. In the movie, once members of Cobb's dream team realize that they agreed to a job that was more dangerous than they were led to believe, they regret their decision. They don't feel guilty about getting mixed up with Cobb. Instead, they regret getting involved with something more dangerous than they had realized. In other words, they regret their decision because it may not bring about the results or consequences they desire.

Likewise, during the Fischer inception job, Cobb's partner in crime Arthur tries to steal a kiss from Ariadne as a way to divert the attention of the projections who are starting to come after them. Arthur may or may not regret stealing the kiss in terms of whether or not it is effective in sparking a romance. It's doubtful, however, that he would feel guilty about what he did. Assuming no romance ensued, Arthur may have simply wished he didn't kiss Ariadne because he embarrassed himself for nothing. In other words, since his action didn't bring about what he had hoped for, Arthur may now regret that kiss.

Guilt thus has a moral dimension that regret does not necessarily have. We can regret decisions or actions that have no moral dimension whatsoever. There was nothing "morally" right or wrong about my grad school decision or Arthur's stealing a kiss. Moreover, we can regret morally wrong things for either moral or non-moral reasons. Just think of the difference between members of the dream team regretting signing up for the inception job because they might land in Limbo (no reason to feel guilt) versus regretting the job because they come to realize that inception was morally wrong (they would have reason to feel guilt). In addition, the moral dimension of regret, which entails feeling guilt, allows for the possibility of feeling badly about an immoral action regardless of whether or not a person is caught or whether his or her decision or action brings about undesirable consequences. Members of the dream team could have regretted their decision because they recognized that what they were doing was morally wrong, regardless of whether the job might land them in Limbo.

Cobb, as we know, regrets many moments in his life. He feels responsible for his actions, and he feels badly for the pain and suffering he has caused. When people don't feel badly for their transgressions we think of them as monsters or sociopaths, particularly if their actions are especially egregious. Cobb's regret over what he has done to his wife and children leads us to assess his character as morally better than a person who would feel no regret at all.

Notice, however, that Cobb doesn't regret everything that he has done wrong. He does not regret choosing a criminal lifestyle in which he involves others. Only Cobb's father-in-law, Miles, appears to care about the fact that inceptions and extractions are forms of thievery. In one scene, Cobb's father-in-law makes clear that he "never taught [Cobb] to be a thief," and Cobb responds, "No, you taught me to navigate other people's minds. But after what happened there weren't a whole lot of legitimate ways for me to use that skill." Because he is convinced that he became a criminal of necessity, Cobb doesn't feel badly about his immoral work. As for the others he has dragged into this corruption, Cobb might tell himself that because they freely chose to join him, he shouldn't feel guilty. Even if that is true, however, Cobb still misled them and put them in harm's way simply so that he could advance his own interests. Cobb is not a heartless monster, but he only regrets inception in the case of Mal because of what happened to his once very happy family as a result of the inception. In other words, Cobb regrets what he did because it didn't bring about his desired outcome. It does not appear that Cobb feels regret (or guilt) for the morally right reasons.

Descartes on Regret

Descartes believes that if we act resolutely we have nothing to regret. Even if we do wrong, "if we always do whatever reason tells us, even if events show us afterwards that we have gone wrong, we will never have grounds for repentance, because it was not our fault."[7] As Descartes sees it, the only thing we should ever regret is being irresolute, which amounts to being irrational or indecisive: "[N]othing causes regret and repentance except irresolution."[8]

Like any good Catholic of his day, Descartes believes that humans are rational creatures of God who were created imperfect yet absolutely free to choose between good and evil. Descartes also recognizes that we sometimes act on emotions such as anger, love, hatred, joy, and sadness, which can get in the way of our ability to act rationally. He does not, however, think that our emotions are inherently bad or to be avoided at all costs. In fact, he thinks that emotions (or "passions," as he calls them) contribute to being virtuous, or morally excellent. It's just that they can sometimes lead us astray.

Above all for Descartes, moral virtue requires being resolute, which means that we fully embrace the freedom of the will and deliberately apply our minds without being overly influenced by the emotions. "Virtue, I believe, consists precisely in sticking firmly to this resolution [to carry out whatever reason recommends without being diverted by emotions or appetites]; though I do not know that anyone has ever so described it."[9] Resoluteness also requires that once a person decides on a particular course of action (or inaction) he or she must stay the course—don't flip-flop, dilly-dally, waffle, or wrangle. A resolute person is strong and steadfast. Even if resolute deeds bring about unintended bad consequences, there should be no regret. Instead regret should be reserved exclusively for those who act irresolutely, that is, who fail to act according to the recommendations of reason. Descartes believes so strongly in the virtue of resolve that he thinks that even if we act irresolutely, but bring about *good* consequences, we should regret our lack of resolve: "There would be more ground for repentance if we had acted against our conscience, even though we realized afterwards that we had done better than we thought."[10]

Descartes' view that regret is only appropriate when we act irresolutely, regardless of whether or not our actions bring about good consequences, may sound counterintuitive. After all, Cobb regrets his inception of Mal because of the result, losing his wife and his kids. Descartes, though, would tell Cobb that he should only feel badly if he acted irresolutely, regardless of what happened as a consequence of his actions.

So why does Descartes hold this view? When we feel regret (or guilt) we feel responsible for our misdeeds, wishing that we had never done what we did. Cobb is sad that his wife is dead, and doubly sad—or regretful—because he thinks he caused her death. But Descartes believes that the only thing we can be held responsible for are our thoughts, because our thoughts are the only things we can control: "We are responsible only for our thoughts, and it does not belong to human nature to be omniscient, or to always judge as well on the spur of the moment as when there is plenty of time to deliberate."[11] When we are figuring out what to do and how to act, often we need to make snap judgments. Even in cases in which we have time to deliberate, we may still go wrong because we can't have eyes everywhere, nor can we predict all future consequences of our actions. Given these indisputable facts about the nature of action as well as ourselves and our world, Descartes believes that we shouldn't regret our misdeeds as long as we did our very best to judge well at the time we needed to act, and then carried out our chosen course of action with constancy and resolve. For Descartes, the best kind of person—the virtuous person—is the one who acts resolutely, regardless of the consequences of his or her actions. Good or bad, it makes no difference.

How does Descartes defend such a view? Praise or blame can only pertain to that which lies within our control, and for Descartes, only our thoughts or desires are within our control. Actions are informed by our thoughts or desires, from which we form judgments about what we should or should not do. Therefore, actions should only be considered virtuous in terms of whether or not they are taken with the right thoughts in mind, which amounts to doing what "we judged best at the time when we had to decide to act."[12] To Descartes' credit, he is not suggesting that virtue requires that we do *whatever* we deem to be the best course of action, and do it with gusto. In fact, Descartes has fairly strict requirements for how we accustom ourselves to forming good judgments in the first place. This formation involves a rigorous program of intellectual exercises that are outlined in his two most famous works, *Discourse on Method* and *Meditations on First Philosophy*. We won't get into all the details, but suffice it to say that Descartes is confident that over time we can train ourselves to make better and better judgments, or become more and more resolute. A good part of his confidence stems from his belief in God and God's infinite goodness. Since God is ultimately good, Descartes believes that we are born with a kind of guarantee that as long as we are properly using our God-given intellectual faculties we can and do arrive at the truth. In other words, even though God did not create us perfect, God still gave us the ability to perfect ourselves. In fact, it is this confidence regarding the likelihood of our success that helps to get us into the habit of acting resolutely, or virtuously. At times we may be quite unsure about what to do, but we need to act anyway. In these cases the best we can hope for is to act with determination and resolve on what we have discerned to be most probably the best course of action. Being resolute requires that once we undertake a course of action we stay the course that reason recommends, even if it may cause us harm.

Well-Placed Regret

Sagelike Ariadne tells Cobb to let go of his regret and guilt because Mal's suicide was not his fault. At the time, Ariadne didn't know the idea that drove Mal to commit suicide was a result of Cobb spinning her top in the safe of her subconscious. Even knowing that, however, Descartes would still agree with Ariadne's assessment. Cobb might have suspected that Mal's belief could persist into *the real world*, and maybe he suspected that it would give rise to suicidal thoughts, but Cobb could not have controlled her actions. So, Descartes would suggest that he has nothing to regret in that regard. Cobb also regrets leaving his children, but Descartes would also say he should not regret this. He did the best he could in the short period of time he had to make a decision.

Descartes would still insist, however, that Cobb has plenty to regret. Cobb was irresolute. One aspect of being resolute, or virtuous, is that we apply our minds properly to figure out what should or should not be done. We must not be swayed by passions or desires. So even if Limbo was an accident that resulted from experiments with shared dreaming, Cobb was wrong to allow himself to be controlled by impulse and desire when he decided to stay there. Drunk with his own power, Cobb tells us, he enjoyed feeling like a god who could create his own reality—the dream world that started the problem in the first place.[13] He (and Mal) should have left then and there, before things got out of hand. Cobb shouldn't regret incepting Mal—that was the best he could do, given the circumstances, and he couldn't control the way she reacted—but he should regret how he let his passion for godlike power dictate his decision to stay in Limbo.

Descartes would also say that even when Nolan's characters regret the right thing, they do so for the wrong reasons. Cobb regrets his decisions because of their consequences— because they led to the death of his wife and the absence of his children from his life—not because they were fueled by passion, or a lack of virtuous character. If he was not virtuous and had been fueled by passion, yet somehow saved his wife and never lost his children, he would regret nothing, despite the fact that he should. Descartes would have Cobb feel regret for being irresolute or irrational, regardless of how things turned out. Hence Cobb's regret is not ennobling, for it is not felt for the right reasons or directed toward the right objects.

Cobb is no tragic hero. Compare him to Piaf. She avoids regret altogether by resolving to live a life that few would be able to survive. Cobb, on the other hand, had a good life. He was very happy with Mal, in *the real world*—clearly in love, with two beautiful children, a home, and so on. But it wasn't enough. Swept up by his desire to be with Mal forever, Cobb came to regard himself as a god who could create a new reality. Piaf, on the other hand, accepted the harsh realities of her tragic, mortal existence and embraced her past. Realizing that she could not control the misery and pain that was inflicted upon her, the Little Sparrow did the best she could. She resolved to survive, and for this she rightly had no regrets. Cobb, by contrast, is not tragic but merely flawed. Like us, this imperfect protagonist has moments of his life that he regrets. Unlike us, however, Cobb believes that he is capable of reinventing the past—of turning painful memories into dreams—so that he can avoid feeling the pain of regret.

Cobb fails to realize that what's done is done. Descartes believed that although we do not have control over future consequences of our actions and decisions, we do have control over the kinds of persons we are. Virtue, or resoluteness, requires being thoughtful and reflective, not impulsive. Resoluteness requires that we work hard to make sure that we are making the right decisions in the first place, without being overly swayed by passion; we must stay the course reason recommends, even if this may cause us harm. We should try to anticipate the consequences of a proposed course of action, but Descartes recognizes that some of what happens as the result of our decisions and actions is out of our control. Thus we should not feel regret for the outcomes of our decisions, but only for how we came to form those decisions in the first place. Cobb thus acts contrary to Descartes' views when he tries to re-form his memories to avoid his feelings of regret.

Ultimately, Nolan's deeply Cartesian movie "mal-places" regret. Not only does the main character regret the wrong things, but he regrets things for the wrong reasons. Nolan has us focus on the consequences of actions as if we should only regret our actions when we get caught—that is, when they do not bring about our desired outcomes. Instead Descartes believes that we should habituate ourselves toward being resolute and only regret being irresolute, or irrational, regardless of consequences. In this way, well-placed regret can be ennobling.

Postscript

The movie critic Andrew O'Hehir, in *Salon*, said that "Nolan has inherited some of Kubrick and Hitchcock's worst tendencies, most notably their defensive, compulsive inclination to work everything out about their stories and characters to the last detail, as if human beings and the world were algebraic or geometrical phenomena requiring a solution."[14] The fact, however, that there is so much discussion and downright confusion about the characters and story line suggests that Nolan did not offer enough detail. Although he resolutely chose a potentially rich theme for his movie, he treated the topic in a superficial manner. That is regrettable.[15]

NOTES

1. For the purposes of this chapter, I am not going to weigh in on the debate as to whether or not *the real world* (where they plan the inception, where Cobb doesn't wear his wedding ring, where Mal committed suicide) is a dream or not. If *the real world* is a dream, which is an interpretation that some, including the editor of this book, favor, then there is an issue as to whether or not Mal really committed suicide—or actually woke up. I don't think this matters for my discussion. Whether or not Cobb's reality is a dream, he believes that Mal did commit suicide, for which he feels responsible, which is the important point for my discussion.

2. Ariadne also helped Theseus by providing him with a thread so he could find his way back *out* of the labyrinth. She was also abandoned by Theseus. The *Oxford Classical Dictionary* (Oxford, UK: Oxford University Press, 1996) entry for Ariadne describes her myth as "centered on marriage and death."

3. Interestingly, Marion Cotillard, who plays Mal in *Inception*, won an Oscar for playing the legendary French chanteuse Piaf in the 2007 French film *La Vie en Rose*.

4. Carolyn Burke, *No Regrets: The Life of Edith Piaf* (New York: Alfred A. Knopf, 2011), p. 199.

5. Burke, p. xi. Here is a link to a a video recording of Piaf's performance: http://www .youtube.com/watch?v=vn5SWXwbqRs.

6. Monique Lange, *Piaf*, trans. Richard Woodward (New York: Seaver Books, 1982), p. 180.

7. CSMK III 258; AT IV 266. CSMK III refers to John Cottingham, Robert Stoothoff, Dugald Murdoch, and Anthony Kenny, trans., *The Philosophical Writings of Descartes: The Correspondence*, Vol. III (Cambridge: Cambridge University Press, 1991).

8. CSMK III 267; AT IV 295.

9. CSMK III 258; AT IV 265.

10. CSMK III 269; AT IV 307.

11. CSMK III 269; AT IV 307.

12. CSMK III 269; AT IV 307.

13. Of course, Mal helped Cobb to create the city in Limbo, and she may have enjoyed this godlike feeling as well. But the movie and this essay focus attention on Cobb and his feelings of regret, not Mal.

14. Andrew O'Hehir, "'Inception': A Clunky, Overblown Disappointment" (*Salon*, July 14, 2010), www.salon.com/entertainment/movies/andrew_ohehir/2010/07/14/inception.

15. Special thanks to Jason Grinnell for planting the idea for this paper in my mind and subsequently commenting on my work. I am also grateful to Kevin Meindl for his helpful feedback.

"YOU'RE JUST A SHADE": KNOWING OTHERS, AND YOURSELF

Daniel Forbes

I can't stay with her anymore, because she doesn't exist. . . . I wish more than anything, but I can't imagine you with all your complexity, all your perfection, all your imperfection. Look at you. You're just a shade. You're just a shade of my real wife. And you were the best that I could do, but I'm sorry . . . you're just not good enough.

—Dom Cobb

You think inception is impossible, don't you? It's not. In fact, I can succeed at inception with you even if you're aware I am attempting it, despite your best efforts to protect your thoughts. My mission is to introduce an idea into your mind—a simple one, one that will take hold of your being so intensely that you will think it is your own. The concept will have rational implications, but I'll need to distill it down to its emotional essence in order for it to be effective. I will require several dream levels to make inception happen. On the first level, I will convince you that you never *really* know anyone else, only yourself and your perception of other people. On the second level, the idea takes a simpler, more deeply emotional form: you're inescapably, unavoidably, *alone*. On the third level—where things get really interesting—I'll convince you that you can't even know yourself. That's going to leave us in a pretty strange place, and we'll need a pretty powerful "kick" to escape back to reality. It'll be tough, but I guess I'll just have to improvise when we get there.

Mission Planning

Other chapters in this book have examined René Descartes' famous "dream argument" where he entertains the possibility that although it seems he's in a stove-heated room pondering philosophy, he really is just dreaming about it.[1] But let's leave the skeptical question of whether or not he can know he is dreaming aside—it's not a simple enough idea for inception—and instead ride this idea down to an even deeper level. Unlike a team effort requiring an extractor, an architect, a forger, and a point man, Descartes' version of the thought experiment is a solo project. He's focused on the question of whether or not he can trust his own conscious perceptual awareness as a truthful source of information about reality. In fact, Descartes clearly thinks this is something he *has* to do alone—for how could another person help you evaluate the reliability of your own conscious perception if you're not even sure that person exists?

There's more to the dream argument than questioning the truth of our perception, however. Descartes wasn't the first to consider it. (You might say that he, too, experienced inception.) The ancient Greek philosopher Plato (c. 428–347 BCE) in his dialogue *Theaetetus* also ponders the significance of dreaming, although with a slightly different spin. Rather than a philosopher reflecting by himself, we have a philosopher, Socrates, in conversation with another person, Theaetetus.

> Socrates: Suppose someone asks us, just as we are at present, whether we are asleep and all our thoughts are a dream, or awake and talking to each other in the waking world. What evidence could we give that would prove our answer?
> Theaetetus: Truly, Socrates, it's a real puzzle what evidence would be enough to prove it. . . . When we are asleep, there is nothing to prevent us from believing that we are having the very same conversation with each other. And when we dream that we are reporting a dream, there is quite a bizarre similarity between such experiences and *really* reporting a dream.[2]

If Descartes is dreaming, then he's not really where he thinks he is, but at least he's still doing philosophy. He could wake up from the dream, and if he can manage to remember what he was thinking about (dreams are so hard to remember), he can still feel like he got something philosophically useful from the experience. But if Socrates is dreaming, not only is he not where he thinks he is, he's not even having a real conversation in the first place. The character of Theaetetus would be merely a memory or figment of his imagination, and Socrates would be just an old man, filled with regret, doing philosophy alone.

We can get a clearer sense of Plato's concern by looking at a quote about dreaming from an even earlier ancient Greek philosopher, Heraclitus (c. 540–c. 480 BCE), who said, "For the waking there is one common world, but when asleep each person turns away to a private one."[3] (It seems that Plato may have been a target for inception, too.) Heraclitus isn't wondering whether or not he's dreaming, and isn't worried about whether or not what he perceives is real. Rather, he seems to be making a different point about why we value waking experience over dream experience. The problem is not so much that what is perceived in a dream is not real, but that dreaming by its very nature is *private*. You might dream of having a deep conversation at a café in Paris, or of collaborating with a skilled team to plan an inception, but in fact you are *alone*, living in your own little dream world. The dream argument suggests that the interpersonal interaction and companionship we treasure could simply be an illusion.

In the world of *Inception*, however, we have a way to address this worry: shared dreaming in which different individuals not only can occupy the same dream space,[4] but also open their subconscious to exploration by others. In this way it is possible for there to be a real conversation—and even real collaboration in a sort of "dream heist"—within an unreal dream space. Dreaming doesn't have to be a solo project anymore.

"You're Keeping Her Alive": The Problem of Projections

There's a complication besides the fact that dream-sharing technology is not real . . . yet. In *Inception* there are characters in the dream space that do not exist outside of it and yet play significant roles in shared dreams—the "projections" of individuals inhabiting the shared dream space. These projections, while they can be threatening to those in the dream space, often don't have much personality or individuality. Dom Cobb populates Ariadne's first shared dream of Paris with many passers-by, and Robert Fischer creates "militarized" projections to defend his subconscious. There are other projections that seem more lifelike, however, because they represent specific individuals. Robert Fischer projects his godfather, Peter Browning, when he is not present, and projects his dead father, Maurice Fischer. Cobb, of course, projects an image of his wife, Mal—an image that not only embodies Cobb's memories and guilt but has the ability to actively interfere with his attempts at extraction and inception. None of these projections are real individuals. Rather, they are the imaginary creations of someone in the dream space.

This complication spells trouble because Cobb and his team treat Mal as a *real person*. This isn't surprising since she appears in a sense to have a mind of her own, seemingly intentionally thwarting Cobb's extraction attempts. So in practical terms she is just as real as any participant in the shared dream. But if projected persons can function like anyone else inhabiting the shared dream, then it's impossible to tell who is real and who is merely a projection. It's possible that *all* of the persons in what seems to be a shared dream are just projections. Shared dreaming might not really be shared—you still might be alone.

It gets worse. Despite his insistence that she is just a projection of his subconscious, Cobb at times seems to see and treat what he consciously recognizes to be a projection of Mal not only as a real person, but as a specific real person—his wife, Mal—as if in some sense this projection is the same person as the one whom he lost. In fact, it's clear that in some sense he wants to *make her real*, as he tries to change his past by making his memories dreams, and making the dreams his reality. Cobb's desire to live in his dreams embodies Heraclitus's worry about dreaming because Cobb intentionally turns to his own private world and turns his back on the world shared with others. So forget about whether or not Cobb can distinguish dreaming from reality. Let's ask a more emotionally charged question, a question centered on Cobb's desire to make Mal real again. Cobb would like the Mal that he knew to live for him again. *But did Cobb ever know Mal in the first place?* If Cobb's experiences of Mal in some sense never represented her truthfully, then perhaps *no one has ever been real for him*. Welcome to dream level one.

Is Consciousness "Windowless"?

Some philosophers have argued that experience is *completely* private, that you never really know anyone but yourself. The philosopher Gottfried Wilhelm Leibniz (1646–1716) theorized that each human consciousness is a "monad"—a completely separate and self-sufficient being. According to Leibniz, conscious monads are "windowless"—they do not have any way to perceive anything outside of themselves.[5] A conscious monad can perceive only the contents of its own perceptual consciousness and memory, and therefore can never know anything about the world beyond its own perspective. If Leibniz is right, then Cobb (and each of us) is a conscious monad whose perspective *is* the world for him. In a sense, the entirety of every conscious monad's life must be private, every bit as much as a dream is private. So for Leibniz there's not much of a difference between a dream and waking life.

To get a sense of what it means to talk about consciousness being "windowless," imagine a real scenario where Mal stabs Cobb in the chest (not unlike Cobb's projection of Mal does toward the end of the movie—"Does this feel real?"). If we think about such a scenario in terms of conscious perceptual experiences, what has happened here? In Mal's conscious experience there is an intense feeling of anger, a sensation of her arm moving, and a feeling of resistance in her hand as she pushes in the knife. But Cobb's conscious experience is entirely different. He sees a blur of motion, then feels a stabbing pain in his chest, and finally experiences emotions of surprise and hurt that someone he loves would do this to him. Whose experience is the *true* one? Neither, or both. They're simply different. But since Mal cannot truly experience Cobb's perspective, and Cobb cannot truly experience Mal's, these experiences never mix or overlap. What Mal experiences is known by Mal alone, and the same goes for Cobb.

According to Leibniz, each of us is this way: we each have perspectives that are forever private, impossible to share for the simple reason that consciousness cannot be shared. There are no "windows" through which I can see what it is like to be you, and no window into which you can look to see what it is like to be me. My life is a sort of movie playing out inside my own mind—and I'm the only person in the audience. The same is true for you, of course, as well as for every other conscious being. Everyone lives in their own private world.

If Leibniz is right, we never really "know" anyone else, but can only speculate about what others think and feel. Since it is impossible for anyone other than Mal to know her perspective, what Cobb "knows" about Mal's perspective is only what he can extrapolate from his own. If Cobb tries to understand what Mal is going through when she stabs him, he will reflect on his own experiences and memories—what it is like to feel angry, what it is like to stab something with a knife—and then construct an imaginary notion of what Mal must have been thinking, feeling, and experiencing when she lashed out. If Cobb hasn't had an experience that is similar to Mal's, however, then his extrapolation will be unreliable. The bottom line: the things Cobb (or any of us) thinks he might "know" about Mal or about others are merely his projections. So you never *really* know anyone else.

Leibniz's theory of conscious experience is pretty compelling, and a bit scary. It has taken us to the edge of the second dream level, but it's still not quite emotionally intense enough to achieve a successful inception. We need to go deeper to introduce a more powerful idea. Plug yourself in again so that we can go down to the next level.

Is Shared Privacy an Oxymoron?

Despite the eeriness of the idea that we never really know anyone else, there is nevertheless something comforting about Leibniz's idea that our conscious experience is perfectly private. The possibility of shared privacy—a scenario that would blow up Leibniz's theory more completely than explosive charges demolishing a heavily guarded Alpine installation—is not really as pleasant as we might think. If you could really open your perspective for others to share, or others could open their perspective to you, how would you know which thoughts or feelings were yours and which belonged to someone else?

Basic to a sense of identity is having attitudes, ideas, experiences, and perspectives that belong to you alone. If you can't determine to whom experiences and thoughts belong, then you don't even know who you are. In short, shared privacy would blur our sense of identity so much that *sharing* would no longer be meaningful—we have to be different persons in order to share. Cobb would like to hold hands with Mal, not "share" the experience of her hand. Perhaps "knowing" another person is not something we would really want. Maybe we really *need* to keep our conscious experience "windowless" and private so that we can maintain a clearly defined sense of self.

So we're now at level two: you're unavoidably, inescapably, *alone*. The people you *think* you know are only projections of your own reflections and memories, and things you think you know about them are merely the results of your extrapolations. Will this simple idea take hold? Will you be able to accept it as your own? Will it change everything about you? Perhaps we need to go even deeper.

Can We Still Feel the World through the Walls?

Leibniz's theory has a basic problem because it rejects our beliefs about causal relationships between individual beings. Sure, there are two very different conscious experiences in the same situation where Mal stabs Cobb in the chest, but it's still the *same* situation—they're not *entirely* living in their own worlds. They are both players in a single event of causal interaction: a moving hand plunges a knife into a chest. While our conscious experiences and perspectives may be private, they nevertheless happen in a world where these experiences and perspectives line up with one another because things interact with one another. What makes this possible are the causal interactions between things in a real, *shared* world.

The philosopher Benedict de Spinoza (1632–1677) agrees with Leibniz that our conscious experiences are inevitably our own perceptions. He points out, however, that technically these are perceptions of events happening in our own *bodies*.[6] For example, Mal experiences motion in her arm because of the contractions of the muscles, the change in position of her arm with respect to the rest of her body, and the feeling of the knife in her hand. Even her experience of anger, which seems intangible, is really embodied: there may be tension in her face and jaw, and in her muscles in general, as her body responds to a general urge to strike out. It's hard to have a concrete idea of what it means to be angry without having a body to express the emotion. Even if we think of Mal's inner awareness of her own anger as something fundamentally tied to a conscious experience, that experience can ultimately be traced to neurochemical events occurring in her brain. In short, what she directly and consciously experiences are the things that her body is doing and the changes it is undergoing.

Because Mal's body is not physically linked to Cobb's body, she can only feel what happens in her own body; as Spinoza puts it, our perceptions say more about our own bodies than about the external objects that causally interact with them.[7] But the fact that our bodies interact with many other things in a world means that there is a causal dimension to our understanding and interpretation of experience. Our perceptions, though they are really awareness of events occurring in our own bodies, nevertheless involve other bodies insofar as they affect our body.[8] So while I directly perceive my own body, in a sense I *indirectly* perceive other bodies because they have an effect on my body. When Cobb feels a wave crash over his face, he's really feeling his face, but he wouldn't feel anything at all if there weren't water splashing against it. So Cobb's perception, while it is *mostly* about the skin on his face, is also *partly* about the world outside his body having an impact on it.

Likewise, while your perceptions of another person are mostly about the effect he or she has on you—and so you may falsely attribute characteristics or ideas to the person that are really based on your own thoughts—your perceptions never-theless indirectly involve them. What Cobb remembers about Mal is largely what she meant to him, and so his projection of Mal is focused on his sense of guilt. As Ariadne points out to him, "Your guilt defines her." But still, there was a Mal who was *not* a projection of Cobb's thoughts and memories and who in some way influenced the formation of the projection haunting his (and others') dreams.

If Spinoza is right, then even if we are trapped within our own consciousnesses, and there are no windows to reveal what's outside, we nevertheless come into contact with a world of other people that influences how we represent them to ourselves. We can feel a world though the walls.

Can We Even Know Ourselves?

This takes us down to the third dream level. It's going to be very strange—like unconstructed dream space. Let's hope we don't get stuck there for fifty years.

So far we've been talking about consciousness, and ignoring the distinction between it and the subconscious. If conscious-ness encompasses what we can readily know about ourselves, the subconscious encompasses what we do *not* readily know about ourselves. We've already asked whether or not we can know anyone else, but when we take the subconscious into consideration we have to ask whether or not *we can even know ourselves*—because the subconscious contains our deepest and innermost thoughts and feelings, and keeps them hidden from us. This is what allows us to "create and perceive our world simultaneously" in a dream; our consciousness perceives what the subconscious creates outside of conscious awareness. This is also why it is often difficult to make sense of our dreams. Dreams express in metaphor and image what is concealed in our subconscious, and since we aren't familiar with these thoughts and feelings, they confuse us. In the dream spaces of *Inception* the subconscious is largely responsible for the weirdness and paradox that confuse the dreamers. And since the subconscious by its very nature conceals the self from the self, it exacerbates the problem of knowing who is who in a shared dream. As we have already discussed, Cobb has a hard time regarding his projection of Mal as a reflection of himself, and often seems to confuse her with the real Mal.

Inception suggests, however, that the "shared privacy" that can take place in a dream space may at the same time be a solution to this very problem of self-knowledge. If we can enter into the imagination of the dreamer, or interact with projections from the memories of others within a dream space, then we can reveal a great deal about ourselves to one another, and others to us. Shared dreaming makes it possible for Ariadne to intrude into Cobb's dreams in order to learn more about what is driving him. She accesses his innermost thoughts and repressed memories by exploring his subconscious. In this way Ariadne engages in a very unusual form of psychotherapy that helps Cobb to uncover thoughts and feelings that he hides from himself.

But does "shared privacy" really give Ariadne any advantage in learning about Cobb by exploring his dreams and memories? There's reason to doubt it. Though the film doesn't explore this, perhaps the mere presence of another person in his dream space distorts the landscape of Cobb's memories as he tries to protect them. Cobb, after all, deep down wants to hide these memories from *himself*—why would he share them with an uninvited visitor? Moreover, Cobb's subconscious imagery is highly symbolic, which is what we'd expect from a dream. For example, he represents Mal's repression of her memory of *the real world* as a safe inside a dollhouse inside another house—echoing the concept of a dream within a dream. These images require Ariadne to interpret Cobb's thoughts such that she must inevitably construct an interpretation of who Cobb is. So perhaps she ends up with an image of Cobb just as distorted as Cobb's projection of Mal.

Ultimately, the boundary between the conscious and the subconscious implies that Cobb may not be who he thinks he is. If Cobb can't tell the difference between an image of Mal that represents himself more than it does Mal, then not only did he not know Mal, he apparently doesn't even know himself. This creates a bizarre situation. If you can't know others and can't even know yourself, then what sense does it make to think of yourself as alone? If Cobb doesn't know himself, then even if the entirety of *Inception* is a dream, we can't be sure whose dream it is in the first place.

Encountering the Other

This leaves us in a pretty strange place, but we don't want to be stuck in Limbo, filled with regrets, waiting to die alone. Is there any sort of "kick" we can use to ride out of this dream space?

Well, we have a sense that we really *do* succeed sometimes in achieving knowledge of ourselves and others, and that our interactions with different perspectives help us to do this. So how can we know other people, or ourselves? Perhaps it depends on what we mean by "know." We can get a better feel for this with the help of Martin Buber (1878–1965).

Buber suggests that we can "know" the world and other people in two very different ways, "experience" and "encounter." An experience converts the event of perception into a representation and generates a relation that he calls "I-It"— a conceptual relation where the perceiver holds something within consciousness as a sort of object or thing to be understood or used.[9] As we've seen, this implies that we've already made something real into an object of our own thought—its representation is now shaped by our expectations, biases, and interests. As Spinoza says, the object is now more about the perceiver than it is about the thing that affected her. This is the problem that faces Cobb with his projection of Mal—again, his guilt "defines her." Cobb has come away from his life with Mal with a projection of what she (and her death) meant *to him*, and the real Mal is mostly left out of Cobb's image of her. As Cobb himself admits to his projection of Mal, "I can't imagine you with all your complexity, all your perfection, all your imperfection." Buber would say that Cobb has "experienced" Mal and so Cobb's relation to the projection of Mal in his dreams is an "I-It" relation. What Mal is to Cobb is a lingering memory, a mere object of thought that he uses to grapple with his guilt.

Buber points out, though, that before there can be an experience there must first be an encounter—an event of entering into direct relationship with a being.[10] Any encounter provokes the conscious self to generate an experience that represents that being—and once the experience has been generated, the immediacy of the encounter is lost. Buber suggests that if we resist the tendency to convert this other being into a representation and instead try to live within the moment of the encounter as long as we can, we participate in a concrete relation that Buber calls "I-You." This involves just trying to *be with* the other, without trying to *know* the other, since an attempt to know the other person will only produce a distorted objectification. As Buber describes it:

> The relation to the You is unmediated. Nothing conceptual intervenes between I and You, no prior knowledge and no imagination; and memory itself is changed as it plunges from particularity into wholeness. No purpose intervenes between I and You, no greed and no anticipation, and longing itself is changed as it plunges from the dream into appearance.[11]

According to Buber, if I try to describe and understand the other person in a reflective or analytical way, then I will begin the process of objectively representing that person in my own thought—and at that point I'm really describing and understanding my own projection of that person, which of course says more about me and my desires than it does about anyone else. Since all that I can ever describe is a biased interpretation of the other person distorted by my desires, the experience of an encounter as an "I-You" relation will inevitably be indescribable.

What's more, Buber contends that the kind of life I live—one that is dominated by experiences, or one that is dominated by encounters—will determine the sort of person *I* am. If I spend my time analyzing the things I perceive in order to objectively understand them and use them for my own purposes, the world for me will become the objects that I have constructed through my own thought. I will have chosen, consciously or unconsciously, to make my thought about *me* by interpreting it in light of my own thoughts, memories, and attitudes. By doing so, I will effectively detach myself from the world that I try to know and *make* myself alone.[12] On the other hand, if I make an effort to focus on the encounter rather than the experience—if I try to live in the moment of being present with another person, without trying to think about what that person may mean to me in terms of my desires—then I stand a chance of *being with* others. It's impossible to *never* objectify what we perceive; objectification is necessary for us to survive and successfully navigate our world. The more we can immerse ourselves in the encounter, however, the less alone we will be.

In the end, when Cobb recognizes that he has to let Mal go, it's clear that he is letting go of a part of himself. Buber's philosophy suggests that Cobb has confronted the fact that he has been clinging to an I-It relationship. It's not clear, however, that he has really "come back to reality." He lets his projection of Mal go in order to return to his children, Phillipa and James—but are they only projections of his own desires as well? Are they objects to which Cobb will cling just as he did Mal? Will Cobb thus recreate the problem that he just escaped? Maybe that mystery is more important than the mystery of whether or not the spinning top falls. Will Cobb seek to encounter the world— or will he instead try to experience and know his children and thus continue to live in a private world?

So that was my attempt at inception. You can never know anyone else because the attempt to know only creates a representation that is more about you than the person you want to know. And because the same thing holds for your conscious mind attempting to know your unconscious mind, you can never know yourself either. But if you can give up on the attempt to *know* others or yourself—that is, if you can refrain from interpreting them through the lens of your desires and interests—and instead can simply *be with* them, then at least you won't be alone.

So, has the idea taken hold? Do you feel like it is your own? Have I successfully achieved inception? Or are we just stuck in Limbo?

NOTES

1. For more on this question, see James Miller's and Katherine Tullmann's chapters in this volume.

2. *Theaetetus*, 158b4–c7. The quote is taken from a translation by Timothy Chappell, *Reading Plato's* Theaetetus (Indianapolis: Hackett, 2004), p. 80.

3. Fragment 22. *A Presocratics Reader: Selected Fragments and Testimonia*, ed. Patricia Curd, trans. Richard D. McKirahan and Patricia Curd (Indianapolis: Hackett, 2011), p. 43.

4. The question of "where" shared dreams would take place is interesting. For more on this question, see Ken Marable's chapter in this volume.

5. *Monadology*, paragraph 7. G. W. Leibniz, *Discourse on Metaphysics and Other Essays*, ed. and trans. Daniel Garber and Roger Ariew (Indianapolis: Hackett, 1991), p. 68.

6. Benedict de Spinoza, *Ethics*, Part II, Proposition 13. *The Essential Spinoza: Ethics and Other Writings*, ed. Michael Morgan, trans. Samuel Shirley (Indianapolis: Hackett, 2006), p. 36.

7. Benedict de Spinoza, *Ethics*, Part II, Proposition 16, Corollary 1. *The Essential Spinoza*, p. 41.

8. Ibid., p. 40.

9. Martin Buber, *I and Thou*, trans. Walter Kauffman (New York: Simon and Schuster, 1996), pp. 55–56.

10. Ibid., p. 62.

11. Ibid., pp. 62–63.

12. Ibid., pp. 74–75.

PARADOX, DREAMS, AND STRANGE LOOPS IN *INCEPTION*

Tyler Shores

Shall we take a look at some paradoxical architecture?

—Arthur

Thinking and dreaming about the impossible spurs our imagination and encourages us to question the boundaries of what is possible. *Inception* is compelling because it takes impossibilities and paradoxes for granted. "In a dream you can cheat architecture into impossible shapes. That lets you create closed loops. Like the Penrose steps. An infinite staircase," says Arthur to Ariadne as he teaches her dream architecture. They pass the same woman, fumbling with her papers, twice as they ascend the staircase—suddenly the camera angle descends to reveal that the next step "up" is also the lowest step of all. "See? Paradox." The Penrose steps are not the only paradox in *Inception*, of course. Consider the very act of dreaming itself: you dream while sleeping, and thus while you are unconscious. Yet you are having experiences, and therefore must be conscious. Dreaming itself seems to be a paradox.

But what are paradoxes exactly? Are they really possible? What might we learn from them? And what other paradoxes does *Inception* invoke? At least one critic wondered if Christopher Nolan's film seemed to run the risk of being "too literal, too logical, too rule-bound."[1] In fact, *Inception* is anything but.

What Is a Paradox?

A paradox might be understood as something that, on its face, seems possible but when examined is logically contradictory. Consider, for example: "There is a town in which all the men are clean-shaven; one of those men is a male barber who shaves all and only those men who do not shave themselves."[2] At first this seems sensible, but upon examination we realize it entails that the barber both does, and does not, shave himself. This is a logical contradiction. And if paradoxes are paradoxes because they are logically contradictory, then they can't exist.

Perhaps, however, paradoxes are more than this: perhaps they are something that seems contradictory, but upon examination is not. Richard Sainsbury suggests something along this line. A paradox is when:

> an apparently unacceptable conclusion [is] derived by apparently acceptable reasoning from apparently acceptable premises. Appearances have to deceive, since the acceptable cannot lead by acceptable steps to the unacceptable. So, generally, we have a choice: either the conclusion is not really unacceptable, or else the starting point, or the reasoning, has some non-obvious flaw.[3]

With both *Inception* and paradox, things are not always as they may appear to be. What seems to be an obviously false conclusion can't follow from unquestionable premises with unfaltering validity. There must be a mistake somewhere. Either the conclusion isn't false, the premises aren't unquestionable, or the reasoning isn't valid. For example, consider the birthday paradox. If you have fifty people in a room, what is the probability that two of them celebrate their birthday on the same day? Since there are three hundred and sixty-five days in a year, it would seem low. Maybe one in seven? Nope. It's actually 97 percent likely. This seems contradictory, but isn't. Once you consider the math, you realize that the conclusion is not as unbelievable as it first appeared. Given the number of ways people can be paired up in a group of fifty, the chances that two of them won't match are very low.[4]

Often, it is vagueness or ambiguity that leads to such paradoxes. For example, suppose I enter the lottery. Can I know that I will not win? The chances are so low, it seems that I can know it. The chances are that low for everyone, though. And not everyone can know they won't win, because someone will. Paradox? Again, not exactly. The resolution comes in simply clarifying our terms. Classically, "knowledge" is defined as justified true belief, and everyone who won't win is justified in believing so—so they know. The person who will win is justified in believing they won't win, too; it just turns out they are wrong. Thus, they don't have true belief and lack knowledge.[5] But if knowledge requires certainty, then it turns out that my initial instinct was wrong; I can't know that I won't win and neither can anyone else. We resolve the paradox by clarifying what we mean by "know." That changes the way we view the paradox, and the seeming contradiction disappears.

We find a visual example in Arthur's hotel dream. One of M. C. Escher's most famous works is a drawing of a set of stairs made up of four 90-degree right angles that seem to be simultaneously ever-ascending and ever-descending. Such Penrose steps leave us with the impression that "there is a conflict between the finite and the infinite, and hence a strong sense of paradox."[6] But the conflict can be resolved with a change of perspective. One of Fischer's projections chases Arthur into a stairwell. We get an overhead camera angle as Arthur appears to run down and away from the projection, only to find Arthur appearing behind him. The camera angle suddenly shifts to reveal a precipitous drop and abrupt end to the staircase. "Paradox," Arthur says before pushing the guard over the edge. The sense of paradox is produced by one's perspective: the illusion of paradox is only successfully brought about when looked at in a certain way. The paradox is resolved when we realize that the appearance of a three-dimensional endless staircase can only be produced in two dimensions. A three-dimensional endless staircase cannot exist.

There is a distinction that we should be careful to make, however, between a paradox[7] and a thing that may well appear to be paradoxical, but ultimately only "grazes paradoxicality."[8] There are many everyday instances of the latter, things that we intuitively grasp as being kind-of-true and kind-of-not-true at the same time. In the opening pages of a book, for instance, you might find a blank page that has the contradictory statement: "This page intentionally left blank." Can a page that includes words describing its own blankness really be blank? It seems not, yet there it is . . . sort of. This paradox is easily resolved when we realize that the meaning of the sentence is, "The fact that there is nothing on this page, besides this sentence, is not an oversight."

Intuitively we should understand that this is different from "The sentence inside these quotes is false." If the sentence is true, it is false; but it if it false, it is true. Contradictions can't be true, yet it is a basic rule of logic that sentences can't lack a truth value. This is commonly called "the Liar Paradox," and it doesn't seem that it can be resolved by clarifying an ambiguity. The sentence can only be understood in one way. (A popular science fiction trope employs such logical paradoxes; Captain

Kirk used it often, effectively, to defeat androids.) Solutions to this paradox have been proposed, but we won't get sidetracked with them here.[9] The point is, the Liar Paradox does not merely "graze paradoxicality."

Why Thinking about Paradox Is Useful

If paradoxes can't be true, or if they merely turn on an ambiguity, what is the point in thinking about them? Often in philosophy what is important is not the answer, but the process of posing the question and thinking about an answer. Appreciating the value of paradox helps us to appreciate the value of philosophy itself. As French philosopher Gilles Deleuze (1925–1995) suggests in his book *Difference and Repetition*,

> Philosophy is revealed not by good sense but by paradox. Paradox is the pathos or the passion of philosophy. . . . Subjectively, paradox breaks up the common exercise of the faculties and places each before its own limit, before its incomparable: thought before the unthinkable which it alone is nevertheless capable of thinking.[10]

For Deleuze, paradox represents both the most enlightening and the most mystifying elements of philosophical thinking at the same time. The kinds of thinking that we find ourselves doing in philosophy can be a welcome change from the humdrum reasoning we rely upon in our day-to-day lives, much in the same way that the gravity-defying, perspective-skewing science fictional elements of *Inception* are a welcome change from our own lived reality. Those same fantastical elements can even whet our philosophical appetites for thoughts that we might not otherwise have opportunity to consider.

For philosophers such as Friedrich Nietzsche (1844–1900), contradictions and paradoxical thinking can have a certain unique value:

Among the things that can reduce a thinker to despair is the knowledge that the illogical is a necessity for mankind, and that much good proceeds from the illogical. . . . Even the most rational man from time to time needs to cover nature, that is to say his illogical original relationship with all things.[11]

Embrace of the illogical, Nietzsche advises us, can be an occasion to shake ourselves free from our accustomed habits of thinking, and lead us to greater insights and what might even seem at first to be "illogical" conclusions. Trying to solve the Liar Paradox, for example, is valuable even if you don't "solve" it. The attempt involves thinking differently about the ways in which we understand ideas such as "true" and "false," which ordinarily we cannot help but take for granted. Paradox, in this way, speaks to our non-rational sentiments—it serves as a way for us to come to terms with seemingly irreducibly complex ideas. Paradox can provide a way to embrace self-contradiction as a means to greater self-understanding, without actually contradicting ourselves.

Arthur's Penrose steps—which seem to be without beginning or end—are a useful metaphor for how we might think about *Inception* as a whole. In *Inception* we have a film that seems to begin in one dream and (perhaps) end in another dream, providing a mazelike, never-ending quality that is beguiling (and perhaps somewhat confusing). This dream-within-a-dream aspect of *Inception* presents us with another paradox: the paradox of dreaming.

The Paradox of Dreaming

Inception is a film about dreams, and dreams are experiences had while sleeping. But how could we be asleep, and thus unconscious, yet at the same time be consciously aware of experiences? This we might call "the paradox of dreaming."

To resolve this paradox, sleep researcher Michel Jouvet, in his book *The Paradox of Sleep*,[12] suggests that there is a third distinguishable mental state between those of waking and sleeping—what he calls "paradoxical sleep"—in which the brain exhibits traits of both mental states at the same time. Such thinking may contradict our long-understood notions of waking and sleeping states of consciousness, but it could resolve the paradox. These states of consciousness may be less distinct than originally thought and overlap in previously undiscovered ways. And this is not the only way to resolve it.

In *Inception*, we find characters within a shared dream who are able to consciously control their own actions while inhabiting the dreams of others. For researchers who study sleep, the ability to consciously control behavior represents a significant distinction between the mental experiences of sleeping and of waking. On the one hand, we have "primary consciousness," which is related to primary, unreflective cognitive processes such as perception and emotion. On the other hand, we have "secondary consciousness," which involves the more complex and abstract thinking associated with activities such as language and self-awareness. For J. Allan Hobson, a longtime Harvard sleep and dream researcher, this has important implications for our understanding of the science of consciousness, and resolving the dream paradox:

> Waking consciousness may consist of . . . secondary consciousness as well as primary consciousness. Primary consciousness has recently been proposed by us to be characteristic of dreaming. Put another way, waking, by including secondary consciousness, is characterized by higher orders of insight, abstraction, and awareness of awareness, precisely those attributes which dreaming normally lacks. Dreams have strong primary consciousness elements. They include a strong sense of self, of self-as-agent, and movement of that self-agent through a perceptual space.[13]

By thinking about consciousness differently—instead of as something that can either be simply "on" or "off"—we can resolve the paradox. Waking involves two kinds of consciousness, but if sleeping only deprives us of one kind of consciousness, conscious experiences can still be had while sleeping. In short, the paradox is resolved when we realize that describing sleep as a state of unconsciousness is too simplistic.

Normally, while dreaming, we serve as the unwitting marks of a dream-con of our own making; we get caught up within the plot of the dream, oblivious to the fact that it is a dream, and are unable to do anything about it until the dream reaches its end. But sometimes we become lucid; we become consciously aware of the fact that we are dreaming, and we are thus able to consciously influence the content of the dream. Cobb and his team experience their dreams in this way. This might sound paradoxical because lucid dreaming would seem to be dreaming that involves, as in our waking life, activity of second-order consciousness such as awareness of awareness. How can we have waking experiences while asleep? But, actually, this only "grazes paradoxicality." It's doubtful that every aspect of second-order consciousness can be experienced in a lucid dream, or can be experienced to the same degree.[14] And even if they could be, such lucid dreams would seem to present no more of a paradox than an experience machine,[15] like the Matrix, for example. If you fed your brain false signals, you could produce "waking experiences" of things that seem real, even though they are not in fact real and you know they are not. In a lucid dream, your brain simply does this to itself; it is its own experience machine.

Strange Loops

In thinking about things such as the Penrose steps and dreams within dreams, we can't help but feel a certain circular, mazelike quality to *Inception*. Douglas Hofstadter, in his fascinating book

I Am a Strange Loop, introduces a new and complicated idea for us to consider in the context of *Inception*'s dreams: the strange loop.

> What I mean by "strange loop" is . . . an abstract loop in which, in the series of stages that constitute the cycling-around, there is a shift from one level of abstraction (or structure) to another, which feels like an upwards movement in a hierarchy, and yet somehow the successive "upwards" shifts turn out to give rise to a second closed cycle. That is, despite one's sense of departing ever further from one's origin, one winds up, to one's shock, exactly where one had started out. In short, a strange loop is a paradoxical level-crossing feedback loop.[16]

Hofstadter further elaborates by describing another M. C. Escher illustration, called *Drawing Hands*. In this drawing, a right hand and a left hand appear to be drawing each other into existence, a never-ending loop in which the beginning and ending points are indeterminable. That sense of appearing to move from one level to another level itself mirrors the central mystery of *Inception*—Cobb has moved up and out of Limbo. Or has he? His attempts to get out may have landed him right back where he started.

A strange loop, as Hofstadter describes, consists of a hierarchy of levels that are inextricably linked to one another, much in the same way that actions at one *Inception* dream level are linked to other levels further down. Where the "strangeness" comes in, however, is in the fact that in a strange loop the hierarchy is tangled; the difference between higher and lower, up and down, becomes confused, blurred, or indistinguishable, and the ending point paradoxically becomes the starting point. When planning out the inception, Eames and Arthur touch upon aspects of strange looping.

Eames: So now in the first layer of the dream, I can impersonate Browning, and suggest concepts to Fischer's conscious mind. Then, when we take him a level deeper, his own projection of Browning should, should feed that right back to him.
Arthur: So he gives himself the idea.
Eames: Precisely. That's the only way it will stick. It has to seem self-generated.

The plan is an example of what Hofstadter calls "downward causality," which muddles the relationship between cause and effect: an idea caused by Eames and Arthur must seem to be caused by Fischer's own subconscious.

The key to accomplishing this act of idea-altering turns out to be quite similar to what we've already seen in Nietzsche's earlier appeal to irrationality. As Cobb explains: "The subconscious is motivated by emotion, right? Not reason. We need to find a way to translate this into an emotional concept." For the inception con to be successful, they must plant an idea ("I will split up my father's empire") at one level of Fischer's consciousness that will manifest itself as a self-generated thought on a lower level of subconsciousness ("My father accepts that I want to create for myself").

How can one idea be turned into something completely different (or, as Arthur poses that all-important question about human nature: "How do you translate a business strategy into an emotion?")? The answer is found by thinking about another loop, another paradox: the paradox of repetition. Deleuze asks us, how can an idea be the same and different, simultaneously? It can when what changes in the repetition is not the idea itself, but the receiver of the repeated idea: "Repetition changes nothing in the object repeated, but does change something in the mind which contemplates it."[17]

And these are not the only paradoxical loops in *Inception*.

The Paradox of Human Subjectivity

The philosopher and mathematician Edmund Husserl (1859–1938) identifies what he calls "the paradox of human subjectivity: being a subject for the world and at the same time being an object in the world."[18] This paradoxical duality allows us to observe the world, but also observe ourselves as a part of it. The idea of our selves as both objects and subjects of thoughts is part of how the dream worlds in *Inception* are populated:

> Ariadne: Who are the people?
> Cobb: Projections of my subconscious.
> Ariadne: Yours?
> Cobb: Yes. Remember, you are the dreamer. You build this world. I am the subject, my mind populates it. You can literally talk to my subconscious. That's one of the ways we extract information from the subject.

Although this paradox doesn't seem all that "paradoxical," this is a rather important point for us to understand. Instead of the dreamer and the subject being one and the same person, here we find the roles split between two people— Ariadne is the dreamer, Cobb is the subject. The projections are simultaneously objects within the dream and part of the subject. In terms of consciousness, this represents its own loop: the dreamer is aware that the dream characters are part of the dream, yet as things are altered in the dream world, the "people" pay increasingly more attention to that dream interloper's presence. A dreamer becomes aware of his own self within the dream—a moment of self-perception that Hofstadter identifies as a property of strange loops: "a kind of self-referential operation, the twisting back of a concept on itself."[19]

If the architect makes herself too obvious, by tinkering too much with the dream, things could turn out badly.

Ariadne: Why are they all looking at me?
Cobb: Because my subconscious feels that someone else is creating this world. The more you change things, the quicker the projections start to converge on you.
Ariadne: Converge?
Cobb: They sense the foreign nature of the dreamer. They attack like white blood cells fighting an infection.
Ariadne: What, they're going to attack us?
Cobb: No, no. Just you.

But this brings to mind yet another loop. As we learn, Cobb's projections don't just threaten and attack Ariadne; they threaten and attack him. His own projection of Mal challenges his worldview: "No creeping doubts? Not feeling persecuted, Dom? Chased around the globe by anonymous corporations and police forces, the way the projections persecute the dreamer?" Shortly after this challenge, Mal stabs him with a kitchen knife, as she did Ariadne in an earlier scene. Mal's antagonism is a continual obstacle for Cobb throughout the film. In essence, Cobb's mind has turned against itself. What a strange loop.

Paradox, Creation, and Memory

Inception is very much about the things the mind creates, ranging from fantastic, physics-bending displays of cityscapes folding on top of themselves to Cobb's guilt-driven projections of Mal. Cobb describes dream-building as "the chance to build cathedrals, entire cities, things that never existed, things that couldn't exist in the real world." Of course, we build dreams ourselves, but examining how we do so gives rise to yet more loops, and more paradox.

During one of the more provocative exchanges in the film, Cobb and Ariadne discuss the mechanics of creating a dream world, in which invention and discovery somehow become simultaneous operations.

Cobb: Well, imagine you're designing a building. You consciously create each aspect. But sometimes, it feels like it's almost creating itself, if you know what I mean.
Ariadne: Yeah, yeah, like I'm discovering it.
Cobb: Genuine inspiration, right? Now, in a dream our mind continuously does this. We create and perceive our world simultaneously. And our mind does this so well that we don't even know it's happening.

The idea of creating and perceiving something simultaneously seems paradoxical—especially if that perception is discovery. How can I discover something that I myself created? How, if I am creating my dream, can I be surprised by parts of it, and not know what will happen next? As Cobb sketches this idea—two curved arrows, pointing at each other's non-pointed ends—perceiving begets creation, which in turn feeds back into more creative ways of perceiving, and so on. Can the mind be both the subject (perceiving that which it creates) and object (creating the thing that it is perceiving) at the same time? Instead of being a paradox, perhaps this merely suggests that creation is less like a linear process of getting from one point to another, and instead is more like a feedback loop.

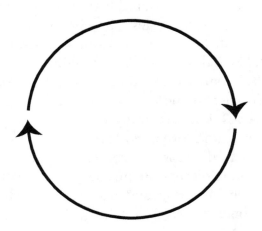

In *Inception*, characters are able to experience the contents of their dream experiences as they happen. For our own (non-lucid) dreaming experiences, we can only experience our dreams as remembered events when awake. In the film, Cobb blurs that line between the contents of memories and created ideas, which, as we find out, spells trouble.

> Ariadne: These aren't just dreams. These are memories. And you said never to use memories.
> Cobb: I know I did.
> Ariadne: You're trying to keep her alive. You can't let her go.
> Cobb: You don't understand. These are moments I regret. They're memories that I have to change.

The reason that Cobb restricts the use of memories—and the reason his breaking of his own rules makes us wonder if he has completely lost his grip on reality—is "because building a dream from your memory is the easiest way to lose your grasp on what's real and what is a dream."

Memory and imagination have a complicated relationship. On the one hand, imagination by its very nature draws upon our remembered experiences, taking what we already know and transmuting it into a newly created and discovered something else. On the other hand, the distinctions between our memories and what might simply be imagined memories seem at times to be indistinguishable. Separating memory and imagination becomes a paradoxical task:

> Paradox is not on the side of memory but of imagination. This is the case because imagination has two functions: one is to bring us outside of the real world—into unreal or possible worlds—but it has a second function which is to put memories before our eyes.[20]

Cobb's rule, "Never re-create places from your memory. Always imagine new places," seems to reverse this relationship.

Imagination becomes part of the inner world of the dreamers in *Inception*.

The solution may lie in asking ourselves: what are memories without imagination? What would imagination be without memories? Like Cobb's loop between perceiving and creating, and like Escher's *Drawing Hands*, it can seem impossible to find that dividing line between where memory ends and imagination begins. Perhaps, despite what Cobb wants to believe, with memory and imagination (and, as we saw before, consciousness) it is too simple to think of them in terms of only two possibilities—either "on" or "off." Even imagination, with its ability to take us from the possible to the impossible, has its limits, as Cobb finally forces himself to realize when he confronts Mal. "I can't imagine you with all your complexity, all your perfection, all your imperfection. Look at you . . . you're just a shade of my real wife and you're the best I can do, but I'm sorry, but you're just not good enough."

Paradoxes and a Leap of Faith

Philosophy can be a venture into the great unknown, and this can be a strangely liberating experience. In thinking about paradox, Søren Kierkegaard (1813–1855) remarked: "It is the duty of the human understanding to understand that there are things which it cannot understand, and what those things are."[21] We feel compelled to think about paradox as a way of thinking about the limits of what we understand. And even when we reach the limits of our thinking, when we contemplate the ununderstandable, Kierkegaard, in thinking about the paradoxes of the finite and the infinite, ultimately felt that a leap of faith was an acceptable conclusion. Significantly, Mal at a pivotal moment tells Cobb: "I'm asking you to take a leap of faith." More significantly still, Mal herself did take a literal leap of faith, when she jumped from the hotel window. Where a leap of faith will take us is the great mystery that thrills us in both *Inception* and in philosophy.

NOTES

1. A. O. Scott, "Inception: Decoding the Mind in Christopher Nolan's Thriller," *New York Times*, July 15, 2010.

2. This is a version of a paradox identified as "Russell's paradox," named after Bertrand Russell (1872–1970). In fact, Russell himself suggested the barber scenario as a way to demonstrate his paradox: the set of *all sets that are not members of themselves* must both contain, and not contain, itself.

3. Richard Sainsbury, *Paradoxes* (New York: Cambridge University Press, 1995), p. 1.

4. Wikipedia has a quite user-friendly explanation of this paradox. See "Birthday Problem" at http://en.wikipedia.org/wiki/Birthday_problem.

5. If we knew who didn't know, we'd know who would win.

6. Douglas Hofstadter, *Gödel, Escher, Bach: An Eternal Golden Braid* (New York: Basic Books, 1999), p. 15.

7. If you're interested in paradoxical food for thought, an excellent resource is Roy Sorensen's very comprehensive *A Brief History of the Paradox: Philosophy and the Labyrinths of the Mind* (New York: Oxford University Press, 2003). Sorensen considers paradoxes "as the atoms of philosophy because they constitute the basic points of departure for disciplined speculation. Philosophy is held together by its questions rather than by its answers. The basic philosophical questions come from troubles within our ordinary conceptual scheme" (p. xi).

8. Douglas Hofstadter, *I Am a Strange Loop* (New York: Basic Books, 2007), p. 101.

9. For a rundown of this paradox, and its solutions, see the *Internet Encyclopedia of Philosophy*'s entry on "Liar Paradox." www.iep.utm.edu/par-liar/.

10. Gilles Deleuze, *Difference and Repetition*, trans. Paul Patton (New York: Continuum, 2001), p. 227.

11. Friedrich Nietzsche, *Human, All Too Human*, trans. R. J. Hollingdale (New York: Cambridge University Press, 1986), p. 28.

12. Michel Jouvet, *The Paradox of Sleep: The Story of Dreaming* (Cambridge, MA: MIT Press, 1999).

13. J. Allan Hobson, "The Neurobiology of Consciousness: Lucid Dreaming Wakes Up," *International Journal of Dream Research* 2 (2) (2009): 43.

14. This is touched upon directly in the film, as Cobb and Ariadne sit in a Parisian café setting, until Cobb directs Ariadne's awareness to specific questions.

> Cobb: Let me ask you a question: you never really remember the beginning of a dream, do you? You always wind up right in the middle of what's going on.
>
> Ariadne: I guess, yeah.
>
> Cobb: So how did we end up here? . . . How did you get here? Where are you right now?

15. For an in-depth discussion of the experience machine idea, you might be interested in Robert Nozick's *Anarchy, State, and Utopia* (New York: Basic Books, 1974).

16. Hofstadter, *I Am a Strange Loop*, pp. 101–102.

17. Deleuze, p. 70.

18. Edmund Husserl, *The Crisis of European Sciences and Transcendental Phenomenology* (Evanston, IL: Northwestern University Press, 1970), p. 178.

19. Hofstadter, *I Am a Strange Loop*, p. 60.

20. Richard Kearney, *On Paul Ricoeur: The Owl of Minerva* (Aldershot, Hampshire, UK: Ashgate, 2005), p. 155.

21. Søren Kierkegaard, *The Journals of Kierkegaard*, ed. and trans. Alexander Dru (Oxford, UK: Oxford University Press, 1939), p. 194.

APPENDIX

A Safe Full of Secrets:
Hidden Gems You May Have Missed

One thing that makes *Inception* so amazing is that after watching it a fifth time, you realize that all the vexing questions you had the first time don't matter; you missed too much. "Does the top fall?" Who cares! Even if it does, Cobb could still be dreaming. There are many secrets, hidden in the safe, that you may have missed. We scanned the movie, the script, special features, interviews, and the Internet. Here is a list of a few cool things we discovered. (For details on abbreviations and sources check out "The Key to the Appendix: Unlocking the Safe" at the end of this appendix.)

The Music

"Non, Je Ne Regrette Rien" (No, I Regret Nothing), sung by Edith Piaf, is the song the dreamers use to signal the end of a dream and to synchronize the kicks during the Fischer inception.

The signature ominous theme of the film is a composition that replicates what "Non, Je Ne Regrette Rien" sounds like slowed down (as a dreamer would hear it in an accelerated dream). In fact, "all the music in the score is subdivisions and multiplications of the tempo of the Edith Piaf track."[1] (HZ)

The original running time of "Non, Je Ne Regrette Rien" is 2 minutes, 28 seconds. The running time of *Inception* is exactly 2 hours, 28 minutes. (IMDB)

Marion Cotillard, who played Mal in *Inception*, won an Oscar for portraying Edith Piaf in *La Vie en Rose*. (IMDB)

How Incepting, Extracting, and Shared Dreaming Work

The briefcase used for shared dreaming is a PASIV (Portable Automated Somnacin IntraVenous) Device. Our characters use Model MV-235A. (SS)

During shared dreaming, the dream being shared has to "belong" to someone. During the Saito extraction, the first level of dreaming (Saito's apartment) belonged to Cobb's first architect, Nash; the second level (Japanese Mansion) was Arthur's. During the Fischer inception, the first level (Kidnap) dream is Yusuf's, the second (Hotel) dream is Arthur's, and the third (Snow Fortress) is Eames's.

Kicks, which take you out of a level of dreaming, usually occur on the level above the dream to be exited. Cobb being dunked in Saito's apartment (first level) wakes him from the Japanese mansion dream (second level). Arthur being tipped in the chair in *the real world* wakes him from the dreams the team is using to test the effects of Yusuf's sedative. If a kick within a dream can, by itself, kick one from that dream, we never see it happen. Regardless, a kick within a dream cannot get you back to *the real world*. According to Arthur, while there is "still time on the clock, you can't wake up from within a dream unless you die."

A single kick from above cannot wake one from a level of dreaming while under a sedative as heavy as Yusuf's. Otherwise, the van hitting the bridge barrier would have woken (at least) Arthur from his hotel dream, and back into Yusuf's kidnap dream. Apparently, what is needed is two simultaneous kicks—one from above and one on the level to be exited. This is why Yusuf's dream must have a kick that can "penetrate all three levels," that can be synchronized with kicks on the other levels. Fortunately, since the team missed the first such kick, Yusuf's dream had a second—the van hitting the water.

Brain function accelerates during dreams, according to Arthur, so that it seems like more time has passed in a dream than actually has passed in *the real world*. "Five minutes in the real world gives you an hour in the dream."

Yusuf's sedative, which our dreamers use during the inception, compounds the effect of brain function acceleration by—according to Yusuf—"about 20 times normal." It is impossible to get, however, the suggested nice and neat 10 hours/1 week/6 months/10 years distribution for the dream levels in the inception using that number. Compounding 10 hours of sleep by 20, gets the following:

x20	Years	Months	Days	Hours
Plane	0	0.0137	0.42	**10**
Yusuf	0.02	0.274	**8.33**	200
Arthur	0.46	**5.4795**	167	4000
Eames	**9.13**	109.59	3333	80000

The way to get closest to the dream times in the film is to assume 1 hour of the 10-hour flight is not spent dreaming, and compound the effect of Yusuf's sedative by twenty-one:

x20	Years	Months	Days	Hours
Plane	0.001	0.0123	0.38	**9**
Yusuf	0.022	0.2589	**7.88**	189
Arthur	0.453	**5.437**	165	3969
Eames	**9.515**	114.18	3473	83349

Only a couple of hours (at most) have passed in Yusuf's dream, when the dreamers return to it. It doesn't take them long to get to the warehouse, or from the warehouse to the bridge, and Cobb and Arthur don't spend a lot of time interrogating Fischer. Cobb does say Eames has an hour to spend with Fischer, to extract information from him, but it is unclear if he even uses it all. If so, given dream time acceleration and the effects of Yusuf's sedative, only about six minutes have passed on the plane by the time the inception is complete.

The dreamers still have about a week to spend in Yusuf's dream after they wake up in the submerged van; you can't wake up from within a dream until the clock runs out, the clock on the plane would have only ticked off a few minutes, and dying will send them down to Limbo until the sedative wears off.

Limbo is no one's dream; it is simply "unconstructed dream space" that anyone can inhabit and (with time) manipulate.

It is unclear where one goes upon waking from Limbo. One does not automatically awake in reality. Ariadne and Fischer went back to the level from which they descended into Limbo—Eames's snow fortress dream—but this was also the "closest" level with an active dream in it. If Saito and Cobb simply went to back to the level they left, they would go back to the empty level of Eames's dream and would have nearly ten years to spend there remaking it. If they go back to the closest inhabited level, they would go to Yusuf's dream;

however, since their bodies are underwater in the van, they would likely die and just go right back down into Limbo. Where Cobb and Mal went, upon waking from Limbo after fifty years, remains a mystery.

It is raining in Yusuf's dream because he needs to urinate; he drank too much free first-class champagne.

Eames "forges" the distracting sexy blonde in the hotel dream. While in the elevator with Saito, as the blonde, Eames's layered reflection reveals his identity (a few layers down).

The violent projections in the Snow Fortress are Fischer's. He is the subject.

Saito is ninety when Cobb finds him in Limbo (SS, p. 216), so Saito spent at least forty years in Limbo.

Cobb spinning the top in Mal's dollhouse safe, according to Nolan, symbolically represents Cobb's inception of Mal—an event that happens off screen. (NN, p. 15)

How Totems Work

A totem can only tell you that you are not in *someone else's* dream, Arthur tells us. Why? Totems work in the following way: if you are in someone else's dream, they create all the physical objects in the dream—including your totem. So, if you use your totem in someone else's dream, it will behave as they expect it to. If they do not know the special way it behaves in the real world, they cannot make it behave as you know it should. So, if it does not behave as you know it should, then you know you are in someone else's dream. However, since you know how it should behave, your totem cannot tell you that you are not in your own dream. If you are the dreamer, the dream version of your totem (that you create) would likely behave as it should in the real world.

Arthur's totem is a loaded die; only he knows how it will fall in the real world. A dreamer would produce a non-weighted die.

Ariadne's totem is a bishop chess piece. It is not clear how its movement is unique, but given what she does with it in the film, it's likely that she has weighted it such that when it tips over, it will roll and come to rest in a particular way—perhaps, with the bishop's hat facing down.

Eames's totem seems to be a poker chip—although there is no indication of how it works.

Saito and Yusuf do not appear to have totems.

Cobb's totem—the spinning top—is not reliable. For one thing, since it was originally Mal's and Cobb told Ariadne how it works, it cannot tell him whether he is in one of their dreams (or a dream they designed). Further, for a totem to work, its movement has to be unique in the real world—not in a dream. No one knows how Arthur's or Ariadne's totems are actually weighted, thus no one knows how they would behave in the real world. Yet, everyone knows that tops fall, and that is how Cobb's top behaves in the real world. Any dreamer, if Cobb spun his top in their dream, would dream of the top falling.

Cobb seems to misunderstand, at one point, how totems work. As Cobb and Mal are arguing, in their kitchen, about whether they are still dreaming, Cobb asks, "If this is my dream, then why can't I control this?" It looks like he is holding the top as he says this, and is thus suggesting that his inability to keep the top spinning by sheer will is evidence that they are not dreaming. If so, this is not consistent with the rest of the facts just mentioned about how totems work; you do not see if you can "control" your totem to see if you are still dreaming. You see if your totem behaves as only you know it should in the real world. However, careful examination reveals that Cobb, in fact, is holding nothing when he says that line. (BR) Further, the original line in the shooting script is "If it's my dream then why can't I control it? Why can't I stop this?" (SS, p. 140) He is not wondering why he can't stop the top; if the top wasn't stopping, they would know they were in someone else's dream. On the other hand, since the content of a dream is determined by the dreamer, Cobb is trying to prove that they are not in his dream by showing that he cannot control the content of their surroundings—he cannot stop the dream, or their argument. Since dreamers can control their dreams only when they are lucid—only when they know they are dreaming—Mal's response is enough to defeat Cobb's argument. "Because you don't know you're dreaming."

The Characters

"Cobb" means "dream" in Urdu, Sanskrit, Hindi, and Punjabi. (HM) "Cobb" may be a reference to a character in *The Prisoner*, a British television series Nolan wanted to adapt for the big screen. (RB) As spelled on his plane ticket, Cobb's first name is Dominick (with a "k"). (BR)

Ariadne, in Greek mythology, guided her brother Theseus through the labyrinth to defeat the Minotaur. The Labyrinth was circular. Recall the maze Ariadne drew to pass Cobb's test.

"Mal" is French for "bad." One line in "Non, Je Ne Regrette Rien," even uses the world "mal" in reference to "bad things" the singer has done, that she does not regret. (IMDB) "Mal" has similar connotations in Spanish and English, because of its Latin root.

"Arthur" can mean "rock" in English. Arthur is especially grounded in reality, and attempts to keep Cobb that way.

"Saito" in Japanese is "purifying flower." (MQ) Saito cleanses the impurities from Cobb's record. Saito's company is called "Proclus Global." (GN) Proclus was a Greek Neoplatonist philosopher who kept the school at Athens alive, somewhat like Saito keeps the energy industry alive by preventing the Fischer empire from monopolizing it.

Eames is likely, given the emphasis in architecture in the film, named after Charles Eames and Bernice Alexandra "Ray" Eames, a married couple who made major contributions to modern architecture and furniture. (IMDB)

"Yusuf" is Arabic for "Joseph." In the Bible, Joseph was known not just as a dreamer but as a dream interpreter. These gifts brought him fame and recognition as well as misfortune. (IMBD)

Stephen Miles is Cobb's father-in-law. Stephen's wife, Marie Miles, looks after Cobb's children. (SS)

Robert Fischer may reference chess champion Bobby Fischer (IMDB). The name may also reference the Arthurian legend of the Fisher King, whose kingdom physically changes to parallel his wounds. (TVT)

Maurice Fischer is likely homage to graphic artist M. C. (Maurits Cornelis) Escher. (IMDB)

The names of the characters—**D**om, **R**obert, **E**ames, **A**rthur/**A**riadne, **M**al, **S**aito—spell DREAMS. (IMDB)

Phillipa and James, Cobb's children, were played by two sets of child actors; one set for the end of the film, one set for the rest. (IMDB) They wore different clothes. (BR)

• Younger (dream) three-year-old Phillipa was played by Claire Geare. She wears a short-sleeved pink dress with a two-inch pleated frill trim at the bottom and brown shoes.

- Older (end of the movie) five-year-old Phillipa was played by Taylor Geare (Claire's older sister). She wears a pink dress with shoulder straps that has an eight-inch pleated frill trim at the bottom and a waistband design. She is also wearing a white T-shirt underneath the strapped dress and pink tennis shoes.
- Younger (dream) twenty-month-old James was played by Nolan's son, Magnus. He wears a short-sleeved plaid button-down shirt that contains reddish-orange, brown, and yellow vertical stripes, khaki shorts, and brown sandals with no socks.
- Older (end of the movie) three-year-old James was played by Johnathan Geare (brother to Claire and Taylor). He wears a short-sleeved button-down plaid shirt that contains red and brown vertical stripes. He is wearing dark khaki shorts and white tennis shoes.

Inception Is an Analogy

Inception is an analogy for movie-making. The role of each inception team member parallels roles of a movie-making team. (NN, p. 19)

- Cobb, who orchestrates everything, is the director.
- Ariadne, who designs the dreams, is the screenwriter.
- Saito, who bankrolls the whole thing, is the production company.
- Arthur, who organizes and sets everything up, is the producer.
- Eames, who pretends to be Peter Browning and the Sexy Blonde, is the actor.
- Yusuf, who has the technical savvy to enable them to produce the dreams, is the special effects expert.
- Robert Fischer, the mark, is the audience.

Inception implants ideas. Just as inception implants ideas into its target, so too does *Inception* implant ideas into us.

Inception is an analogy for human psychology; there are many ways to look at it. For example:

- Cobb is the id, which seeks out the fulfillment of desires (relive his memories, be with Mal, be with his kids). Cobb never follows his own rules and just does what he wants.
- Arthur is the ego, rational and reality based. In a healthy psyche, it controls the id—like Arthur attempts by trying to talk Cobb out of risking inception.
- Ariadne is the superego, the critical and moralizing agent that considers right and wrong and the effects our actions have on others. She helps Cobb through his troubles, for the sake of the others.
- Eames, the forger, can be seen as our creative nature.

If the entire movie is Cobb's dream, one might interpret each character as a different part of Cobb's psyche.

Things You Might Have Missed

The window in the Japanese mansion bedroom suite resembles the Legendary Pictures logo. (BR)

The artwork in the Japanese mansion dream is a projection of Saito's subconscious. Saito is partial to "postwar British painters."

The Japanese mansion dream starts to collapse when Cobb shoots Arthur in the head, thus waking him up, because it was Arthur's dream.

The goal of the failed extraction that begins the film was to find "Saito's expansion plans" and deliver them to Cobol engineering.

If you look in the background while Eames is elaborating on the details of what ideas they will incept on each level, during a "practice version" of Yusuf's dream, you will see that Ariadne had been folding the city in half.

The caged elevator floor buttons have Cobb's memories ranked, ending with the worst in the basement—Mal jumping from the hotel window. He says they are moments he regrets, but the memory on the top floor—of a family trip to the beach—seems pleasant enough.

Cobb's memory is not dependable. Flashbacks show him being young with Mal as they laid their heads on the train, yet they had spent fifty years in Limbo. Later, his memory revises as we see elderly images of them, in Limbo, including a brief but memorable shot of their elderly hands locked together as the train track is vibrating. During the "cage elevator" dream with Ariadne, Cobb even indicates that he tries to change his memories.

Cobb and Mal stumbled into Limbo while experimenting with multilevel shared dreams, according to how Cobb recounts the events to Ariadne.

Mal and Cobb build sandcastles in order to build their city in Limbo; as they knock one down, you can see its corresponding building crash in the background.

3502 is Cobb and Mal's anniversary hotel room number. The train that barrels into the sedan Cobb is driving and that brings Mal and Cobb out of Limbo is 3502. The taxi that Arthur, Eames, and Saito get into is 2053. (IMDB)

Yusuf flips off the projection that was shooting at him when he reverses the van and breaks through the bridge barrier. (BR)

5-2-8-4-9-1 are the numbers that Fischer arbitrarily gives as the combination to his father's safe. The "fake" (too short) phone number given to Fischer by Eames (as the sexy blonde) is 528–491, and the two hotel room numbers in Arthur's dream are 528 and 491. The combination for the small safe beside Maurice's deathbed is 5-2-8-4-9-1, and it seems that is the combination for the large safe in the snow fortress's "antechamber," as well—but it's hard to be sure.

On the riverbank, as Fischer talks to Browning (Eames in disguise), Browning's body is briefly blocked from view. When it returns, it is Eames, undisguised. (BR)

Ariadne is fiddling with her bishop totem on the plane, after the inception; apparently, she performed a reality check after waking. (BR)

Chess references in the film abound: a black-and-white tiled floor in Saito's apartment bathroom (BR), Ariadne's totem, and Robert (Bobby) Fischer's name.

Cobb's wedding ring never appears in scenes where he is in *the real world* (not counting the flashbacks of before Mal jumped). This includes the end of the film; watch closely as he passes his passport to the agent. (BR)

Standing next to Miles, as he waits for Cobb at the airport, is a chauffeur holding a sign with the name FISCHER. (BR) Other names are also seen, but seem to have no significance.

Significant Lines You May Have Missed

"If I jump, would I survive?" This is Mal's first line in the film, when we meet her at Saito's mansion and she and Cobb are overlooking a drop down to the ocean. Of course, if she was right and they were dreaming, Mal did survive her jump from the hotel window.

"I don't like trains," says Cobb, right before he gets off the train in Kyoto. Later, we find out why.

"Couldn't have peed before you went under?" Arthur quips as the team rescues Yusuf from the rain of his dream.

Eames adds "Bit too much free champagne before takeoff, hey Yusuf?" "Ha ha, bloody ha," Yusuf replies. It's raining in the dream because Yusuf has to pee.

"Good-looking fellow, I'm sure." This is Browning's reply to Saito, when Saito says to Browning, "I see you've changed," thinking he is Eames in disguise, and then claims to have mistaken Browning for a friend.

"Couldn't somebody have dreamt up a goddamn beach?" Fischer remarks, after he and Saito fall to avoid the avalanche. Ironically, a beach is likely how Fischer entered Limbo.

"Well it's not me that doesn't get to go back to my family, is it?" Eames replies to Cobb when Cobb admits that Mal shot Fischer because he "couldn't kill her."

Cultural References

"Downwards is the only way forwards" is a line used in *Dante's Inferno* to drive the characters deeper into the levels of hell.

A spinning top is used in Clifford D. Simak's 1953 novel *Ring around the Sun*. (IMDB) Characters can travel to millions of alternate earths by looking at the spinning top and wondering where the colors go. (CS)

"Don't think about elephants" references a work on cognitive semantics titled *Don't Think of an Elephant* by George Lakoff. (IMDB)

Penrose steps reference a lithograph print by the Dutch graphic artist M. C. Escher; it is also known as *Ascending and Descending* or the *Infinite Staircase* and was first printed in 1960.

The blonde that Eames poses as in the hotel dream may be a reference to "the woman in the red dress" that Mouse creates in training simulations in *The Matrix*.

Clues That *The Real World* Is a Dream[2]

Exiting limbo: When Fischer and Ariadne awake from Limbo they only go one dream level up, to the Snow Fortress. According to Cobb, he and Mal entered Limbo when experimenting with multilayered dreaming. Wouldn't they have simply gone one layer up, to a lower level of their original multilayered dream, when they exited Limbo?

Perpetual spinning top: At the beginning of the film, elderly Saito spins the top. We flash back, and spend the rest of the movie getting back to elderly Saito . . . and the top is still spinning. When the top spins and doesn't fall, we are in a dream—and the top was spinning the whole movie!

One-dimensional characters: The other characters are all too one-dimensional for *Inception* to be a good movie. Ariadne, Eames, Arthur, Saito don't even have last names. This makes perfect sense, however, if they are all projections of Cobb's subconscious.

Dream jumps: There are many editing jumps in *the real world* that mirror those in dreams. During Cobb and Mal's first conversation in the film, they jump mid-sentence from inside to outside. A similar jump is seen during Cobb and Ariadne's first conversation. In Paris, Cobb stands outside Miles's classroom. Suddenly, without opening the door or making Miles aware of this presence, Cobb is sitting in the classroom. Another "dream cut?"

"Come back to reality": Cobb's father-in-law, Miles, implores him to do so when Cobb reveals that Mal won't let him design dreams anymore.

PASIV absurdity: How the PASIV Device works is absurd; you can't control the brain through the arm in the real world. Even how the device hooks into the arm is always just out of frame.

Dream forging in *The Real World*: In Mombasa, Eames produces forged poker chips out of thin air. The script specifically says he was down to "his last two chips"; he loses them but then "mysteriously produces two stacks of chips." (SS, p. 76) Cobb even recognizes them as forgeries. "I see your spelling hasn't improved." Is Eames "dream forging" in *the real world*?

Mombasa chase: The chase scene in Mombasa has many dreamlike elements. The overhead view makes it look like a maze. Agents (projections?) are around every corner, and pop out of nowhere. Cobb can't stop the restaurant owner from drawing attention to him. As he runs away, the walls close in around him, and Saito appears out of nowhere to rescue him.

Cobb/Cobol: The company chasing Cobb is named "Cobol." The similarity indicates he might be chasing himself.

Magic newspaper: As the team plans the inception, the newspaper articles in Cobb's folder about Fischer and his father change without Cobb turning the page.

Cobb's addiction: Cobb can't sleep or dream unless he is hooked into a PASIV Device. Is he addicted, or could it be that he can't sleep or dream or his own because he is already sleeping and dreaming?

Mal's call: "You know how to find me. You know what you have to do." Mal continually says this to Cobb in his dreams. Is she calling him down into Limbo, or to commit suicide to find her up above in reality?

Ariadne's step: While in Cobb's memories, Ariadne steps on the champagne glass just like Cobb did. Is this because she is Cobb—or, at least, a projection of his subconscious?

Mal's jump: Before Mal jumps, she is oddly in the window of another room *opposite* Cobb, instead of on the ledge outside their suite. (She is not in the suite's bedroom; the same living room furniture is behind them both.) Cobb doesn't seem to recognize the oddness, as he motions for her to come toward him, across the empty space between them, to come back inside. "It's only when we wake up that we realize something was actually strange."

Fischer's training: Fischer's subconscious is trained and attacking the team, yet Fischer's training didn't show up in Arthur's research. Was Arthur not diligent enough, or is the team actually in Cobb's dream, and it's Cobb's subconscious that's attacking them (just like Mal does)? After all, the attacking projections show up at the same time the menacing train does, and we know the train is a projection of Cobb's subconscious.

Forged theft: In the hotel dream, Eames (as the sexy blonde) lifts Fischer's wallet without actually touching him; it seems he just forges the wallet and gives it to Saito. No big deal; they are dreaming, after all. However, Eames also lifts Fischer's passport, in *the real world* on the plane—yet he clearly has no opportunity to do so. Watch closely; Eames's hand only touches the back of Fischer's arm—but then *poof*, he has the passport. Is this more *real world* dream forging?

Inexplicable paintbrushes: At the end of the film, when Cobb spins his top, the number of paintbrushes in the glass inexplicably multiplies.

Cobb's kids: At the end of the film, even though Cobb's children are older, wearing different clothes and played by different actors—they are still in the exact position he always dreams them in. In addition, they say they are building "a house on the cliff"—just like Saito's mansion. In fact, that is what they were building on the beach as Cobb washed up on the shore below Saito's mansion. Are subconscious dream elements still popping through?

Running time: The running time of the song they use to signal the end of a dream, "Non, Je Ne Regrette Rien," is 2 minutes, 28 seconds. The running time of *Inception* is 2 hours, 28 minutes. (IMDB) Could it be—when the time is up, the dream is over?

Unanswered Questions and Plot Holes

Why does Fischer not recognize Saito, his main competitor?

How does Saito have enough power to eliminate Cobb's charges with a single phone call? Sure, he could pull a few strings—but a single phone call to lift, instantly, such serious charges?

Why doesn't Cobb move his children out of the United States? In fact, if Cobb's father-in-law Miles teaches in Paris, and his wife Marie looks after the kids in the States, why wouldn't they just move the kids to Paris—that way, Miles can live with his wife, and Cobb can live with his kids? "Extradition between France and the United States" is enough of a "bureaucratic nightmare" that, at the least, Cobb could visit his kids in Paris.

Overlap with Nolan's Other Films

Nolan's film *Following* overlaps significantly with *Inception*. *Following*'s antagonist, Cobb, is a con artist/thief. He takes an apprentice under his wing, tells him "everybody has a box . . . that's sort of an unconscious collection . . . that tells something very intimate about the people." (RB) This idea is repeated in *Inception* when extractors create a safe, and the subjects place their secrets in it.

Handheld objects, or ways of keeping track of reality—like totems—appear in many of Nolan's films: Leonard's tattoos (*Memento*), Bruce's arrowhead and his father's stethoscope (*Batman Begins*), Harvey Dent's coin[3] (*The Dark Knight*) and Borden's ball (*The Prestige*). (RB)

Leg injuries are common in Nolan's films: Mal shooting Arthur in the kneecap, Angier falling through the trapdoor in *The Prestige*, and Batman dropping Maroni in *The Dark Knight*. Cobb even thought that Fischer was supposed to have knee surgery. (RB)

Inception is the third Nolan film in five years where Cillian Murphy's character spends on-screen time with a cloth bag over his head. The other two are *Batman Begins* and *The Dark Knight*. (MQ)

Making the Movie

The flight attendant was played by Miranda Nolan, first cousin to Christopher Nolan. (IMDB)

"You mustn't be afraid to dream a little bigger, darling." Tom Hardy (Eames) ad-libbed "darling." It was just supposed to be "Arthur." Nolan liked the change, so it was kept. (TH)

The large opposing mirrors Ariadne creates are not in the shooting script. They were included after visual-effects supervisor Paul Franklin was inspired by a set visit to the Pont de Bir-Hakeim in Paris, a bridge with a series of repeating iron arches reminiscent of a hall of mirrors. (CF, p. 49)

Saito's medieval Japanese castle was based on Himeji Castle in Japan. (CF, p. 42)

The "folding Paris" scene was inspired by Chicago's drawbridges seen by Nolan and Franklin during the filming of *Batman Begins*. (CF, p. 46)

The Snow Fortress exterior was based on the Geisel Library at the University of California, San Diego, designed by William L. Pereira. (IMDB)

Oliver's Arrow was *Inception*'s production codename. It was inspired by Nolan's son Oliver. (TB)

Ariadne's hair was put into a tight bun in the hotel sequence so that the filmmakers didn't have to deal with figuring out how her hair would move in zero gravity.[4] (IMDB)

The Key to the Appendix: Unlocking the Safe

The following citations denote where and how the information in the appendix was derived. If an entry has no citation, it is an original observation by the contributors or by the editor of this book.

IMDB: The Internet Movie Data Base Inception page, found at www.imdb.com/title/tt1375666/.

SS: *Inception: The Shooting Script by Christopher Nolan* (San Rafael, CA: Insight Editions, 2010).

NN: "Dreaming/Creating/Perceiving/Filmmaking: An Interview with Writer/Director Christopher Nolan," interviewed by Jonathan Nolan, the preface to *Inception: The Shooting Script*.

BR: Information thus denoted was derived by careful observation of the movie on Blu-Ray.

HZ: Hans Zimmer, quoted in Dave Itzkoff's "Hans Zimmer Extracts the Secrets of the 'Inception' Score," in the *New York Times, Arts Beat,* July 28, 2010.

GN: Refers to the prequel graphic novel, *The Cobol Job,* which can be seen in the special features of the Blu-Ray disk.

HM: Kathryn McKenzie Nichols, "The Hidden Meanings of Inception" in *Yahoo: Entertainment,* found at www .associatedcontent.com/article/5729508/the_hidden_ meanings_of_inception.html?cat=2.

RB: Richard R. Barrett, "Thoughts on Inception or, Christopher Nolan and Cobb Salad," found at http:// leitourgeia.wordpress.com/2010/07/21/thoughts-on-inception-or-christopher-nolan-and-cobb-salad/.

MQ: MovieQuotesandMore.com, "Inception Trivia: 'Dream within a Dream,'" found at www.moviequotesand more.com/inception-trivia.html.

TVT: TV Tropes "Film:Inception," found at tvtropes .org/pmwiki/pmwiki.php/Film/Inception?from=Main .Inception.

CS: Clifford D. Simak, "Book Review—Ring around the Sun," found at http://guysalvidge.wordpress.com/2.

NOTES

1. Online, this article includes a video that plays Piaf's song and the *Inception* score side by side, http://artsbeat.blogs.nytimes.com/2010/07/28/hans-zimmer-extracts-the-secrets-of-the-inception-score/.

2. For more detail on these clues, see "The Editor's Totem" as well as Jason Southworth's and Ruth Tallman's chapters in this volume.

3. Of course, Dent's coin was not Nolan's idea.

4. The editor thanks Lance Belluomini, who contributed a great deal to this list.

CONTRIBUTORS

The Architects

Adam Barkman is an assistant professor of philosophy at Redeemer University College. He has written books, including *C. S. Lewis and Philosophy as a Way of Life* and *Through Common Things*, and has edited others, including *Manga and Philosophy* and *The Philosophy of Ang Lee*. If inception is possible, Adam wouldn't mind being convinced that he's Batman. Of course, his wife, Ashley, would definitely be able to convince him otherwise.

Lance Belluomini received his BA in philosophy from the University of Arizona and did his graduate studies in philosophy at the University of California, Berkeley; San Francisco State University; and the University of Nebraska-Lincoln. His philosophical interests include ethics and the philosophy of popular culture. Lance can't stop watching *Inception*. This would explain why he keeps daydreaming about opening safes and vaults. And yes, the combination is always 528491.

Kimberly Blessing is chair and associate professor of philosophy at Buffalo State College in Buffalo, New York. Her areas of interest include early modern philosophy, especially Descartes, meaning of life, and philosophy of religion. Kimberly coedited

Movies and the Meaning of Life: Hollywood's Take on Philosophy. She also contributed articles to *The Daily Show and Philosophy* and *Metallica and Philosophy*. Though she does have some regrets, Kimberly does not regret contributing to this volume, and she knows *Inception* fans will not regret reading it.

Albert J. Chan is constructing dreams as an assistant professor of philosophy at St. Ambrose University, in Davenport, Iowa. He specializes in business ethics and enjoys blogging about the mazelike layers of cinema, culture, and corporate morality at mondaymorningbusinessethicist.com. Albert still can't believe Christopher Nolan did not win an Oscar for Best Original Screenplay. Most likely, a corporate spy planted a resilient "kingly speech-type" idea deep within the Academy. Each NFL football season, Albert also seeks honor and redemption from a Seattle Seahawks Super Bowl championship. But his hometown totem falls short every time, reminding him he is living in the real world.

Keith Dromm teaches and writes on such topics as the philosophy of film, ethics, and the philosopher Ludwig Wittgenstein. He is an associate professor of philosophy in the Louisiana Scholars' College at Northwestern State University, in Natchitoches, Lousiana. He has contributed chapters to other Philosophy and Pop Culture volumes, such as *The Office and Philosophy*. And he makes millions of dollars doing these things . . . in his dreams.

Scott Daniel Dunbar is an assistant professor in the Department of Religious Studies at the University of Prince Edward Island, Canada. He has taught courses on Asian religions and philosophy at Canadian universities for over a decade. He is fascinated by the transmission and reinterpretation of Asian philosophy in popular culture, and has previously written about the influence of Asian thought on the movies *Star Wars: The Phantom Menace* and *The Matrix Revolutions*. He enjoys "sleep research" and wonders whether he is dreaming that you bought this book.

Bart Engelen is a postdoctoral fellow of the Research Foundation–Flanders (FWO). He is currently affiliated with the Centre for Economics and Ethics of the K.U. Leuven (Belgium). Bart publishes on topics in political philosophy, ethics, and the philosophy of economics. He has coedited *Denkbeelden*, the first Dutch book to introduce philosophy by means of films. Bart is living evidence that positive emotion trumps negative emotion every time.

John R. Fitzpatrick is a lecturer in philosophy at the University of Tennessee at Chattanooga. His areas of research and teaching include political philosophy, ethics, and the history of philosophy. He has published two books on the nineteenth-century British philosopher John Stuart Mill. He has contributed a chapter in *House and Philosophy* and is working on two other popular-culture book chapters. John is not sure that the technology in the film *Inception* will ever exist, but the idea that others can manipulate you into doing stuff while you think it was your own idea is quite plausible, since he is reasonably sure that it has been done to him.

Daniel Forbes is an assistant professor of philosophy at West Chester University of Pennsylvania. He earned his PhD in philosophy from the University of Georgia. His research focuses on the history of early modern philosophy, particularly the metaphysics and epistemology of Spinoza. He also has research interests in American pragmatist philosophy, process philosophy, and philosophical pedagogy. This is his second attempt at incepting ideas about philosophy in popular culture, having contributed a chapter in *Vader, Voldemort and Other Villains: Essays on Evil in Popular Media*. Dan got into the study of philosophy because he thought it would offer him the chance to build cathedrals of the mind. These days he sometimes thinks he should settle for a comfortable bungalow. But then he remembers Eames's advice: "You mustn't be afraid to dream a little bigger, darling."

Charles Joshua Horn is a doctoral candidate at the University of Kentucky. He specializes in early modern philosophy (Descartes through Kant) and is writing his dissertation on the nature of compossibility in the philosophy of Leibniz. Josh is primarily interested in how the history of philosophy informs the contemporary debate in the analytic tradition. He contributed a chapter to *The Legend of Zelda and Philosophy* called "The Triforce and the Doctrine of the Mean." Josh thinks that the Descartes estate should sue Christopher Nolan for copyright infringement.

David Kyle Johnson is an assistant professor of philosophy at King's College, in Wilkes-Barre, Pennsylvania. His specializations include metaphysics, logic, and philosophy of religion. Kyle is the editor of *Heroes and Philosophy* and the coeditor (with William Irwin) of *Introducing Philosophy through Pop Culture: From Socrates to South Park, Hume to House*. He is a regular contributor to the Philosophy and Pop Culture series, with articles on *South Park, Family Guy, Battlestar Galactica, The Hobbit, Batman*, and *The Office*. He hosts a podcast at philosophyandpopculture.com. Kyle owns a replica of Cobb's spinning top, which he keeps in his office. He kind of freaked out once when he spun it, answered an e-mail about editing this book, and then looked down to see it still spinning, flawlessly, without wobbling, in exactly the same place—for what had to have been another thirty seconds. (True story.) His arm is still bruised from all the subsequent pinching.

Clint Jones earned his BA in philosophy from Transylvania University, in Lexington, Kentucky, and is currently a doctoral candidate at the University of Kentucky. His dissertation focuses on the origins of violence and justice in society. His primary interests are in social theory, twentieth-century continental philosophy, and environmental philosophy. But he often finds himself sidetracked by projects that have nothing to do with anything he should be working on. These include coaching debate at his alma mater, writing poetry, and campaigning for political offices. However, this is especially true where inception is concerned because he believes it's possible. He's currently in the market for a good chemist. If you know one, let Clint know, as he really doesn't want to travel to Mombasa.

Daniel P. Malloy is an adjunct assistant professor of philosophy at Appalachian State University in Boone, North Carolina. His research focuses on issues in ethics. He has published numerous chapters on the intersection of popular culture and philosophy, particularly dealing with the illustration of moral questions in movies, comic books, and television shows. Daniel suspects that his recent string of nightmares has been the result of disappointed extractors who've found no valuable information—they now know the names of some of his students and the *Gilligan's Island* theme; much good may it do them.

Ken Marable is a doctoral student in philosophy at Michigan State University and a visiting professor at Alma College, in Alma, Michigan, where he received his BA. Ken specializes in philosophy of mind, bioethics, and psychology. He sees metaphysics, ethics, and science as three layers all informing one another. The richest knowledge is found in studying all three rather than any one in isolation. Recently, he tried to fold his city with his imagination; he quickly returned to failing to fold laundry in a timely manner.

James T. M. Miller is a doctoral candidate at Durham University (Old Elvet, Durham, U.K.) researching the relationship between thought and language and its consequences for metaphysics. He is also interested in philosophy of science and the relationship between scientific theories and truth. James is pleased to be able to contribute to a book about a film that shows big-money Hollywood blockbusters can be intelligent, and so hopes that it is not all some dream—or if it is, that he can just stay in the dream.

Tyler Shores is a graduate student from the University of Oxford (Oxford, U.K.) and also has a BA from the University of California, Berkeley, where he created, and for six semesters taught, a course on the Simpsons and philosophy (inspired by William Irwin's book of the same name). His research interests include philosophy and literature and the impact of digital technology on the experience of reading. Tyler has contributed to other volumes in the Philosophy and Pop Culture series on *Alice in Wonderland*, *30 Rock*, and *The Girl with the Dragon Tattoo*. He has also previously worked at Google and on the Authors@ Google lecture series. Tyler sometimes can be seen walking backward up stairways, in the hopes of one day discovering that the Penrose Steps are in fact real.

Michael Sigrist teaches philosophy at George Washington University and lives in Washington, D.C. He has written on philosophy of religion and metaphysics, but specializes in phenomenology and philosophy of mind, having written a dissertation on Edmund Husserl's theory of consciousness. He admires Husserl's work very much, but will acknowledge that reading Husserl can be an effective way to slow down the passage of time. On Michael's last trip to Limbo he was able to finish all of his articles, build the house of his dreams, prepare a gourmet dinner each night, and direct his own screenplays. He's more than a little jealous that Christopher Nolan seems able to do all that in the real world.

Jason Southworth is an ABD graduate student at the University of Oklahoma, Norman, and an adjunct instructor of philosophy at Barry University, Miami Shores, Florida. He has written chapters for other Philosophy and Pop Culture volumes on *Batman*, *X-Men*, and *Stephen Colbert*. Lately, he has been having a reoccurring dream in which he no longer has to put cutesy tags at the end of his bio.

Ruth Tallman is an assistant professor of philosophy at Barry University, Miami Shores, Florida. She is pleased to be able to use *Inception* as an entryway into discussing great philosophical concepts with her introduction to philosophy students, and she hopes that now we can all finally stop talking about *The Matrix*.

Andrew Terjesen has a PhD in philosophy from Duke University and was a visiting assistant professor at Rhodes College, Washington and Lee University, and Austin College. His main interests in philosophy have been in the moral psychology of empathy, Chinese philosophy, and the works of Adam Smith. In addition to publishing work on those topics, he has also produced a number of essays on the philosophical aspects of popular culture, including contributions to books in this series on *Avatar, Battlestar Galactica, The Girl With the Dragon Tattoo*, and *Green Lantern*. He will be attending law school in the fall. Though he insists that this is not the result of an inception orchestrated by his parents, Andrew will not deny that he hopes a law degree will resolve his daddy issues.

Katherine Tullmann is working toward her PhD in philosophy at the City University of New York Graduate Center. She received her MA in philosophy from the University of Missouri–St. Louis and her BA from Truman State University, Kirksville, Missouri. Katherine's current research interests include philosophy of art, emotions, and consciousness. In her free time, Katherine enjoys running up and down Escher's stairs and trying to make her way through the mazes of New York City so she can get to class before the projections catch her.

Dan Weijers is an assistant lecturer in the philosophy department at Victoria University of Wellington. By the time this book hits the shelves, Dan should have just gazed upon his newly minted PhD for the first time (outside of his dreams). Dan researches happiness, well-being, and the meaning of life from interdisciplinary perspectives. He says: "Yes, that is just as interesting as it sounds." Dan is a founding coeditor of the *International Journal of Wellbeing* and has published articles and book reviews about happiness in philosophy, psychology, politics, and economics journals. Dan's personal tips for happiness include: watching *Inception*, talking about *Inception*, reading blogs about *Inception*, watching *Inception* again, reading this book (especially his chapter), and avoiding brain-melting generic Hollywood action films at all costs. Dan's totem is his lucky pair of socks (no one else has ventured close enough to know exactly how they smell).

INDEX

The PASIV (Plenary Alphabetized
Subject Index for This Volume) Device

utopia, 265–275
  defined, 266–267
  desire and, 268–270, 271
  dystopia and, 266, 267–268
  heaven as, 272–273
  idyllic hope and, 266–267,
    269, 271, 273, 274
  Limbo as, 265–266
  perfection and, 271–272

Village Voice, 47–48

Waking Life (film), 102
Wall Street Journal, 48
Walton, Kendall, 51–52, 53,
    55, 57
Weber, Max, 266
wedding ring
  epistemic angst and, 81
  the real world and, 2
Wittgenstein, Ludwig, 242

Yogācāra, 282–283
Yusuf
  dreaming and, 234, 236
  epistemic angst and, 79,
    83–84
  ethics and, 126–128, 130
  extended mind theory and,
    181–183
  faith and, 263
  "Full Dream" interpretation
    and, 34, 38
  hedonism and, 111
  intentionalism and, 18
  the real world and, 1, 5, 6
  time and, 199, 201, 206, 212
  utopia and, 268–270, 273
  See also film devices

Zeus (Greek god), 131–132
Zhuangzi, 287
Zimmer, Hans, 209

CPSIA information can be obtained
at www.ICGtesting.com
Printed in the USA
BVHW082253210619
551688BV00011B/50/P

9 781118 072639